God's Presence in the Life of an Ordinary Woman

An Autobiography

Kitty McCaffrey

WestBow
PRESS
A DIVISION OF THOMAS NELSON

WestBow Press books may be ordered through booksellers or by contacting:

WestBow Press
A Division of Thomas Nelson
1663 Liberty Drive
Bloomington, IN 47403
www.westbowpress.com
1-(866) 928-1240

ISBN: 978-1449-7-5589-8 (sc)

Library of Congress Control Number: 2012912167

Printed in the United States of America

WestBow Press rev. date: 7/30/2012

This work is dedicated
to
the many people who have
invested in the making of
this ordinary woman.

Appreciation to
Carole Bogard and Rose Butler
my friends who
encourage me every day.

Many thanks to my friend Sara Douce for editing the
manuscript.

I suppose that there will be those who will think, "Well, who is she to write a book about herself?" They have missed the point. Let me make it clear. I am absolutely nobody, and I am everybody. It's the simple people, just every day ordinary people, who make an effort to allow Jesus Christ to rule their lives who should try to help those around them along their way. Check this out in the Bible. We ordinary people make mistakes, we sin, and we have major weaknesses. But we should all strive to be a blessing to every other person as we come in contact with them. This book is part of my effort to encourage any reader with their journey through their many struggles and victories. I'm full of hope!

Part 1

FROM WHENCE I CAME

Chapter 1

My Hometown

My hometown was a beautiful town when I was growing up. I think of it now as a village. The home folks then were the "salt of the earth". Good people; hard working people; law-abiding people; church-going people.

The beautiful flowers and trimmed lawns made our town special. The mill people kept their yards mowed and trimmed, and they worked in vegetable and flower gardens ten months out of each year. I thought that this was the German in them. Years later when I spent time in Germany, I felt right at home. I enjoyed the same type of beautiful flowers and lawns. The rich folks hired yardmen who worked weekly to make sure that their employer had the prettiest yard on the block. I thought when I was little that all of America was like this. Little did I know!

The population has changed little in the almost fifty-seven years since I left there, but the make up of the population has changed. Most of the factories have closed. Downtown is very different. People now shop in the malls on the Hickory Highway. The wonderful people seem the same.

The town was so crime free that no one locked their doors. At least, the poor people didn't lock their doors. Maybe that was because they didn't have any thing worth stealing. I wasn't in the know about the rich people in town. Maybe they locked their doors. Migrant workers from the fields below our house or someone down on their luck could knock at Mom's back door on Saturday morning and offer to chop wood or fix something or pick up the apples which had fallen from the apple trees along the side of the garden. In return, Mom would cook their breakfast which they ate on the back porch. They ate like they had never tasted bacon, eggs, and biscuits before. There was no fear in helping a stranger. In the whole time I lived there, I can't remember a murder. The police mostly picked up drunks and threw them in the jail for the night to sober them up. That was it.

Newton, North Carolina, was an industrial town then. There were many factories – hosiery mills, glove mills, children's clothing mills, cotton mills spinning cotton into thread, textile mills weaving thread into cloth, furniture factories, and many others. The large majority of the population worked in these mills. Many factory workers lived in homes owned by the factory owner. These homes were on streets of white wooden houses near the mill that owned them. You had to work in that mill to have a house. We called them mill hills, although they were not necessarily on a hill. These mill workers were the "low class" of the town. Others were included in the "low class". I think anyone who had a dirty job, like the trash collectors and grease monkeys at the service stations, would be among the "low class". The store owners and employees were considered the "middle class" in Newton.

We were the county seat of Catawba County, so we had a Court House Square which was in the middle of town. On the square around the courthouse, there were about twenty-four to thirty stores. We had two pharmacies (then called drug stores), a Belks, Dellingers and Carpenters and Moritz and Smithys (locally owned department stores), two dime stores (even back then the dime stores were just a joke; hardly anything cost a dime), several very nice dress shops (Taylors and Lucy Lou's), a men's clothing store, a furniture store or two, a café, and others came and went. Some of these stores were on the side streets off the square. Of course, this was all before Walmart, Kmart, and Target built the big discount stores on Hickory Highway.

There was a group of stores in North Newton. A service station, a grocery store, a dime store, a fabric store, and a hardware store. Almost

4

everyone who lived in North Newton worked in some factory and walked to work. These stores were very convenient for these people who generally did not have a car.

The mill owners were the elite of the town. The "Upper Class". In school you could actually tell the difference by looking at the kids' clothes. Of course, they had memberships to organizations that the mill workers had never even heard of and didn't care to. They belonged to the Country Club. They lived in South Newton or in the small elitist town of Conover to the north of Newton. I remember three factory owners who lived near the schools. Their homes were the beautiful large brick homes which differed from the white clap board two story homes of the rest of the town. Cars were a real teller also. Most of the mill workers did not own cars. All mill owners had fine cars. Lawyers and physicians were considered "Upper Class" also.

There was, you might say, "A church on every corner." Within a mile of the Court House square on Main Street alone there was a Baptist church, a Methodist church, a Reform church, a Lutheran church, and a Presbyterian church. I don't know if it was a fact or something I felt, but I think most of the town was Lutheran. However, there were Southern Baptist, Free Will Baptist, Pentecostal Holiness, Methodist, Presbyterian, and many churches representing denominations I had never heard of. Most of the church buildings were large and beautiful. St. Paul's Lutheran Church, the second oldest church in the state, is just outside Newton.

My Southern Baptist Church at that time was one block off the Court House Square. It was crunched in between the town's only fire station and a China shop. It was a red brick structure with gorgeous stained glass windows. Every time I entered the church I took care to study the beautiful windows and remembered the Bible stories which they represented. I've lived in many places and traveled extensively, and I've never seen more beautiful windows than those in my little home church. When a new building was built on the bypass, I don't know what happened to those gorgeous windows. In church, it was hard to tell the classes apart. Of course, the mill people wore their Sunday best to church. School was a different story.

Newton was located on the western edge of the Piedmont section of North Carolina. We were in the foothills, maybe twenty miles from real mountains which we could see in the distance. I loved the hills. It was like they spoke to me; today they still do. Living in Florida now forty-four years, I can truthfully say that there has not passed a day that I haven't thought of the beautiful North Carolina mountains. When I've had the chance to go back, I always remember the scripture, "I will lift up mine eyes unto the hills, from whence cometh my help. My help cometh from the Lord, which made heaven and earth." Psalm 121:1 There is no wonder that I did so well my first four years in college in those hills. The water is different in the hills. The beauty around you inspires you. The very air is different. The word that comes to mind is "heavenly".

A neat thing about Newton which I didn't realize when I was living there was that we had the four seasons. Every winter we enjoyed a snow or two. When I was little, Daddy would carry me on his back when it snowed, and sometimes my feet would drag the snow. So the snow was rather deep at times. By the time everyone was cursing the snow and the mess which followed it, we would see the crocuses popping through with their beautiful yellows and purples. We knew then that the tulips and daffodils of spring would follow. There was a definite spring with warming weather and many flowering trees such as dogwood and pear and apple and cherry. As the weather warmed, the town would seemingly come back to life. Summer would usually be a steamer with showers many afternoons. The yards would come alive, and the gardens gave us much of what we ate. We, the people I knew, did not have air-conditioning, but maybe a fan which moved from room to room as we moved, carrying a rag to mop the sweat. By the end of July everyone was tired of the heat of summer. But at the end of August, autumn began. This was the most beautiful time of the year. The town had hundreds of sugar maples which turned red, yellow, and orange. The gums turned red. People would walk by the school and other places to see the leaves. People who had cars would invite Mom and me to ride up into the mountains on Sunday afternoons just to see the leaves. I still miss this change of seasons.

We had a library and a newspaper and plenty of grocery stores. Of course, we had a post office and a jail.

There were only two school buildings in town. The large and beautiful elementary school was a three-story building with the best auditorium and stage you could find any where in those parts. The high school building which housed the middle school and the high school was right across the street. It was crowded in the fifties when I was a student.

This area of the country has its own special language. I have jokingly named this language Newtonian. I don't think that I can write the words. After I permanently left my hometown, I would return yearly. Mom would say, "K'Dean, you better go down to the gas station to get some gas. It's about nighttime." No, you can't hear it in my writing. They pronounce the long " a" and the long "i" in a drawn out flat kind of way in the bottom of their mouths. I would immediately fall back into their speech patterns as soon as I walked back into my mother's house. If I forgot and used my own adopted language, Mom would point out that I was trying to act high-flutin'. Once my cousin and her husband visited when I was home at Mom's house. She had started teaching. Something came up about when it was appropriate to send a misbehaving student to the office. I responded to her question. Her husband howled and said, "Listen. All that college, and she can't say "awfice". He was making fun of the way I pronounced the word "office".

On the way back to my home, I could easily switch back to my own dialect. When I was assistant principal of a large high school on the beach near Jacksonville, Florida, a secretary was assigned to make the announcements first thing in the morning. Occasionally she would have an appointment or be running late, so the principal would tell me (the only female administrator) to make the morning announcements. Invariably, as I patrolled the hallways after making the announcements, several kids would point out to me, "Hey, Ms. McCaffrey, you sound like a Hill Billy on the speaker." At first I was taken aback by these observations. But I learned to smile and reply, "That's because I AM a Hill Billy." A Hill Billy is really a person who speaks the language of Billy Shakespeare and lives in the hills. Yep, I am surely a Hill Billy.

Newton was and is a special place. No matter how many places I live or how long I stay away, I will always remain proud of the education I got there in the schools and in my church. Although I was able to dodge the factories, I know that the factories were a major part of the town and that the mill workers were among the finest people on this earth. The town has traditions which provide sweet memories. I will always remember with fondness the wonderful people who grew me. They were caring, loving souls who nurtured me beyond belief. I would have a very thick book if I tried to list the names of these nurturing saints. I have spent my whole life making sure that these people were not disappointed in me.

Chapter 2

My Father

My father was a good-looking German. He looked like Alan Ladd, only taller. He had a wonderful personality. Every body liked my dad. His thinking was ahead of his time. He seemed to be in the wrong place at the wrong time. He knew it, but he didn't let that bother him.

His father had left his mother with seven children, and Dad was the oldest. Interestingly Grandma had a boy, five girls, and then another boy. First was my dad, then Dorthola called Bid, then Thelma, Mary, Blanche (my favorite), Lola, and then Uncle Ed, a very spoiled baby son.

The family left Virginia to come to North Carolina and settled in the mountains near North Wilkesboro. Grandma made and sold moonshine and worked as a mid-wife. From these proceeds she fed herself and seven children. Of course, it was imperative for each child to quit school as soon as possible to help with the work. My dad finished the seventh grade. Around that time at age twelve he was on the back of a truck carrying family made moon shine out of the mountains when Revenuers began chasing them. Dad was bumped off the back of the truck and rolled down the mountainside. They found him the next morning with a broken leg. Grandma set his swollen leg and didn't do such a great job. Dad's broken leg was from then on about one inch shorter than the other. When I first saw the movie "Thunder Road", I was shocked. The movie is exactly how I had imagined the environment where my dad grew up.

If you watched my dad walk on most days, you couldn't tell that he had a problem leg. So this didn't bother my daddy, until he wanted to go into the army in World War II like all the other guys, but he was declared 4F because of his leg. So Dad left home and spent three years living in Wilmington, building ships for the war.

He was already grown when he moved with his family to Newton.

He immediately found a job at Burlington Industries which turned out to be a great decision. He worked himself up to being a Weave Teacher. He taught many young men to thread the looms, repair the looms, and to work hard. All of these young men loved my dad and felt beholding to him. Dad was sent to Mexico one whole year to help open another textile plant for Burlington Industries. Another year he was sent to Red Springs, North Carolina to help man a new factory. His employers wanted to send him to England for a year. He didn't go, but I don't know why.

Among her many skills, my grandmother Hester (Dessie) made wine, brandy, and white light'ning. She not only used her own products, but taught her children to drink from an early age. She also sold the stuff. I don't remember ever seeing my grandmother that she wasn't smiling. I'm not sure whether the alcohol had any effect on her good-nature. This never sat well with my mom who had brothers and a father who drank, but she herself was a teetotaler. She brazenly emptied every bottle she found into the red clay of our back yard. It's a miracle that our back yard didn't have a permanent problem with alcoholism. Surely my dad did.

Yes, my dad surely had a thirst for alcohol. But the thing I remember most about my dad was his thirst for knowledge. He should have lived in the computer age. He would have sat at the computer all of his spare time. I can see him now getting excited about something he was learning and drinking his whiskey out of a Mason jar...until Mom came home from work.

Dad worked the third shift (11 PM – 7 AM) his whole life. He would reach home, eat a plate of eggs covered with ketchup, some kind of meat, home made biscuits, and coffee. Then he would sleep till around 2 PM. Mom would reach home around five. So Dad had about three hours a day to do his thing. His thing was to read. He read about fourteen books a week.

When I was home, he would bargain with me, promising some great treat IF I would be quiet, so he could read. This forced me to read also because I wanted to please Dad, and reading was a quiet activity. This developed into my love of reading which is still with me today. Mom didn't believe in drinking carbonated drinks. So frequently Dad would take me to Lingerfelt's grocery just up the street to get a RC Cola and a moon pie when he finished a book. This was heaven – having Daddy's attention, having the treat, but most of all, having the secret with my dad.

On every Saturday, Dad would take me to town. The library was then in a two story house on the Court House square. There were doctors' offices down stairs. There was an outside staircase to the second floor where a lady in town had started a library. Daddy wouldn't go up those steps. No, it wasn't because of the steep stairs and his leg. It was because Daddy hated the wonderful lady who ran the library. Daddy's real name was Elza Delmore Hester. I can't imagine where Grandma found such a name. The librarian drank a lot. She frequently would have been stumbling around by noon. She loved Daddy. The problem was that she called him Elsie. Daddy hated that, so he would send me up the steps with a huge brown paper bag of returned books. This began when I was about five, so dragging that bag was a big chore. On top of the bag Daddy always placed a list of books I was to bring back down the steps. He sat on the bottom steps waiting anxiously, like I was bringing him a bag of hundred dollar bills. The librarian would find the books, and no doubt she would sign the card Elsie. She would walk me to the door, help me out, and scream in her loudest alcoholic voice, "Good afternoon, Elsie. Enjoy all those books". Daddy would cringe, and I would look down all those steps and wonder how I could get that heavy bag of books down to Daddy. Some days I had to make several trips. Daddy was always patient with me. We were like two bank robbers out on a spree.

Daddy also belonged to a book club. I remember vividly how

excited he would be to open the packages of books. I still have some of those books. He read Chekov's plays, all of Steinbeck, Hemingway, and Faulkner. Of course, Zane Grey was a favorite. The day *For Whom the Bell Tolls* arrived in the mail, I saw the excitement in Daddy's face as he pulled the book out of the package. He was sitting in a rocking chair on the front porch. He pulled me right in front of him and made his bargain, "Kitty, if you will give me three hours to finish this book, I'll treat you to a big surprise." He lay down on a metal glider in the side yard under a huge oak tree. I grabbed a book and climbed onto the lowest limb of that tree to read. I could see Daddy as he enjoyed his book. The treat was that he took me to a baseball game that night. I know for sure that Daddy never dreamed of being a character in this book. Somehow I figure that he is smiling as I write. I am glad that he doesn't have to deal with the fact that books are going out of style.

Many days Daddy would move from the bed in the house out to a metal glider in the side yard. I didn't know anyone who had air-conditioning, so the bedroom would get steamy hot in the afternoon. About noon he would make his move without interrupting his sleep with talk. Usually there was a cool breeze in the side yard. If he slept past two hours, I felt that it was my responsibility to wake him up. I could have yelled, "Daddy! It's time for you to get up." But I was a creative, nature-loving child, so I would catch a June bug. A June bug looks like a huge cockroach, but he can fly. I would tie a string to his leg. There lay Dad on his stomach in his jeans exposing his full bare back. I would set the bug near his belt and pull the string till the bug was forced to walk up his back. That always worked to wake him wide awake. He always said the same thing when I did this, "That wasn't funny, Kitty." But it was funny. It was hilarious.

With all of his good looks, fun-loving ways, many interests, and intelligence, Daddy had habits which were beyond Mom's comprehension. Daddy loved to shoot pool. Some Saturdays he would leave the mill at seven in the morning and go straight to the pool room. He would drink liquor and shoot pool until Mom would go "show herself", screaming for him to get out of there and get home. He also loved to gamble. A woman in town had poker and pinochle games going in her home twenty-four hours a day seven days a week. Daddy loved to gamble there. Frequently he would lose a week's wages before he left. My thought has always been if you are good at gambling and win on a consistent basis, then gamble. If you begin to lose, quit. Dad had no such insight. I knew then that insight is not always available to those with habits.

Daddy helped very little with the expenses of the family. He bought a couple of pieces of furniture. Mom paid for the rest. Most Saturdays Daddy would take us out to eat, but Mom paid for all of the groceries. Mom saved and paid cash for our first house when I was about three. Daddy gambled and bought liquor and helped his mom.

He never owned a car, which was a good thing. We walked everywhere. It was sixteen blocks to the library, seven blocks to school, and fourteen blocks to church. All of my life in Newton I walked these distances every week many times. I never thought of there being life on the southern side of the courthouse square. I was about nine when Daddy almost died. He had an appendectomy at the hospital in south Newton. They gave him ether when he had a cold. He developed pneumonia, so they rocked his bed for about three weeks. My Uncle Carl and other relatives who had cars drove Mom and me to visit Dad every day. We drove through South Newton, a real adventure for me. People actually lived south of the courthouse.

Dad was a sweet drunk. He was never mean or violent. That didn't matter to Mom. His drinking drove Mom crazy. When I was about five, Daddy showed up one day "drunk as a skunk". He was staggering and drooling and slurring his words. He staggered to his rocking chair between his radio and the laundry heater (a stove, used to heat the room, which had a flat top where you could keep things like kettles of hot water). He fell asleep and began to fall toward the heater. I ran over to him to push him back in his chair. He was heavy. It was very sad to see my dad like this. Mom grabbed me away from him and said, "No, no, let him burn. He'll get a taste of hell." I was too young to understand her anger, but I knew that no matter what my daddy did, I loved him. Years later, alcoholism was accepted as a disease. Then he was just considered a sot.

By the age of seven, I began to realize the mismatched marriage that I was a result of. Dad loved his liquor and his cards. Mom hated these things and was frustrated with Dad because he wouldn't change. In those days the prevalent belief was that you could change a person by being a good example and praying for them. Mom believed these precepts and was always frustrated by my daddy's refusal to change. Once he didn't drink or gamble for three years. Ordinarily Dad wore black leather boots, a black leather jacket, jeans, and a dress shirt. Mom bought him two beautiful suits. Dad and Mom attended church every Sunday during that wonderful three years. Mom was so happy that she smiled all the time.

Dad loved ball of any kind. We had a great stadium in Newton. Years after Dad was gone, the Yankees had a training school in Newton in the spring and summer. Dad organized a baseball team at work and asked other mills to organize teams, so that they actually had a mill league. This was before any Little League or stuff like that was heard of. Dad took me to games. He also tossed the ball around with me in the side yard as Mom screamed, "She's a girl. She's not supposed to be playing boys' games." This was another of my mom's beliefs that she stuck to till the day she died. Now that I'm grown I wonder if Dad yearned for a son because I was not only a girl, but I was really a klutz. I wanted to be the best pitcher, the best catcher, and the best runner. I just wasn't. Daddy pretended not to notice. His patience was amazing.

Finally it happened! When I was ten, I came home from a piano lesson. Little did I know that this day was to become the saddest day of my whole life. Mom said, "Sit down and eat!" I could tell that she was beyond angry about something. I asked, "Aren't we going to wait for Daddy?" She turned from the stove, ran across the kitchen, and screamed at me, "He is gone. Don't you ever mention his name in this house again." The pupils of her eyes appeared to be bright red, and her body was trembling from the top of her head to the bottom of her feet. I was more than scared. I put the food into my mouth, but it stayed there. I couldn't swallow. I didn't want Mom to beat me when she was this angry, but I felt that it was coming. She left the room and didn't come back until after Aunt Lola brought Daddy to the front door. She had a car. Daddy got his clothes and the radio and left without a word. Thank goodness, he didn't take the piano which he had bought for me when I was six. Mother came to the kitchen door and told me to stay in the kitchen, so I didn't get to see Dad. I wanted to ask him if he was taking me with him. I began slowly to understand that he was gone, and I was left with a very hurt mother. All of the fun and excitement left my life when he walked out of that front door. It was eight years before I began to recover....to truly smile again.

This was all a mixed bag for me. I was very happy that Dad had escaped. I understood why he left Mother, but why did he leave me? He left mother's restrictions, her screaming, and her constant efforts to turn him into something he couldn't or wouldn't be. Aunt Lola drove him to a boarding house Grandma Hester was running in the Burlington Industries mill village in Marion, a town about thirty miles away. He might as well have moved to China.

Daddy sent money every month for a couple of years for me, but no matter how she struggled, Mom sent the money back. Every year for five years Daddy sent Christmas presents to Mom and to me. She sent them back unopened. The sixth year Mom was not home when the package came. I opened it. Dad had sent me a red sweater (it fit) and an amethyst ring (my birthstone). I still have these items today. It caused such a stir in the family that Dad never sent another package.

I saw Daddy three times after he left. I also paid the price. One Saturday as I was stocking at the dime store where I worked in downtown Newton when I was fourteen, Daddy and Aunt Blanche walked up, and we talked briefly. As soon as I got home, Mother was ready with the belt. The more I refused to cry, the harder she hit. She beat me until she was exhausted and had to quit. I was badly bruised. The next morning she didn't want me to go to church. I went anyway.

When I was a sophomore in High School, Marion High School played Newton-Conover in football. I went to the game. At the half time, I went to the concession stand. I was standing in line when someone tapped me on my shoulder and said, "Hey, you!". I turned to see Daddy smiling. We talked the rest of half time. When I got home, Mother was waiting with the belt. Some nosey person had already called her. No matter how many times she hit me, I refused to move or to cry because I knew for sure that I did not deserve to be beaten for talking to my daddy.

When I went to Mars Hill, I went home one weekend. A friend drove me back to school on Sunday afternoon. We had to go within a block of Daddy's house in Marion. We stopped to see him. He had remarried and had a two-year old son. He came to the front porch, and we talked again briefly. He told me that he was proud of me. That one remark from my daddy seemed like riches given to me from a real King. When I reached Mars Hill, I went to the mountainside behind the dorm and thanked God that Mother was not there to beat me. I knew that my seeing Daddy hurt Mother. It was one of the saddest parts of my life that I never learned to handle.

For years I idolized Daddy which placed a great divide between my mother and me. She could not understand my feelings for my dad. She had no memories of good times with her own dad. I put Daddy on a pedestal and actually worshiped him. Of course, I was careful never to mention his name in front of Mother because that was her rule. This was my secret, but she could tell. Her own brothers and sisters discussed him freely with me when Mother was not around. Mother's neighbors did the same. Mother told me so often that I was nothing but a damn Hester. This meant that I was like my daddy. She said it so often that I had to teach myself not to show the hurt because I knew that she meant it in a mean way. I began thinking to myself, "Thank you, God." Frequently I was told that I was just like my father by the people in town who knew him. They meant it as a compliment. Thank God I had the insight to differentiate between the two.

I awoke one morning when I was twenty-eight with what I initially thought was a nightmare, but when I was fully awake I realized it was a vision. It was a man in a casket. I could only see his chin down to where the bottom part of the casket covered his lower body. He seemed to be in his early to mid fifties. I could see his hands clearly. I slipped out of bed and went downstairs in the cold to wait for six o'clock. At six o'clock every morning my husband's father got up and read the newspaper. My father-in-law and I had a good relationship. I called and asked, "Dad, are you okay?" He seemed fine. I thought I was going crazy.

About four that afternoon, Mother called and asked to speak to Jack, my husband. She despised Jack, so I thought this very strange. She told him to stay by the phone that she had some news which would upset me. Jack was very dark with that Pembroke (a branch of the Lumbee and eventually declared part of the Cherokee Nation) Indian blood flowing through his veins. When he handed me the phone, he was snow white. As he handed me the phone, my mind ripped through the list of mother's brothers, for I already knew a man had died. Mother said with no feeling at all, "Kitty, your father died this morning at four o'clock."

Daddy had a valve to close on his heart as he stood at Burlington Industries teaching a young man to thread the loom. He was fifty-four, way too young to die. But fifty-four years of smoking five packs of Old Golds and drinking daily probably tallied in at seventy-five to eighty years. How I wish I had been with him more in my adulthood!

I attended his funeral against Mother's wishes. As soon as I heard he was dead, I headed out of Raleigh to Newton, three hours away. Jack wouldn't do funerals, so I drove alone. Maybe this was the reason he gave our babies to research centers. Along the way, I repeated in my mind the events of the morning. I should have known it was Dad because being a weave teacher, Dad kept his nails and cuticles perfect. He never had a hangnail or imperfection of the cuticle because it would have hindered his work.

When I got to Newton, Mother began screaming at me that I was not to go to the funeral. I was determined to go. There was snow on the ground. She used that as a reason I shouldn't go. She said that my presence would cause trouble. She went on and on with invalid reasons. She kept saying she wouldn't let me drive alone. She said that I was too upset. So I told her to stop it. I was going. This was rare; I never stood up to my mother. But now I was twenty-eight years old. Enough was enough! I announced that I would ask Aunt Helen to go with me. Finally Mother and I left for the funeral.

Mother insisted that I sit near the back of the church. I told her to take a seat. Then I marched up that aisle alone to see my dad in that casket. I didn't think I could do it. But I did. As I looked down at Daddy, I saw myself lying there. I knew that simply having his blood flowing through my veins was an honor and a hardship. Daddy was so very laid back, always rolling with the punches. I'm not sure that he knew the punches existed. He had his mind in a book most of the time and in a bottle the rest of the time. At times he balanced the two at once. My mom was so opposite. She worried about everything. She was uptight about everything in her life. I never saw her relaxed. When she saw a challenge, she attacked it with super energy. With the genes of these two in me, it's no wonder that I have such an uncontrollable personality. It's very important that I trust in God who guides me.

The family hadn't come in. The church was in Marion, Daddy's town. The church was packed. Although Dad had left Newton eighteen years before, half the church was filled with people from Newton which hurt Mother. When the funeral was over, one of the three Workman boys who had been our neighbors in Newton ran out and told Aunt Blanche that I was there. She came back into the church to get me to go to the graveside. Mother was emphatic that I would not go to the graveside. One of the Workman boys told me to go on. They brought Mom and let her sit in their car.

This was the first time and last time I ever saw Virginia, my little sister. She looked like a little Kitty. It was the second time I saw my brother, Joey. He was about twelve. My heart cried for them. Now Joey and I talk about once a year on the phone.

People told me so much that I was just like Daddy that the year I was fifty-four, I tippy-toed around all year. I moved very carefully. I knew that I would die before the end of the year. He didn't have a gray hair in his head when he died. I was sad because I was sure that I wouldn't have gray hair like old women have. I believed strongly that when all my hair turned gray that I would become elegant. It would be proof that I had earned a seat in the rocking chair on the front porch. Little did I know that folks wouldn't even have big front porches or rocking chairs by the time I was old. This ruined my plan for retirement.

It was not until about 1984 when I was in my fifties that it hit me. It hit me so hard that I had to pull the car into a gas station and vomit. I had taken eight days intensive training in Substance Abuse Prevention taught by faculty members of the Miami Medical School at the Blue Ridge Assembly grounds right outside Asheville, North Carolina (my beautiful hills). I was working with a group of Duval County School Personnel to start a Substance Abuse Prevention Program for the Duval County Schools.

Later the same year a group of educators from Glenbeigh Institute came to the University of North Florida to do more training. I was sent for a three-day study. The first day we had a three hour session in the afternoon about one's place in the family unit. I had never heard this information before.

On the way home I stopped and sat for an hour on the side of a gas station thinking about my family. I had been idolizing a scoundrel. Daddy was a sot (common word back then), a non-believer, a gambler who contributed almost nothing to the welfare of our family. He was a dead-beat Dad right there in our own home sleeping with my mother. I can only remember a couple of encouraging words he ever gave me. This brilliant man threw away a loving wife and child. He did not use the fine mind which God provided him, but threw it into a bottle of booze. All the good wages he made, he gambled away. Oh, Daddy, what a waste! I sobbed for hours. No, I may look like him, but I'm not like him. That's not me. How have I come to be me? I'm not sure, but I have some ideas.

Don't get me wrong. I will always love my daddy, simply because he's my daddy. I'll never forget his patience and his way of bargaining to get his way. He rarely showed that he was actually the boss. He treated me like a pal. I wanted to cooperate with him. Oh, yes, I wanted to please my dad. I will always treasure the time I had with him. I also greatly appreciate the traits he passed on to me. They are some of my best traits.

I thank God everyday that I have been able to take these traits to a different level than my dad was able to do. So often I used Daddy's approach of behavior control when I found myself telling my students, "This lesson will be hard today, but if you try and do a good job, we will read a good play tomorrow." That was Daddy's method of bargaining, a great behavior management tool. Dad had never heard the song from *Sound of Music* which says, "A spoon full of sugar makes the medicine go down", but he certainly understood it. Other teachers often questioned me about why my students liked me and how I had so few discipline problems. I never tried to explain that I was using my dad's skills of bargaining in the classroom. It would have been too hard to explain.

Yes, I love him dearly, but I no longer have him on a pedestal. He's no longer my idol.

Chapter 3

Father's Family

Dessie Hester was a character. She was very dark complected, with black hair and dark eyes. She seemed to be a Cherokee, but she was German through and through and proud of it. Back then being German stood for cleanliness, honesty, hard working, and smart. This was before the Austrian madman took over Germany and almost destroyed the world.

She supported herself and her family in many ways. She never took a hand out from welfare. I don't know that there was such a thing back then. As already said, Grandma made and sold alcoholic beverages and was a midwife. When the family moved to Newton, her house was on the street behind the street we lived on. There was a path between her backyard and our backyard, a real shortcut. I wasn't allowed to go to Grandma's house. One day when I was three I slipped off and made my way to Grandma's. She was so happy to see me. She laughed and laughed at my adventurous nature. Mother found me there, broke a switch from a bush, and switched my legs all the way home. The path was well-worn simply because my dad went to see his mom every day.

Across the street from my house there was a huge CCC Camp. President Franklin Delano Roosevelt set up these camps for young men whose families could not afford to feed them. These camps were part of the Civilian Conservation Corps section of his New Deal. Research shows that these boys planted trees, built parks, drained swamps. and restocked rivers. Each boy was paid $1.00 per day and given free board and job training. I don't know what the boys did in Newton, but I know there were lots of them. They lived in Newton for about three or four years. Some of them married Newton girls.

Grandma Hester got a contract to do their laundry. This was before washers and dryers existed as we know them today. Washing was soaking these clothes in tubs set up on benches, scrubbing them on a washboard, throwing them in a tub of rinse water, and wringing the water out by hand. Drying was hanging them to dry on the line, and then ironing them. This was for more than a hundred young men. It took Grandma a better part of a week to service this job. I never saw anyone helping her. I never saw a frown on her face nor did I hear a complaint come from her lips. I did see her reddened hands, and I watched her lather tons of lotion on those hands when she finished.

When I was five, Mother was forced for a while to leave me with Grandma Hester during the day because Grandma Hendrix was sick. My cousin Barbara Jean, Jimmy Stokes, and several other kids played house or doctor under her high back porch within her sight as she did the laundry. What fun to play with my cousins and neighborhood friends!

Finally Grandma got a job living with and taking care of an elderly Waldensian couple in Valdese, North Carolina. This little town is in the mountains at the very bottom of the Blue Ridge. It had been settled in the nineteenth century by a group of Waldensians from the hills of northern Italy. This elderly couple was called No No (which means Grandmother) and Bo Bo (which means Grandfather). Two summers they invited me to spend the summer with Grandma there at their house. Mother let me because she had no one to take care of me while she worked. They had grown children who had families and lived on the same street. These children ran the town and the wonderful Waldensian bakery which was located on Main Street and caused the whole town to smell like fresh baked bread. It was a delight to go to the bakery and get a loaf of unsliced bread straight out of the oven. This was Sunbeam bread. My Aunt Bid lived across the street. She had a daughter, Barbara Jean, a few years older than I. Aunt Bid and her husband owned a restaurant on Main Street. The street where they lived was right behind the Main Street.

At the end of the second summer staying there in that wonderful place, Bo Bo and No No gave me a collie puppy. I named him Bo Bo to Bo Bo's delight. This was a wonderful dog. But he was a bad dog, and Mom hated him. He loved chasing her chickens. This angered her. After all, she raised chickens for the eggs and the meat. After growing up and looking back, I have wondered why she didn't have those chickens in a pen rather than running around the yard. She gave Bo-Bo away. It broke my heart.

Eventually Grandma began running a Boarding House in Marion. Although I never saw her during this time, there's no doubt in my mind that Grandma did a good job running this establishment.

When she was on her death bed, she sent for Mother. As much as Mother hated my grandma, she asked someone to drive her to the hospital. Grandma asked her daughters to leave the room, so Mother and Grandma had a private talk. Mother did not let me know that Grandma was sick or that she died. I was married and living in Raleigh, so I knew nothing about this until after Grandma had died and was buried. She had cancer, but the doctors said that she died of Bright's Disease (a kidney disease).

The situation between my grandma and my mother was a good example of major differences in their upbringing. Both were smart, strong women who worked hard. But there was no understanding between them. I suspect that neither of them tried.

I remember Grandma Hester with pleasant thoughts and attribute my sense of humor (without the alcohol) to her. I can still see her face smiling as she worked. What a jolly woman with a hard life!

I only saw Grandpa Hester once. He came to Newton to see his children. He came to our house on a Saturday morning to see Daddy who was asleep. Mother had a small tub of water on the kitchen table and was bathing me. I must have been young – maybe three. I felt the cold air on my wet body before I saw who had opened the door. Of course, I had no idea who this man was. I just knew that I was so embarrassed that a man was seeing me naked. When Mother told me that he was my grandfather, I didn't care. I wanted him to go away.

He came to the tub and flicked water up into my face. After that he disappeared into never-never land, never to be seen again.

When Daddy left, he had two sisters living in the rural area near Newton. I was not allowed to see them. However, they decided to give me China and Crystal every Christmas. Some Christmases I would receive one covered vegetable bowl. Some Christmases I would receive five water glasses – one from each aunt. Actually at ten I didn't understand why they would give me such gifts. Mom was not happy about the gifts, but she allowed me to accept them. By the time I was eighteen and had a closet full of boxes of these gifts, I realized their significance. They were saying, "We remember you with fondness." Later I realized that no one I knew had China and Crystal. They were saying, "We expect you to have a better life than we have had." I felt obligated to live up to that expectation. And I have. These dishes are in the China cabinet in the dining room as I write this book.

In adulthood I visited some of these aunts. After I moved away, every time I went back home to see Mother, I would drive out to see Aunt Mary. She was a wonderful woman. Everyone said that I looked just like her. She wanted children and had many miscarriages before she finally had a girl and then a boy. She and Uncle Dwight lived in an old farm house which had been his parents' home place. I enjoyed visits to see Aunt Mary and Uncle Dwight. Every visit was special and thought back on many times afterward. She had the best sense of humor I've ever known, and I believed that she inherited that from her mother. Once many years after Aunt Mary had died, I was walking through a mall in Hickory. A young woman rushed up to me and said, "Are you Kitty?" By the time I answered, "Yes," she had my hand and was pulling me across the Mall. We reached a dark complected young man who was white as snow. He could hardly speak. He finally said, "Do you know who I am?" I responded, "Of course, I know who you are. You look exactly like your daddy." And he said, "And you look exactly like my mother." It was Mac, Aunt Mary's boy. His wife told me that he saw me, and at first he thought that I was his mother although his mother had been dead for years.

Vicki, Aunt Mary's daughter, married and moved to Raleigh when I lived there. We were together some, and she always reminded me that I looked like her mother. I like to think that I have Aunt Mary's sense of humor also. Sometimes when I get tickled and begin laughing, I think of her.

Aunt Blanche was the person in Dad's family that I could talk with the easiest. She moved to Miami with her family. I visited her several weekends and enjoyed learning to know her. She had a wonderful family with a loving husband and three children – a boy and two beautiful girls. Aunt Blanche was a delightful person and encouraged me every time I saw her. Once she saw a Hester woman who was Kenny Rogers's mother on Oprah. She wrote to this woman and found that she was her first cousin. Aunt Blanche was very excited that we're kin to Kenny Rogers. Who would have dreamed?

Aunt Blanche had been living up North when she met and married Charlie Hagopian, an Armenian. He and his brother saved every penny till they had enough to move to Miami, Florida, to open a chain of laundromats. After a few years, they purchased some swamp land, drained it, and built a mall. Finally Charlie and Aunt Blanche opened a Fedders franchise which serviced air conditioners and heaters all over Dade County and surrounding counties. The big hotels kept them busy.

They purchased a ranchette in Davies and had horses, goats, and rabbits. When we visited, Uncle Charlie spent a lot of time with my boys riding horses and playing with the other animals. He gave each boy a rabbit to bring home on one visit.

I also visited Uncle Ed who lived in Marion. Uncle Ed was the baby and was very spoiled. It took him a long time to grow up, simply because he was so smothered. He finally married a good woman who had a daughter. She seemed to be perfect for him. He and his family were very kind to me.

Daddy's family began poor as poor can be. Grandma was hardworking, but barely struggled through. But she gave her children the courage to persevere and the ability to make a joke about any and every thing. Laughter is therapeutic, you know. She gave them the courage to hold their heads high and keep going. This side of my family was very important in the making of Kitty McCaffrey. I didn't get to see them much since I was only ten when Daddy left, but their genes speak to me daily.

$Chapter\ 4$

My Mother

Mary Louisa was a pretty woman. Although she had the beautiful name Louisa, no one knew because she was always called Louise, even by her mother. Although her weight was up and down, she was basically petite in stature more than half her life. She had beautiful hair, especially when it turned pure white when she was about twenty-five. Her nails were perfect. Mother's skin was free of blemish even in her eighties. She would sigh as she told me that I had "Hester skin". I knew that I had "Hester skin" , and I knew that she was saying something unpleasant to me.

Mother was always careful about her appearance. She didn't really have the money for clothes. It was fortunate that she could sew. Not only could she sew, but she could look at a picture, then cut out a pattern of the dress she was looking at, cut the material (frequently flour sacks), and sew the dress. She could hang the dress, freshly ironed, on the closet door ready to wear in a few hours. So she had nice looking clothes. She always had a "store-boughten" dress for Sunday.

Lucy Lou had been a classmate of Mom's. She owned the nicest dress shop in town. Women from many towns around would come to her shop to buy their clothes. Most of the women in Newton couldn't afford to buy any thing in her shop. She would send for Mom and tell her to look at this dress or that dress. Then she would give Mom a stack of old fashion magazines. Mom would look at those dresses and copy them. Lucy Lou had a knack for fashion, and she taught my mom like Mom was a student.

Sadly, my mother didn't fit into her family. Grandpa was strict German – a no nonsense man. Actually he was a mean little man. My grandma was half Dutch and half German. Mother was the spitting image of her paternal aunts. She had a fiery temper and didn't think a split second about telling you off. All seven of the other children in the family were just like Grandma's Dutch side of the family. Mother didn't get along with any of her siblings. She would do more for the women at the mill than for her own sisters. Something bad would happen to Mom, and she would become bitter dwelling on the unfairness of it forever. Talking to Mom about anything would mean listening repeatedly to her grudges.

Mom had many ridiculously cruel things happen to her through her life. She would be hurt; then came the anger. She couldn't let go of either.

Eventually the hurt and the anger became bitterness that never went away. So sad! There were no group meetings to attend, no books to read about such feelings, no professionals to talk to. Of course, I was handy. She often took her frustrations out on me. Most of the time I stood still during the beatings and closed my eyes. Most of the adults back then spanked or beat their kids. Mother was an expert punisher. The most amazing thing about these constant punishments was that early in life I realized that many of my punishments had nothing to do with me or my behavior. It was just something that my mom needed to do. How I knew this, I don't know. It was a "God thing"! Knowing this helped the pain like a soothing salve.

It was two years after they were married that I was born. It wasn't like a teenage girl showing her immaturity by having a baby. Mother had definitely thought through her feelings. She often told me that she had not wanted children. This was very, very rare thinking back then. Of course, I began wondering why I was on earth. I knew nothing about sex or using protection then, so I didn't understand how I got into this family where I was not wanted.

When I was a young adult, I studied a religion which believed in reincarnation. Their idea was that a baby along with the help of sages was allowed to pick a family on earth where they would be placed. The child was to pick a family where they could learn things which would make them better with each life. If this was true, I wondered why I had chosen this mother and father. What was I to learn from this experience? Was I learning what I needed to learn?

Mother worked at the Newton Glove Mill which was just a few blocks from our house. She sewed gloves. She was blind in one eye, but she didn't let that bother her. I understand that she was one of the fastest sewers in the mill. The mill was owned by one of my grandfather's friends.

Grandpa Hendrix was working building roadways when the Great Depression hit. Of course, they stopped building roadways, so Grandpa was out of a job. There were eight children in the family. The older four were married and had children of their own. Mother was number five. The younger three were too young to work. Mother was in the eleventh grade which was the senior year at that time. She was so near finishing highschool that the local furniture store which gave cedar chests to all of the graduates gave her a chest. She used it till she died, and I still have it.

The school house had burned when Mom was beginning high school, and the classes were held around town wherever a space could be found. When the new building was finished, Mother's class planted the beautiful maple trees around the edge of the school yard. She mentioned this often, so I believe that at the time she was vested in her education. I believe that finishing high school was probably the first goal she had.

She was working a couple of hours a day at the glove mill after school. Grandpa made her quit school a couple of months before she was to finish. He made her go to work full time in the Glove Mill. Mother resented this her whole life. She grew up believing that if you do good and follow the ten commandments, every thing in your life will be good. She couldn't bring herself to even think that being able to have this job was fortunate. All she could think about was that this was unfair. It was unfair. About mid-way through my life, I learned that fair is only something that comes to town in the fall. I wish I had known that when Mom was alive because she dwelt on not having her diploma her whole life. She became bitter distancing herself from educated people. She didn't like writing me letters because she said that my penmanship was better than hers. It was. So what? She had several opportunities to finish high school, but she never had the courage to grab the chance. I've heard the phrase "wallowing in your own misery". Yes, that was what Mom dwelt on her entire life. Witnessing this inability to grab either of several opportunities to finish high school although she wanted it so much caused me to know that I would never turn down an opportunity to learn. If I have passed up an opportunity, I don't realize it. My willingness came from God. It wasn't easy to grab these opportunities. It was often hard, very hard.

So she worked fifty-five years for the Glove Mill. When she retired, the President of the company (by then the mill was owned by a big corporation up north) flew to Newton and took Mother out to dinner. After the meal, he presented Mother with her lump sum retirement which she invested.

Mother may not have had a diploma, but she was very smart. She worked hard and saved and paid cash for two homes during her life. Except for the very rich, few people can say that they paid cash for a home. She had good taste and purchased beautiful furniture. She bought sterling silver and stored it. She had nice China and Crystal just like the rich folks. These things were not gifts. She always paid cash for every thing she bought. She saved and paid cash for a car. I tried to explain to her that paying cash up front was not always good. She couldn't bring herself to believe me, although her own experiences gave her grief at times.

During the war when Daddy went to Wilmington to build ships, Mother had it hard as most of the women in our little town did. The male population of the town existed of boys under seventeen and old disabled men. We had to have ration books to buy sugar or oil or gas. Things made of anything rubber or metal or nylon were not available. Mom used her ration book to buy sugar which she stockpiled for Christmas. At Christmas she made cookies and candy for everyone. But this meant that we didn't have anything sweet for eleven months out of the year. I was so glad when the war was over.

Once a military man from Morris Air Base (the government took over Charlotte Municipal Airport and turned it into an air base) in Charlotte came to our door and told Mother that our tin roof was unacceptable. He said that during the air raids our tin roof shined brighter than a star. During air raids, we had to pull the new shades at the windows. Mother had to buy and install either dark green or black shades for the whole house. The air raids were very frightening. The sirens blasted the warning for everyone to ready for a raid. Then we would hear many planes flying overhead. Mother didn't have the money to get a regular roof, so she climbed up on top of our house and painted the whole silver tin roof black by herself.

Some of the factories in America had to close during the war because there was no gas to ship the product, or perhaps the raw material for the product was not available. No mills closed in Newton. The hosiery mills had to switch from nylon to rayon, but they made do. Nylon was used for parachutes, so citizens could find nothing made of nylon. Rubber was not used for civilian products. Gas was not available, so people parked their cars. This didn't affect us because we walked anyway.

Although Mother was hard-working and very smart, I began questioning her parenting skills in my own mind when I was very young. The punishments were harsh compared to the crime. It was like punishing a teen who stole a candy bar with life in prison. To Mom, wrong was wrong. In her mind there were no degrees of wrong. As hard as I tried, I couldn't please her.

One of her least favorite habits was her attitude toward snacks. She would lift the food on to your plate at mealtime. Huge servings. If you didn't eat every bite, she would put your plate into the warming closet which was an enclosed cabinet over the stove which kept food warm. In the afternoon when it was time for your snack, she would pull out what you didn't eat from the last meal. That was your snack. I think this affected my dislike for left-overs in adulthood. Both Grandmothers were good at coming up with biscuits and honey or peanut butter and jelly or ice cream for snacks. Daddy was fantastic with the secret moon pies and RC colas. He frequently shelled peanuts as fast as I could wash them down with a Cheerwine. Mom had no clue what constituted a decent snack. As smart as she was, I couldn't understand her difficulty with this concept. But she was a woman to be admired.

In 1946 when Daddy finally left, we had a well off the back porch and an outhouse out by the vegetable garden. We had an icebox on the back porch. A delivery man would deliver a huge block of ice in the spring and summer and put it into the big ice box weekly. It would last part of the week. Most people had milk and butter delivered, but Mother helped Mr. and Mrs. Watts, an old couple up the street, churn, so they gave Mom milk and butter for her helping.

Mother had just installed a kitchen sink, but there was no water in it. We had a big wood burning stove in the kitchen. Mother would buy a cord of wood at a time. Daddy would chop the wood in an appropriate size for the stove. My job was to stack these pieces of wood into the wood shed which was about fifteen feet from the back door. The shed would keep the wood dry. There was a huge box which Daddy built behind the stove. Every Saturday morning before Dad got up, I had to fill up the wood box carrying wood from the shed. The only time Daddy ever hit me was a big surprise. One Saturday when I didn't fill the wood box, Daddy asked me why. I said, "I'm scared of the bugs and spiders." Daddy said, "Fill the wood box, Kitty, the bugs aren't any worse than every other Saturday morning." I looked him straight in the eye and said, "No!" He smacked me across the face. I was deaf for about three hours. He almost knocked my head off. He felt so bad that he filled the wood box himself. Every Saturday after that, I filled the box without saying a word. I could only carry six to eight pieces of wood at a time, so it took me about thirteen trips to fill the big box in rain, sun, or snow. I hated this chore. But I never said, "No," to either of my parents again. I often wondered why I couldn't have a brother.

After Daddy left, Mother just could not chop the wood, so her first project after Daddy left was to purchase an oil stove for the kitchen. Big improvement! Uncle Carl brought her oil for the stove every Saturday morning. Next she dug a ditch from the kitchen sink to the road in front of our house, and she paid a man to hook up the sink and lay the pipe. We were hooked up to city water. Mother filled in that big well by the back porch by herself. This was amazing that my mother could do this all alone.

Daddy had rented a plow and horse to plow the garden every spring. She fought that red clay, digging with a mallet and a hoe, to do her gardening or to fill in the well and the outhouse. She was very careful not to ask for help unless she actually couldn't do it herself. Smart and hard-working woman!

The outhouse was a major problem. It had to be moved every year. That job took a man. Our house had a long hallway through the middle of the house from the front door to the back porch. There were three rooms on one side of the hallway and two rooms on the other side. These rooms were used differently according to the season of the year. In winter we lived in two rooms because only two rooms were heated. In summer we used the whole house. Of course, on Thanksgiving and Christmas, we heated the living room. Every room in the house except the kitchen had a fireplace. Mother built a room in the back of the hallway and made a bathroom. She bought a commode at the hardware store in North Newton and used my wagon to pull it to its new home in the back of our hallway. She then hired a plumber to hook it up to the city sewage. We were in heaven. She disassembled the outhouse and filled in the hole with dirt. She wore a smile on her face. Eventually she purchased a sink for the bathroom. She had to pay a man with a truck to deliver the new used bathtub which had legs. She let me be the first to have a bath which was a cold water bath. I felt like a princess. Before this there were baths in a huge tin tub in the kitchen or on the back porch. It took her all spring and summer and autumn to save for a hot water heater. But by winter we had hot baths. Of course, there was no heat in the bathroom. Finally she bought a second-hand heater.

A sailor could not out curse my mom. Since she was angry most of the time about one thing or another, she "cussed" a lot. But cursing was not allowed in our home. If I ever said, "Darn, golly or heck", Mom would smack me across the mouth. Therefore, I grew up hearing one language and speaking another.

Another inconsistency in my upbringing was going to church. Mother took me to the Cradle Roll of the First Baptist Church when I was six weeks old. Until I was about three, she delivered me there every Sunday morning where Ms. Coulter and Ms. Sharp would teach me little songs which I sang all week. I still sing these little songs often. It was hard for Mother. We lived more than fourteen blocks from the church. Mother had to walk and carry me. All of a sudden, she stopped attending church.

By age three, I was the apple of many an eye. When Mother didn't want to go, someone from the church would pick me up. From the time I was six weeks old until I was ten, I never missed a Sunday and got

Perfect Attendance Awards. There was a period of three years that Dad and Mom attended. I thought this was perfection. When I was ten and Daddy left us, I refused to go on Father's Day, but every other Sunday I was there. Clearly, God was handling my life here. Mother wanted me to go to church because she had the idea that attending church would make me a better person. She also wanted me to wear the clothes she made me, so that she would receive praise. What it really did was to give me people who encouraged me and treated me like their own daughter. I don't think that these people knew what was going on inside my home. Yet they unknowingly supplied my every need. God used them to drive me to church, to feed me, to allow me to play the piano, to teach me the scriptures, to give me organ lessons, and to love me. They sent me to Summer Camp and supplied things that could never have happened if I hadn't attended church.

When I was fourteen, Mother bought a television. It was the second one in town. For a while, it was the only one in town. A postman bought the first television. He had very young twin sons. One Saturday morning they were lying on the floor in front of the TV watching Hopalong Cassidy, a popular cowboy in those days. The boys had received Hopalong Cassidy holster sets for Christmas. Every show had Hopalong dropping his gun, fighting, and eventually retrieving the gun. However, on this particular morning, when Hopalong dropped his gun, one of the twins whipped his gun out of his holster and yelled, "Here, Hoppy, use mine," as he threw his gun straight into the screen. I was very popular when Mom bought the TV. More popular than I had ever been.

At age sixty-five Mother decided to learn to drive, so she purchased a brand new blue Buick Skylark and had it delivered to her house. Then she called me and told me she needed me at home, a three hour drive away. She wouldn't tell me why. I was teaching in Raleigh, so I drove home that weekend. When I pulled into the driveway, I thought she had company. As soon as I opened the door, she walked toward me with the keys in her hands saying, " No, No, don't sit down. We're going out in the country, and you are going to teach me to drive." So I drove the new blue Skylark out into the country as she asked and put her behind the wheel. It was major scary. I was tired. I had taught that day and then driven the three hour drive to her house. It was beginning to get dark. The country roads were too curvy and too narrow. So I had the bright idea of going up on the Hickory Highway to one of the big discount stores. The parking lots were way too large, so there was plenty of empty space along the edge. All weekend I took Mom out driving many times. She didn't improve one iota. After several weekends of no improvement, I refused to return. Mother hired a driving teacher. It took her almost a year and three tries to get her license. It was a joyous day when she succeeded. Now that was persistence!

Although Mother used tough love on me before psychologists coined the term, I learned valuable lessons from her. Once when I was sixty-five and Mom was near death I asked her, "Mom, why did you make my life so hard?" Mother had a very clear mind till the day before she died. She quickly answered me without thinking about her answer, "Well, Kitty, hardships build character!" I was shocked at this answer and have often heard her voice repeating this wisdom since her death. I have frequently thought of using tough love with my two sons, but frankly I haven't had the guts to try it. Yes, that's a good word. My mother was gutsy! Although she couldn't feel it, she was much wiser than I would ever be.

I'm not sure if I would ever have learned to play the piano except for one of Mom's favorite admonishments. She told me constantly that anger was an instrument of the Devil. Then and now I wonder why she would say this to me so often. She was the one with a temper. Looking back, I think that she may have been trying to figure out herself when she would project onto me. She seemed to really believe that anger is an instrument of the Devil. When I felt angry, I practiced the piano. I practiced a lot. Years later in adulthood, I realized that this warning did not come from the Bible. A Greek monastic theologian Evagrius of Pontus came up with eight offenses in the Fourteenth century. Pope Gregory the Great reduced these eight to seven, and they are now known as the Capital Vices or Cardinal Sins or the Seven Deadly Sins. They are listed differently in different research. One list is pride, envy, anger (wrath), sadness (sloth), avarice (covetousness or greed), gluttony, and lust. I never heard my grandmother or anyone else say these words. I have often wondered how my mother ever knew that anger was an instrument of the Devil. However, I now believe that she was correct because anger leads to many other sins such as rage, vengeance, murder, and such. As one of my sons once said to me, "Mother, do you know how irritating it is to find that you are always right". I can't say that I am irritated that Mom was right so much of the time; however, I am amazed.

When Mother was eighty-three, she was prescribed medicines which caused bleeding ulcers. Her neighbor found her on the floor in a pool of blood. She stayed in the hospital a month and then physical therapy a month. She was told that she had to go to a nursing home. She refused to go. I drove up to convince her, but there was no convincing her. I gave her a choice of a nursing home in Newton or coming to live with me in Florida. She hated Florida, so I had no doubt that she would choose to go into a nursing home. The doctors said that she could not make it to Florida. She chose Florida. My younger son came. He made a bed for her in the back of my Explorer, and he drove us to Florida.

She didn't do well in Florida. She fell six times in the first three months she was here. I took her to the ER after each fall to be checked. Finally when I took her to the ER to be checked out after her sixth fall, the police were called. I was told that I was not providing my mother a safe environment because we had carpeting and dogs. Strangely, the dogs were never near Mother when she fell, and she was never on the carpeted area when she fell. She would go reeling backward with me right beside her. She was diagnosed with Parkinson's.

She was placed at Brooks Rehabilitative Center. One Saturday in late morning I was told that Mother would be released at 1:00 PM. Her insurance was running out. She would have to go into a Nursing Home. I had always heard that the Nursing Homes had long waiting lists. I had seen Nursing Homes on Old St. Augustine Road. I lived right off this street. I knew that I would need to be near. So I went from one to another. I covered six of the nine. Each told me to go to River Garden. I didn't know where River Garden was. I finally found a small sign and a driveway which went back into a stand of woods. When I reached the manager's office, she showed me the long waiting list. She said that it would be months, maybe a year before Mother could get in. The CEO came walking by the door just as I began crying. He stopped. When he heard the story, he said to the manager, "You know the next name on that waiting list is my mother's. We have a room on rehab which has just been vacated. It's being cleaned as we speak. Let Ms. Hester have that room and put my mother's name at the end of the list." When this happened, I was fully aware that it was a "God thing." I went to the hospital and got Mom. When she found out that I was putting her in a home, she threw the sheet at me, bit me, spit on me, and used every profane word ever heard by mankind in the loudest voice she could muster. I got the impression that she was unhappy. If the scene hadn't been so pathetic, it would have been funny.

I had to have power of attorney for Mother to stay in the Nursing Home. She wouldn't sign the papers. Come to find out, she hadn't signed a check in years; Aunt Rose had been writing checks for her. Finally, the lawyer we had hired to do a Trust for both of us came. He brought his secretary as a witness. Mother was in a wheel chair. He got right down in Mother's face and said, "Mrs. Hester, you don't seem to realize what a fine daughter you have who is trying to provide the best care for you." I was shocked when Mother came up out of that wheelchair and responded to him, "No one needs to tell me how fine my daughter is. I've known that since the day she was born." I rushed into the hall as soon as Mom finally signed "the damn papers". As I slid down the wall to the floor, I was sobbing. I had never heard Mother say anything good about me before. It was about time! When I got over the initial shock, I began laughing.

I visited Mother every morning before I went to school and returned to help with her supper every day after school for two years. Most days I took her outside for a ride in her wheelchair. One day after she had been there for about a week, she said to me, "Kitty, I think you have put me in a Catholic Home." I promised her that I hadn't. When she insisted on and on, I told her, "No, Mom, it's a Jewish Home." It was the nearest place to my house and considered the finest facility in North Florida. I took her home with me some Saturdays. And we went for rides on Sunday afternoons. I carried food from my kitchen to her often. She loved the sausage biscuits which I took to her almost every Saturday morning.

I found humor in the fact that Mother hated Jews although she had never known one; she hated Catholics although she had never known one; she really hated Blacks although she knew none personally; of course, she hated all foreigners and wanted them sent back where they came from; she really hated fat people. Fat people were bound to be dumb because they weren't taking care of their own bodies. Here she was in a place run by Jews about a block from the biggest Catholic Center in Jacksonville. Almost every nurse was Filipino or Russian. The food personnel and nurses' aides were Black. I was wondering just how much hate Mother could dish out. She surprised even me.

About two weeks after Mother became a resident at River Garden, I dropped by, as usual, after school. She was not in her room, and I was told that she was having a bath. The bathroom was right across the hall, although she had a sink and toilet connected to her private room. As I stood waiting, I couldn't believe my ears. My mother was laughing. I had never heard my mother laugh, and she was eighty-four years old. It was difficult to believe this laughter. How wonderful! What a beautiful sound! The reason for this laughter was her bantering back and forth with Angie, a heavy-set black Aide. We both learned to love Angie. She made it easy to love her. I was sure that she was an angel in disguise. She was so patient with Mom.

Mother's sister came down from North Carolina to visit her. She declared, "That woman in that room is not my sister. She's too happy." Over the two-year period that Mother lived at River Garden, she mellowed. My son Charles would visit her and tease her and cut up with her. They were like two kids having fun. I wasn't sure that she had ever had a childhood until she was very old. Pitiful!

Every Saturday night River Garden provided some kind of entertainment. Mom and I went weekly. She would clap and sing and laugh. I considered this a miracle.

Mom made me promise not to ever put her on Medicaid. She thought that it was welfare. Although she had worked her whole life and earned every penny she had ever spent, she wouldn't listen. I promised not knowing if I could keep the promise. She was experiencing congestive heart failure and was near having to do dialysis when her diabetes acted up. Within a few months she died of diabetes, thirteen days before she would have had to go on Medicaid. The forms I filled out for Medicaid were shredded. She lived her life without using Medicaid which was her wish.

There were no siblings. I didn't think I could handle a funeral, but I did. Mother's body was flown back to Newton, a Newtonian coming home. The service was there, and she was buried there just like she wanted. My two sons and I made up the receiving line. People whom I had not seen for fifty years shook our hands. It was a somber event. Not the comic son, but the serious son leaned over to me in the receiving line and whispered, "Have you ever considered the first three letters in the word funeral?" Like Mother, he often hides his sense of humor, but it's there.

The world had lost an amazing woman. She had her faults, but not without reason, which was beyond the understanding of those around her. She made her way alone and did a fine job. She was one of the first independent women I ever knew.

Half of Newton would tell me that I looked just like Mother; the other half would tell me that I looked just like Daddy. They would add that I acted just like Daddy. I knew that wasn't true because I have never smoked or drank or gambled in my whole life. I was forty-two when I had my first taste of alcohol. A coach on the faculty where I worked told me that a pina colada was a sweet fruit drink. He thought he was being funny. He ordered one for me at the end of the year luncheon. My first alcohol at age 40. I loved it, not knowing that there was rum in it. Cute, eh? Mother turned over in her grave. If she had been alive, she would have assured me that drinking that one drink was proof of my being nothing but "a damn Hester".

When Mother passed away thirty-two years after Daddy and I bought the first house I had ever owned by myself, I put up their pictures side by side in my bedroom. Both were in their twenties in the pictures. When I stood back and viewed my work, I had to sit down on the bed to laugh. My mom and dad looked like twins. I had never known that. No wonder people were confused about who I looked like.

Looking back, I realize that it is much easier to see all the ways Mother influenced me. It is certainly easier than realizing them at the time I lived with her. What a woman! Her many, many good traits far outweigh the bad ones when you are at a distance.

I'm not sure how far the distance is. I was trying to get a TV in the bedroom to work the day I moved into my house six months after I thought she was buried. It just wouldn't work. I paced back and forth in the bedroom with the frustration really working on me. I heard a voice behind me. It clearly said, "Tin foil, Stupid, tin foil." I jumped. I was positive that it was my mother because no one else would ever call me stupid. I called my handy son and told him what happened. I had no idea what the message meant. He told me to wrap tin foil around the rabbit ears. I did. How about that? TV.

Chapter 5

Mother's Family

Grandma Hendrix was a major influence in my life.
She was tall and heavy. She and Grandma Hester both wore dresses which hit their ankles with black tie shoes on their feet. Both covered their dresses with a fresh apron every day. Each wore their long straight hair pulled back into a knot on the back of their heads. Both Grandma Hester and Grandma Hendrix were tall, heavy set women. When I was very little, I would try to make them laugh because I had a good view of their belly shaking like a bowl of jelly. I used to think that Santa had nothing on either of them.

Grandma lived just across a field from the mill where Mother and all three of her sisters worked. Grandma usually kept me during the day. Mother would leave me there over night many nights each week during the cold season. I was happy about that. Uncle Allen never moved out of his parents' home. He played with me and loved me. Aunt Rose lived there also. Aunt Helen lived in a house behind Grandma, and her daughter Naomi, my oldest cousin, lived beside her. Naomi had a daughter my age who has always been like a sister to me, and two other children. Mother's excuses to leave me over night with Grandma were "It's snowing", "I don't feel good", "I'm tired", or "I have errands to run after work". This worked for me instead of against me. I was left with Grandma during my chickenpox and measles and every cold or sniffle,

Grandma had chickens, a black walnut tree and a pear tree. I have a precious memory of the huge lilac bush outside Grandma's kitchen window. When I think of it, I see the beautiful lavender blossoms, and I can actually smell the fragrance wafting through the window. Grandma had a kitchen table with a chair at each end and long benches on each side. Her eight children walked to her house every day at lunch from the different mills where they worked. She cooked for all of them. Children always ate after the adults, so most days I ate after the adults had gone back to work, and Grandma would be washing the dishes.

Every morning she baked six pies – apple, peach, pecan, cherry, or blackberry. Mother supplied apples from the trees in our back yard. Grandma would send me to the field to collect blackberries. Aunt Helen supplied the pecans from her tree. Ms. Giles next door supplied peaches from her tree. When there was no fresh fruit, she would make chess pies and egg custards. She cooked on a huge wood burning stove. She would sing while stringing the green beans and rolling the crusts for the pies. I would sing with her. Grandma and I made a great pair.

Near the end of Grandma's life, Mom would drop me off at Grandma's house to stay till school started. It was thought that a child who eats breakfast every morning would make a healthy child. Mother would make me eat breakfast at home. Then Grandma would make me eat breakfast at her house. About forty minutes before school I would walk through Grandma's back yard, across Aunt Helen's yard, and on to Naomi's house to pick up Kathy and Becky, my second cousins, to walk to school. Naomi always made cream gravy and biscuits for breakfast. She would be sure that I hadn't been fed, so she would make me eat breakfast again. I was a skinny little kids (probably all that walking), so three breakfasts didn't seem to hurt.

Every day during warm weather Grandma would take me to the rose garden in the side yard. She would sing "In the Garden" as she clipped the dead buds from the bushes. I would sing with her. Today I have a rose garden in the side yard. Every morning ten months a year my sweet Shih Tzu Lily and I go to the rose garden, and I sing,

" I come to the garden alone while the dew is still on the roses, and the voice I hear falling on my ear, the Son of God discloses. And He walks with me, and He talks with me, and He tells me I am His own and the joy we share as we tarry there, none other has ever known." (by C.Austin Miles)

Every morning I think of Grandma who loved her Lord. She introduced me to Him and to the love of gardening and cooking. Grandma told me Bible stories, and I knew most of the Bible before she died.

I was standing at the foot of her bed when the doctor pronounced her dead. She was killed by a heart attack when I was ten, just a month after Daddy left. Daddy came to the funeral. Back then, when you were pronounced dead, the funeral director would put you in a casket and leave you in your own living room for a week. Family and friends sat with the corpse every hour twenty-four hours a day. One night I sat in one of the five straight chairs in front of the casket. All of a sudden Grandma's arm shot into the air and flopped back down on her stomach. It frightened me so much that I ran out of the room. Uncle Allen assured me that she was just waving good-bye to me. It didn't look like good-bye to me. Uncle Allen did not realize that I wasn't a baby anymore because he wanted me to stay innocent. I was growing up fast at this point.

After the funeral, Mother gathered all of my belongings out of Grandma's house. We headed home. When we reached our house, she stopped me on the porch before we entered the house. She stood in front of me with one of her hands on each of my shoulders, and said, "IF you are going to live here, you will clean the house and cook the food. I don't like to clean or cook, so you can do it." This really meant to clean every room every week. The living room was opened every Thanksgiving and Christmas. I was allowed to practice the piano in the living room. However, I had to take down the lace curtains, take them outside and shake the dust out before putting them back up, dust the furniture, and clean the floors. I frequently wondered where the dirt was that I was supposed to be cleaning. The front bedroom was the same; never entered, but cleaned once a week.

I was not allowed to work on Sunday, and Mom only cooked on Sunday when I was at church. She didn't teach me to cook. I was thankful that I had observed my grandmother preparing food for years. Mother allowed me to plan the meals. She seldom complained about anything, except when I accidentally cooked something that reminded her of Daddy. She expected the meal to be on the table when she arrived home from work. Many times I would harvest vegetables from the garden out back. It was in this period that I learned to burn green beans. I would try to cook them too fast. Often I would bury them somewhere in the back yard or later flush them down the toilet. I learned to love that commode. Do you know how hard it is to clean a pot where you have burned beans? And how to get rid of that hateful smell! Then I would hurry to pick squash or some vegetable which would cook quickly.

The "IF" I was to live here kept ringing in my child's mind. If I didn't live here, where would she put me? I missed Grandma as much as I had missed Daddy. I lost both of them within two months.

Grandpa Hendrix was a different story. How he ever hooked up with a wonderful woman like my grandmother is beyond me. He rarely said anything to anyone unless it was to correct them or to yell at them. Grandpa was a very small man. Later in life, I realized that perhaps his size had influenced his behavior. He did not know how to carry on a conversation. He had a brother and two sisters. He seemed to be close to them. Summy lived in Newton, and Grandpa visited him daily. Uncle Summy was a very nice man. Aunt Lena lived in Charlotte, and Grandpa would visit her when he could get someone to drive him. Aunt Lena was an old-fashioned Southern lady...as gentle as a well-fed baby. Aunt Bert married at fourteen and went with her husband, a railroad man, to Sanford, Florida. Grandpa visited her about once every three years or so. Aunt Bert was a fire-ball; my mom was just like her.

Grandpa was mean to everybody except my Grandmother. He watched his P's and Q's around her. The older Grandpa got, the meaner he got. He left me alone until he lived with Mom and me after Uncle Allen died. The plan was for each of the five children who lived in Newton to take Grandpa for three months at a time. Grandpa had been with us for seven months, and no one else would take him. I was moving to Raleigh, and Mom couldn't handle him alone. This was a real problem. He had four children with homes in Newton who did not want their father. Such a sad situation! He made his bed with his cruel ways. He went into a nursing home where he died of a stroke. Don't forget, folks, that hitting anyone you can reach with your walking cane may cause a stroke.

All of my aunts were kind to me. Aunt Helen understood how Mother was treating me. She never said a word, but she knew. Every chance she got, she made it plain that I was special to her. I'll never forget her rose bush. I've never seen another like it. It was a yellow climber beside her carport. Her entire carport roof and one wall was covered with yellow roses from May to October.

She was married to a man who could not read a word, except he could read the Bible out loud. Every time I went there, he wanted to read the Bible out loud to me. Regretfully, Aunt Helen dipped snuff, and her husband smoked cigarettes. In the winter they heated two rooms and sat and dipped and smoked all day long. She spent about a month living with me in Florida every winter after her husband died. She would take the bus and show up. Mother, of course, didn't like this at all. She died of emphysema in her eighties. She only had one child, Naomi who was married before I was born. She was probably the most special person in my life during the time I lived in Newton. Certainly Naomi and Aunt Rose gave me the most support.

My favorite was Aunt Rose. She did everything for me that Mother would allow, but she was careful not to cross Mother. She gave me my first cross on a chain and my first locket which I still have. She was beautiful and generous and loving. Aunt Rose was always there for me until she passed away. It's a wonderful thing to know that there's someone who understands every thing you do. Someone who loves you no matter what. She had two daughters. The oldest, Barbara, was like a sister to me. Joda was many years younger than I, so I never learned to know her very well until she was dying at Bowman Gray Hospital. I would call her every Sunday when visiting hours were over, and I knew that she would be lonely. We talked many hours before she died. I felt like I was blessed that we became phone friends. One night I called. When she answered, she told me that she didn't feel like talking or listening. She died that night. She was forty-three when she died. Aunt Rose was devastated. Aunt Rose had a hard life, but many of her problems she caused herself. I loved her anyway.

Shirley, the baby in the family, was the first female in the family to pursue anything beyond the mill. She worked toward a nursing degree at Davis Hospital, but she dropped out to help at home. When I had my tonsils out at ten, my throat bled for weeks. I lost a lot of weight.

Aunt Shirley took care of me while Mom worked. She married and had three children, Linda, Barbara, and Duane. I would say that she and her husband Sam had the best marriage in our family.

My uncles were a mess. They all drank heavily and, like Daddy, smoked packs of cigarettes every day. They loved gambling and shooting pool. Each of them followed their father's example.

Uncle Carl was a big tease. But he hurt me badly. I grew up thinking that he was a comic. He always made me laugh. One day when I was eighteen he came by the house. Mother asked me to play my recital piece for him on the piano. When I finished, he said, "Kitty, you make all of us proud. I'm so happy to see that you have stuck with your piano lessons. And I never thought you would finish high school. We're all so proud of you." He and Mom walked out on the front porch. I picked up a book and began reading by the front window which was open. I really wasn't allowed to be in the living room unless I was practicing the piano or cleaning, so I was actually taking advantage of the situation. Uncle Carl and Mom were just on the other side of the window screen. He said to Mom, "Louise, I can't believe you are letting this girl go to college." Mom replied, "That's not my idea, but what can I do. It's not going to cost her a penny." He replied, "You can put her ass to work in the glove mill. That's what you can do!" I didn't cry. I was angry. I'm still angry today that this man I trusted betrayed me. He and my aunt Gert had a nice home and nice clothes. She seemed to think they were better than the rest of the family. I knew better. Before he died, he apologized, and I forgave him. I realized that he had no understanding of the importance of having an education.

They were just mill folks like the rest of us. Both his daughter Lillian and his son T. C. were always nice to me. They both knew their parents' faults. They both were down-to-earth, loving people with none of the snobbishness of their parents.

Uncle Allen was a fall-down drunk. I saw him once go into DT's (delirium tremens) in the field beside Grandma's house. I was about five. It scared me to death. I thought that he had turned into the Devil himself. His face was all distorted, and he was rolling in the dirt. He had saliva all over his face. His hands and legs were flailing. But when he was sober (maybe that was never) or near sober, he was so much fun. He carried me sitting on his shoulders to Ed's Café and bought me an

44

ice cream in the summer in the years before Grandma let me go by myself. He teased me constantly. He would stand me on his shoulders to reach a ripe pear from the tree in Grandma's front yard. In his room he had twin beds. Since he worked at night and Uncle Joe was in the service, when I took a nap on Uncle Joe's bed, Uncle Allen would lay on the other twin bed and take a nap too. He had a wife. He married Della and came home after the wedding. He never spent a day or night at her house. I've never figured that one out. When he was a teenager, he ran off with a traveling carnival. Grandpa went looking for him and brought him home. He was probably closer to my daddy than any of mother's brothers. It was the bond of booze.

I taught my first year in Catawba, a town ten miles from Newton. I had just bought a car when Uncle Allen went to the dentist and was told that he needed to go to Duke University Hospital. Against Mother's wishes, I drove him. Everybody in the family was mad at me for taking him. Obviously, the whole family had given up on him and his drunken behavior. I never regretted it although it was a hard day. Duke was three hours away. They kept him. I drove home alone. He had mouth and throat cancer.

After a month or so, I drove to Duke to bring him home. Uncle Allen and Grandpa moved to a three-room house outside Newton, but on the way to my school. I would stop every day that year and cook dinner for them trying to make enough for them to have lunch the next day. Aunt Rose and I bought all of the groceries they had that year. Grandpa had a stroke and was in a wheelchair. Uncle Allen had no car and was recovering from cancer.

One day I arrived in the afternoon to cook dinner. Grandpa said, "Kitty, will you check on Allen? I can't wake him up." I checked. He was breathing, but certainly there was something wrong. I called Uncle Carl who had appointed himself caretaker of the two, but seldom saw them. It was snowing, and he refused to come. I called Mom and asked her what to do. She told me to call an ambulance. I did. They came. As they were moving him into the ambulance, he died. Thank God, Mother got a neighbor to bring her, and she was walking down the driveway as this happened. We took Grandpa to Mom's house where he stayed for months.

Uncle Earl drank himself stupid every day on the way home from work. It was a miracle that he could keep a job. His wife didn't work most of the time. They lived in a mill house and had two children. I was never around him much. When I was, he was nice to me. Unlike the other uncles, he was serious. Since he served in World War II, he went to Oteen Veterans' Hospital in the beautiful mountains near Asheville. He had lung cancer. Oteen was an Indian word meaning "chief aim". The Hospital's chief aim was to heal all of the patients who came there. But Uncle Earl died there. He died too young because he did not value his own life. He was the first child to die. Along with my grandma I wondered where this thirst for alcohol came from. I knew that he had no control over his drinking. Alcohol had control over him. I didn't know anything about alcoholism at that time, but I knew that I would never let a drink control my life.

I was Uncle Joe's girl. Uncle Joe was younger than mother. He was a real rascal. When they were little, he walked up behind Rose one day and cut two long curls right off the side of her head. Grandpa was always having to whip him which did no good whatsoever. He quit high school at Grandpa's insistence and went to work in the cotton mill. The coach Dick Gurley went to Grandpa and begged him to put Joe back in school and let him play football. I guess Grandpa, being a small man, was so enamored with the idea of playing football that he consented.

Uncle Joe was the first in the family to finish high school. He got a scholarship to play football at Lees McRae in Banner Elk, North Carolina, a town smaller than Newton and so high in the mountains one could hardly breath.

My mother thought that Uncle Joe was a total waste. She was almost right. If I went to college and wandered the world, she would think the same of me.

Joe went into the Army in World War II. He first fought in France and then was stationed on the island of Aruba. Then there was nothing on Aruba except a gas station, a general store, our soldiers and Japanese soldiers. I still have a postcard picturing the only building on the island. I loved Uncle Joe, and I prayed for him every morning and every night during the war. During air-raids I sat on the floor in the corner of our sitting room and sang "Coming in on a Wing and a Prayer" and prayed for Uncle Joe and Uncle Earl who were both in service. I was five to eight when they served.

When he arrived home, he married one of the "upper-crust" girls in town. The marriage lasted about six months. Then he disappeared which broke my grandmother's heart. I believe now that Uncle Joe suffered from PTS (Post Traumatic Stress) which was not even known then. Occasionally he would mail someone a letter. Finally, when he was near sixty-five, his sister Shirley received a call from a nun in California. She said that Uncle Joe had been in a mission hospital there for several years. He had lost use of his legs. She wanted someone to come get him. No one in the family would go. Finally Aunt Rose flew there and brought Uncle Joe home. She put him in a nursing home. I went to see him as often as I could, although I had moved to Florida by then.

During one visit to the nursing home, I was shocked to see a picture of me when I was five on his bulletin board. I asked where he got it. He said, "Kitty, I carried that very picture in my wallet through France, Aruba, and every state in the United States. I would whip it out and tell people that this was my little girl." He cried when he told me that story, and I cried too. I really loved Uncle Joe, although I didn't understand him. His picture is in my bedroom right now. I have him standing in the lawyers' bookcase which is right beside my bathroom door. Every time I pass him, I think and sometimes say out loud, "Thank you, Uncle Joe, for loving me so much."

As you can see, I was much closer to my maternal relatives just because I was around them more. I know that each of my relatives put a teaspoon or so into the mix before it was eventually stirred. They grew me as sure as Grandma grew her roses; planting, pulling weeds, fertilizing, enjoying, debudding, and cutting back when the cold weather came.

Chapter 6

The Early Years

When I was a child, I was very lonely. I was an only child, but had a dozen or so wonderful cousins and lived in a neighborhood with many kids near my age. In my early teens I loved to play ball and skate and go to church and make homemade ice cream. I loved to play piano and read books. I had a fairly good childhood. But for some reason, I mostly felt very lonely, a loneliness that can zoom down on me to this very day even in the middle of a delightful party or a motivating conference. I don't feel like I belong. This may be because I yearn for my Heavenly Father and my home with Him. I really do not belong.

Until I began school, I thought at the time that I had the perfect childhood. Maybe that was because I was a child with no points of comparison.

I was a cute baby who grew into a cute little girl. I always had a smile on my face. Actually I was a handful. Daddy let me ride on his shoulders, and later on his back. We had to walk everywhere. Mother would complain to Dad, "You're going to carry that girl till her feet drag the ground." There was much evidence that Mother was very jealous of the relationship between Daddy and me. If Dad noticed this, he pretended not to notice.

Our kitchen was a large room with long windows. The windowsill was wide enough for me to sit on. I was somewhere between two and three when I was sitting on the window sill watching the rain. I could say the little jingle, "Rain, rain go away, so little Kitty can go out to play." But the rain wouldn't listen. All morning I was sitting there begging the rain to stop. Mother walked into the room. Mother used every profane word known to every sailor in the world, but she would cringe when Daddy or any other person within hearing distance used one of her favorite words. She acted like the words were hers – only hers. But I was a fast learner. As she walked into the room that morning, I said, "Mommy, just look at that damn rain." When I looked back at her from my place on the window sill, she was gone. When Daddy got home, she gave him a lecture on using profanity in front of the baby. I had never heard a curse word come from my daddy's mouth.

Our schedule was an interesting one for a little kid. Most weeks before I started to school I would stay with Grandma Hendrix Monday through Friday. I loved this. She was such a wonderful inspiration in my life. She was kind. She never raised her voice. She definitely never used profanity. She read her Bible daily and prayed often. She prayed with me and sang little songs with me. We sang "Jesus Loves Me" and "Jesus Loves the Little Children" and "Farther Along" and many others. She cooked three meals a day. She sang with me while she cooked and while she did the laundry. Being with Grandma was the best environment any child could have.

On Friday afternoon Mother would come for me and keep me over the weekend.

Daddy would sleep till noon if he came home at all. So Saturday morning Mother would heat water from the well on the wood stove, enough for the big tin tub. I would bathe and have a brief time to play in the water; then Mother would shampoo my hair and wrap it around rags to make long curls. My hair was very long and thick and heavy. Mother would bathe in the same water. She would heat new water for Daddy. At noon Daddy would get up and eat, bathe, and shave. He would shave by the kitchen window all the while whistling, "There's a Church in the Valley by the Wildwood". Daddy had a great memory. I know that because he knew the words to every song that had ever been written. I would beg him to sing to me, and being the gambler he was, he would bargain with me to let him stop. It was so easy to obey Daddy because I wanted to please him.

Saturday was always the same if Daddy came home after work. After our baths, Daddy and I would walk the sixteen blocks to the library to exchange his fourteen books. Getting fourteen books for the next week, we would walk back to Grandma's house where we met Mother.

Then we would go to the movies in North Newton. The three of us could get into the movies for twenty-four cents because it was twelve cents for adults and kids were free. A nickel would buy a big bag of popcorn and a coke. It wasn't just the movie. Every week we saw a newsreel with the week's news (there were no TVs), a serial (frequently some cowboy series like Bob Steele, Tex Ritter, the Lone Ranger, Gene Autry, or Roy Rogers) or the wonder guys (Superman or Batman),and then the movie itself. You had to go every week to understand the serial.

As soon as we left the movie we would go down the street to Ed's Café where we bought the best hamburgers in the world. I have never tasted a hamburger as good as Ed's. I always had a Cheerwine. Years later in Raleigh, my second year teaching I went into a famous hamburger joint and ordered a hamburger and a Cheerwine. Being a woman who had never tasted any alcoholic beverage, I heard the waitress explain to me in a loud voice, "Ma'am, we don't serve alcoholic beverages." A Cheerwine is simply a cherry soda. I later discovered, to my surprise, that Cheerwine was manufactured near Newton and not very widely distributed. Daddy and I would sit with Mother and discuss the movie. Mother never entered in.

After our hamburgers, we would go to Grandma's house. The whole family would be there. All of my cousins showed up. Grandma had a swing and five rocking chairs on the front porch. The front porch was about two feet off the ground, so many of the men sat on the edge of the porch. The kids all played tag or hop scotch. There was a pear tree in the front yard, so when the pears were ripe everyone got one. The kids would drip the juice from the pear down the front of their clothes while the adults would warn them not to spoil their clothes. This was a great fun time for all.

One Saturday when I was five, Mom and Dad stayed and talked and talked. I was tired, so I decided to go home. It was only about three blocks. The doors were never locked. By the time I reached home it was dark. My problem was that I couldn't reach the string in the middle of the room where I could pull on the light. We did not have light switches on the wall, but a string hung down from a bulb in the middle of the room. I sat down in Daddy's big leather rocker beside the radio and listened to "Inner Sanctum".

The program began with a creaking door opening and then a very scary story. Usually I sat in Daddy's lap to listen to this adult program. When Mom and Dad decided to go home, they couldn't find me. Horror struck the family. They called the police, and many people scoured the town looking for me. When Mom and Dad finally came home, they found me asleep in Dad's chair in the dark. Mother wanted to whip me, but Daddy wouldn't let her. But he didn't laugh. I had given them a big scare.

Many summer days my cousins Kathy and Becky, Glenda Butler, one of Grandma's neighbors, and I played in Grandma's back yard. The same back yard where Grandma would walk out and pick up a hen and ring its neck. When it was dead, she would cut its head off and dip it into boiling water, pick the feathers, and prepare it for lunch. Grandma's back yard was an interesting place.

Uncle Allen played with me like a kid. He had a dozen silly nicknames for me, rode me on his shoulders or back, jumped up behind me to scare me, and grabbed me from behind and swung me round and round. Aunt Rose pampered me more than she pampered her own girls. Grandma showed me love in so many ways. Daddy inspired me with his reading, his singing, and his loving ways. Daddy amused me with his bargaining and surprises. Mother tolerated me because she had no choice. These ways and these wonderful people were my life. Yes, prior to going to school, I had the good life.

Part II

Chapter 7

My Early Schooling

I attended Newton Elementary School. It was a wonderful experience which gave me a sound foundation. Fortunately I had the best teachers a student could have found in the best schools in the United States. I consider my education in Newton a "God thing". After all, who would think that a small town in the foothills of North Carolina could have such fine teachers.

The town had a teacherage which was a huge two story house near the school. Single teachers were expected to live in the teacherage unless they grew up in Newton and lived with their parents. Until the last four decades, real estate was just not available in Newton. The land has been owned for generations by families. These families hung on to their land. So a teacher from outside our county would have had a difficult time finding a rental. Today in old age I can remember clearly every teacher I had.

My first grade teacher was Miss Lena Long. I remember the reading circle and learning to read. I must have been a good student even then, but, of course, I didn't realize that I was anything more than a struggling little girl with pigtails, trying to understand everything the teacher said.

The students in our schools were divided into groups by the alphabet.

There were three groups every year until we reached high school and took individual classes. Each group had about thirty to thirty-five students, and we had three teachers on each grade level, so we had about one hundred students in each grade. This caused the same students to be together each year. From first through eighth grade it seems that I sat every year behind Richard Gurley. I have fond memories of Izzy Jarret, Beth Haupt, Larry Hollar, Frances Long, Juddy Lawing, Wanda Houston, James Jarret, Gail Gibson, and Cecil Hartsoe. They were all part of my childhood.

My pigtails caused me a lot of trouble every year until in the fourth grade. Mom shampooed my hair every Saturday. My hair was so thick and long that it took about six hours to dry. I had long curls on Saturday and Sunday for church. Sunday night she would braid my hair for the week. I hated these braids. It was the lazy way out of combing my hair.

One rainy day Miss Long was allowing five of us to go to the restroom across the hall. She was standing at the door. Charles Hicks yanked my pigtail so hard that I wondered that it didn't take half my head off. As he pulled my hair, he yelled, "Kitty, Kitty, meow!" I chased him around the room. Miss Long rushed to stop us, but we ran right through the reading circle where she had flash cards sitting on the chalk tray. We knocked them over, and they went all over the floor. Both of us had to stand at attention in front of Miss Long while she smacked our hands with a wooden ruler. All of the other students sat wide-eyed at their desks and stared at our punishment. With the whippings I had at home with a belt or a broom stick, I thought these taps with the little ruler a joke. I knew better than to laugh because this woman was trying to correct a wrong. I was wrong to run in the room. I was wrong to knock over the flash cards. Of course, in my mind, this was Charles Hick's fault. Mother was wrong too because she made me wear those stupid pigtails. When I got home, Mother already knew what happened. The whipping I got at home almost caused me to miss a couple of days of school. Seeing the welts on my legs, arms, and back surprised Miss Long. She never hit me again.

Miss Carrie Thornton was my second grade teacher. She was ancient and had taught mother and most of her siblings in second grade. In Miss Thornton's class I learned to love learning. I soaked in everything she said like a sponge soaking up water. She was so gentle and loving. She was like a second Grandmother. She educated my brain; Grandma Hendricks educated my soul. With these two saints working on me, how could I lose? At the end of the year, she retired. Her retirement was a loss for the school system and the younger children who would miss having her.

It was in the second grade that I first realized that there was something different about me. When I stepped onto the playground at recess, the mill kids would yell at me, "Kitty, Kitty, come jump rope with us." A distance away the mill owners' kids would yell, "Kitty, Kitty, come jump rope with us." I would stand on the edge of the playground not knowing where to go. I wondered why there were such distinct groups. It was years and much distance before I understood somewhat. This was the beginning of years of a pull between the two groups. I didn't really like one group more than the other. I didn't feel a part of either. I was smart, but had not a clue. At the time, I just felt odd. Mill kids weren't supposed to be smart. Mill kids were just supposed to stay in school till the state laws allowed them to quit and go to work in a mill. Another difference was that many mill families had four or five children. Sometimes they were not clean and had few changes of clothes. Being an only child, my clothes were always clean. Since my mom could sew, I had nice looking dresses.

I began thinking, "What's wrong with me?" because I didn't figure all of this out until I left Newton. When I lived in Newton, I had no idea that I was smart. No one ever mentioned it. It took years for this to wrap around my brain. I thought most of the children in my classes were as smart as I or smarter. Indeed I now believe that most of my classmates were very smart. I'm not really sure how much drive they had. When you inherit a business and stay in the same town your whole life, maybe there was no need for drive.

To this day, I know that I'm not the kind of smart who just thinks smart. I am the kind who loves to research and read and study and evaluate. I love learning. This gives me a lot of knowledge about subjects I'm interested in, which are many. If I don't enjoy a subject, I'm dumb as a rock. I've been told many times that I have an outstanding memory. Being around the elderly today, I can see why the people around me think I have a good memory. It's a great asset. I often wonder how long this will last. Mom was alert until a few days before she passed away at eighty-six.

Miss Ruby Lee Sharp was my third grade teacher. She was very young and a relative of my cradle roll teacher at church. She was beautiful with blonde hair cut in a page boy hanging down to her shoulders. She wore "store-boughten" clothes. The greatest memory of Miss Sharp was that she enjoyed creative arts and gave us marvelous opportunities to stretch our narrow minds beyond our dreams. Our room was a corner room in the basement of the school. We had window ledges on two sides of the room wide enough to be a desk top. So every child had a desk for their school lessons and an assigned place at the window for art projects. She even had us wood carving. Each child had a set of carving tools which I still have. First, we carved in soap. Then we carved in a hunk of wood. I carved a horse standing on his hind legs. She showed us pictures painted by masters through the ages. We wrote stories and were allowed to share them with the class. This sounds common today, but remember this was in 1945. We learned music beyond what the music teacher taught us. We sang every day. She started the day with the pledge to the flag, a Bible story, and a prayer. Every morning she would discuss the Bible story. She was surprised at the beginning of the year with how much I knew about the Bible. She was definitely a rare teacher in her day. Such an inspiration in my young life!

It was in the third grade that a tradition began which lasted until we reached High School. On rainy days most classes would play games in the classroom. Not our group. We would tell ghost stories – the scarier the better. The star of this activity was Cecil Hartsoe. He was a good boy always obeying the rules. He had a fantastic imagination and told scary stories with all the theatrics of an Alfred Hitchcock movie. Of course, we had never heard of Alfred Hitchcock, but we actually heard Cecil Hartsoe most rainy days for years. North Carolina is known for the many ghosts in their history. Cecil brought them to life. Sometimes he made them up.

Unknown to Cecil, he taught me an important lesson which I used for fifty years. When I began teaching, I would sometimes need a filler for a few minutes. My students seemed to be too sophisticated to be interested in ghost stories, and I knew many. But I told snake stories. Being horrified of snakes, I had many true snake stories. I taught grades one through college. Every age group loved my snake stories. I would look back on those days, and I would pretend to be the great story-teller Cecil Hartsoe. I never tired of entertaining my students for a few minutes once in a while.

Richard Gurley sat in front of me in class. He was the superintendent's son, and his mother had been my mother's Sunday School teacher. A sweeter woman couldn't be found. Mr. Gurley had drawn my uncle Joe back to school when he was a coach and made him a great football player. He had also encouraged my aunt Shirley to return to school when she had quit to nurse her mother. Such a respectable family! Genuinely good people! Richard, on the other hand, was a pest. The whole year not one day did he have notebook paper. He would turn around and look at me pitifully when he begged for paper. I got so I gave him four or five sheets at a time. He would draw airplanes and all kinds of junk on most of them. Mother punished me for using so much paper. But this was my life, and I would not tell her what I did with the paper she bought. This was the beginning of a valuable friendship which lasted till both of us left Newton.

At school we were given little books where we could place stamps which we could buy one day a week. When the book was full, it was turned in for a savings bond. I had bought bonds in the first and second grade, but now Miss Sharp encouraged every student to have a stamp book. For the children who could not afford a stamp, she would give them coins. I must have purchased four or five bonds that year. When Mother passed away fifty-seven years later, I found these twenty-five dollar bonds in her safe deposit box. They had drawn so much interest that each bond was worth several hundred dollars. They had pictures of Donald Duck on them.

One of the most memorable events in my life happened in third grade. It was a day I'll never forget. We had no speaker system, so every announcement was carried by older students from the principal to each teacher. One late morning Miss Sharp received a message to bring all students to the auditorium immediately. We marched in straight lines without speaking a word. Every class was moving to the huge auditorium. When the whole school was assembled, Mr. Wells, our principal, walked out on to the stage. He had placed a straight chair in front of the beautiful velvet curtains. There was a radio sitting on the chair. Our auditorium was built, so that every word spoken on the stage could be heard downstairs and in the balcony without a microphone. Mr. Wells, standing in the middle of the stage, said, "Students, listen very carefully. The President of the United States is coming on to speak to you. He has news for you. You will never forget this day." The President came on the radio. You could hear a pin drop in the auditorium with about 650 people there – even the cafeteria workers. The president's voice boomed out, "Citizens of the United States, I am happy to report to you that the war with Germany is over." No one applauded. There was complete silence. Mr. Wells said, "I want you to follow your teacher back to your classroom, get your things, and go to your home immediately." We did. Walking home, all of the kids were quiet. No yelling! No talking! No running! Every siren in town was screeching. The fire trucks and police cars were flying up and down the streets with their sirens blasting. Every church bell in town was ringing. All of the mills stopped for the rest of that day. I met Mom at home. Mom packed a picnic, and we headed with the rest of the town to the Court House Square. Bands assembled. There was dancing around the square. The people were not quiet long. Shouting was the voice of the day. Mr. Wells was right; this day I'll never forget.

My fourth grade teacher was Miss Ollie Duke. I couldn't forget her, ever. I know because I have tried. She had taught my mother and all of her siblings. They all kept warning me that she was a witch. This is the first teacher I had had whose behavior was beyond my comprehension. All the kids at school hated her whether they had her or not. I often heard kids in other classes saying under their breath, "Miss Duke is a puke." I was always afraid that she would hear them. She demanded that every parent send in the original birth certificate. Of course, she couldn't get away with that now. I can't imagine why she needed to see anyone's birth certificate. We were there in front of her, so she knew we were born. Why did she need to know when we were born? When she saw mine, she called Mother in. Mother never missed work, but she was as afraid of Miss Duke as I was. When Mother got there, Miss Duke showed Mother the certificate as if Mother had never seen it, and said, "We're going to have to change the spelling of her name to Catherine." Katherine was not on the certificate. Mother had never noticed. So my name was Catherine in Miss Duke's class. This was silly. Now I was Catherine, and my nickname was Kitty. I couldn't change my nickname to Citty. So since fourth grade, I have had two different sets of initials. How stupid is that? Some teachers enjoy control.

Howard Little kept sending me notes in Miss Duke's class. I never answered them. When she saw a note being passed to me in class, she gave both of us swats. How unfair! I told Howard Little to never send me another note for the rest of my life. He listened until the seventh grade.

While waiting in line for lunch one day, I was chattering. I may have said three words. Most of the kids around me were talking also. Miss Duke walked up to me, and terror struck my whole body. She said, "Kitty Dean Hester, shut up." And wham! She slapped me across my face with her hand. Maybe because Mother hated her from being in her class or perhaps because Mother didn't want anyone else hitting me, she went to talk to Miss Duke. Miss Duke backed off me after the conference, and I watched my p's and q's in her class.

At the end of the year, Miss Duke retired. It was certainly time. All of my aunts and uncles began to tease me saying, "It took Kitty to get rid of her." Aunt Rose baked a cake in honor of the occasion. Not for Miss Duke, but for me.

Miss Cornelius Setzer was my fifth grade teacher. She was all business and loved history. She lived with her mother across the street from a prominent lawyer in Newton. This lawyer's brother was Hugh Lefler who was a professor at the University of North Carolina at Chapel Hill. This was not the important thing about him though. He wrote a text book on North Carolina history. The book was assigned to the fifth grade. Miss Setzer was beside herself with excitement over teaching this book since she knew the author personally. We must have spent a couple of hours every day studying North Carolina history. I loved it. By the end of the year I was an authority. The book was too difficult for fifth grade, so the year I entered eighth grade the state department had moved the book to the eighth grade. I was happy and became an even more ardent student of North Carolina history. Strangely, at the beginning of my second year working on my Masters at Duke, it was announced that we would have a visiting professor from UNC. I signed up for the course. It was Hugh Lefler who taught a graduate level version of North Carolina history. I was so excited that I could hardly speak. Only two years during my tenure in Raleigh did I get to teach North Carolina history. It was two years of teaching perfection.

Daddy had left in March, 1946; Grandma Hendrix died in May, 1946. At the end of May Mother took me to Richard Baker Hospital in Hickory to have my tonsils out. The ether didn't really put me to sleep. This didn't stop the surgeon. I bit him. I screamed every profane word I had ever heard. Mother sat in the waiting room feeling sorry for another Mother there whose son had screamed and kicked when they came to take him to the operating room. In recovery Mother found out that it was her child who acted up, and because she found out why I was screaming, she didn't whip me. Fact is, she was mad. My throat didn't heal, but bled for weeks. I lost a lot of weight. I had to go back to the hospital.

Mother had no place to leave me while she worked. Grandma Hester had moved out of town; Daddy was gone; Grandma Hendrix had died. Mother sent me to my older cousin Lillian in Mooresville about thirty miles away. Lillian had two babies. The idea was for me to help her. This worked very well until the middle of August. I was pushing the baby around the block in her stroller when my appendix ruptured. Lillian's dad, my Uncle Carl, who was visiting, rushed me to Davis Hospital in Statesville. Dr. Meade did the surgery. It was a serious situation. It was a "God thing" that I survived.

I missed the first week of school in the sixth grade. Then in October I "became a woman". I had no idea what was happening to me. No one prepared me. I thought I was dying. After all, I was still sitting in Daddy's rocking chair on Saturday mornings listening to "Let's Pretend" (fairy stories) on the radio. What woman would listen to fairy tales on the radio? Mother showed me how to use a pad, and said to me the great explanation, "This will happen to you for the rest of your life." Ouch! Oh, no, she must be wrong. Mother never teased, so I was frightened that she must be telling me the truth. I always had severe cramps, so I didn't look forward to this journey into womanhood at all. I would rather be a boy who played ball and pestered girls and wasn't expected to behave.

In the midst of all of this turmoil in my life, a very important thing occurred. I accepted Jesus Christ as my personal Savior. This was no surprise to me because I never remember a day when I didn't know that Jesus was a presence in my life. I simply acknowledged in front of the church membership that I believed and was baptized in the pool in the front of my beautiful church. A boy teenager winked at me just as the pastor was about to dip me into the water. From that point on, I never went near this boy. I was pretty sure that he was Satan in disguise. To this day, I think that this is possible. This boy spent most of his adulthood in prison.

The most important teacher I had in my whole school life was Miss Ruth Hoyle in sixth grade. She not only was the greatest teacher, but she was a kind and understanding woman. She came into my life at the very time when I thought that I couldn't go on another day without someone to care about me. She was good to all of the kids, but she made me feel special. I've heard that people will not remember you for what you say to them or what you do for them. You will remember the people who make you feel good about yourself. I will never forget Miss Hoyle although it's been sixty-five years since I was in her class. She made me feel good about me.

Once I got very sick in school. She asked the principal to cover her class while she drove me home. When she delivered me home, she drove to the Glove Mill and drove my mom home to take care of me. What teacher would do that? Having her at this point in my life was definitely a "God-thing". Just when my young life was falling apart, I was allowed to have contact with Miss Hoyle, the most understanding and caring person I had ever known at that time outside my family.

My grades were average. The teachers in the little town were very good teachers. But their attitude was the same as everyone else in town. A mill kid would grow up to work in the mills. Once in the sixth grade Ms. Booth, our music teacher, became very angry at Howard Little, a mill kid. Howard just couldn't seem to understand what the treble clef had to do with the song we were trying to learn. She was so frustrated that she threw down the chalk which cracked into many little pieces on the floor. She screamed in the highest treble voice, "It doesn't matter whether you understand this or not. You're nothing but a mill kid. And you'll never be anything else." I sat near the back of the room, but when she screamed those words my body seemed to receive an electric shock. I shuddered. "You're nothing but a mill kid. You're nothing but a mill kid. You're nothing but a mill kid." My mind churned with her words for days, and to this day, sixty-five years later, I can hear her voice in my mind. Howard Little, the mill kid, grew up to have a fine military career.

My soul recoiled and recoils today at those words. That judgment that a mill kid could never become anything more was ridiculous, and my child's mind recognized it as such. I didn't believe her. I immediately knew that she had overstepped her bounds. She was wrong. Oh, yes, she was an adult in the day when all adults were right about everything, but she was wrong. Screaming at Howard Little and judging every mill kid with her outburst was unacceptable in my young mind.

Ms. Hoyle must have agreed because she had a startled look on her face when the screaming began. I was happy that Ms. Hoyle stayed in the room for the music lesson. After the music teacher left the room, Ms.Hoyle was very nice to us. She seemed to understand that we all deserved a cup of "nice". Looking back, I know that Ms. Hoyle changed her lesson plan that afternoon. We had games and art and "good" music the rest of the day.

I wouldn't say that our schools were full of teachers like Ms. Booth, but there were enough to keep us mill kids in our place. Then there were the teachers like Ms. Hoyle. We had enough of those who made sure the mill kids were treated with respect. These teachers taught us as if we were just as good as anyone in the class. I believe God places teachers in the very grade and subject where they have the opportunity to reach the most kids. As surely as I believe God gave me my education, I believe that Ms. Hoyle was assigned that sixth grade class that year 1947 – 1948. He put her right where she was needed most.

This incident was indicative of the environment where I lived. It seemed that most people in our little town felt the same way. The pervasive stance on the future of a mill kid caused me to turn off thinking about the future. It was too painful. How could intelligent people in a free country dare to think in such a narrow-minded way! I knew no one to talk to about my feelings. I never heard a word of encouragement from a classmate or a teacher or anyone at my church concerning education because they all expected me to go to work in a factory when I was sixteen. No one thought that education was important for me. I never heard anyone discuss education. Therefore,

I didn't take education seriously. I just worked hard and tried to think of ways to stay out of the factories.

Miss Mary White was my seventh grade teacher. She and her sister were spinsters, but they didn't have to live in the teacherage. They lived in a huge two story white house about a block from the school. Mother and all of her siblings had Miss White. What happened is vague in my mind. I know that my uncles pretended to fuss at me for getting rid of Miss White because she was one of the best teachers ever. That was three of their teachers who retired or left when I had them. Miss Carrie Thornton, Miss Ollie Duke, and Miss Mary White.

Ms. Holloway was my seventh grade teacher for the end of the year. She had just lost her husband and was very unhappy.

I began to be shy, introverted, and ashamed in front of the other students. I wanted to evaporate. Many things happened to embarrass me.

One day I wore a beautiful dress to school. Mom had made it out of flour sacks. She would buy two fifty pound bags of flour to get two bags that matched. She would have to take my wagon to the store because she couldn't carry that much flour. I'll never forget that dress. It was a pink and green check. A wealthy girl in my class was in the restroom the first time she asked me where I bought my dress. She never said that she liked it, so I thought she was making fun of me for wearing flour sacks. I ran out of the restroom. But she asked me many times during the rest of the day. That night Mother answered the phone. I knew that it was the girl's mother. I heard Mother say, "Oh, I made that dress." When the mother inquired where she bought the fabric, I heard Mother say, "It was a piece of material I've had around the house for a while." How clever was my mom! Was it possible that Mother understood?

The seventh grade was not a good year. I became aware of boys or boys became aware of me. I never figured out which. Richard, the pest, began acting strange like he knew something I didn't know. So what! I was sure that I knew something he didn't know. I felt awkward. I felt like I was supposed to know something I didn't know. I was glad when seventh grade was over.

At Christmas in the seventh grade a friend of Mother's who managed a dime store on the Court House Square hired me to stock the counters during Christmas holidays. I was just thirteen, but could work during a holiday. I did a good job and was happy to make thirty-three cents an hour. I worked all day during the time off from school. I walked two blocks up Fifteenth Street to Main Street where I took the bus downtown for a nickel, and the same back in the evening after dark. Our streets were safe. The bus stop downtown was a half block from the store. I had to walk two blocks home when the driver dropped me off at Fifteenth Street. This was nice to be able to hand my salary to my mother who needed it for our expenses. But it set the stage for Mother to expect money every week from me. This proved a hardship at times. After Christmas I had to stop work because thirteen year olds could work only during holidays.

In February I turned fourteen. Then I could legally work. I began working every Friday afternoon and all day Saturday at the other dime store on the square. I liked to work. One Saturday before Easter the manager put me behind the candy counter. There was a strange man watching me all day. He made me nervous. I knew everybody in Newton, and I was sure that this man did not belong in my store. The candy counter was especially busy that day. At the end of the day when I checked out, the manager told me to go to his office. The strange man was there. He was an inspector for the chain. He said, "Girl, you can eat more jellybeans than any human on earth. Every time you weighed a customer's order, you popped two or three into your mouth." I was horrified. He continued, "You ate all of our candy profit for the day. I don't have to say more because I'm sure you're going to be sick. That will be your punishment." The inspector and the manager had a big laugh. I ran for the bus. I didn't get sick, but I never pop a jellybean that I don't remember how scared I was that day. This was stealing. I knew it, and I was ashamed. I still love jelly beans.

Soon after this, I got a job a couple of stores down the street at Belks. I loved this job. Mr. Brumley, the owner, liked me. I don't know why. He was a quiet man who never had any expression on his face. The only reason I know that he liked me was that he trusted me. I started on the balcony selling fabric. His office was on the balcony, so he could see me working every time he glanced up or exited or entered his office. One day he moved me to shoes. I could make more money in shoes. The shoe manager was very arrogant. Old dirty men would come in with dirty, smelly socks. He would refuse to help them. He would make me wait on these men. Sometimes these men wanted engineering boots which were the highest priced shoes in the department. When this happened, the shoe manager would pout the rest of the day. I was paid $3.33 for three hours on Friday plus eight hours on Saturday plus commission. In shoes my commission was higher than my salary. Mr. Brumley knew that he could move me to any department where an employee was absent. He liked my flexibility. On holiday weekends he had me gift wrapping. He even let me dress windows when I was older. There were three large windows out front. I stayed at Belks till I went to college. Even in college Mr. Brumley asked me back to gift wrap at Christmas and Mothers' Day. He was good to me, and I loved working for him. When I went to work, I never knew what I would be doing.

The summer between seventh and eighth grade Mother decided that I could stay home alone during the day. I couldn't have any visitors. This was funny because I couldn't have any visitors when Mother was home either. It rained three weeks straight that summer. Finally we awoke to sunshine. In the early afternoon five or six kids from up the street stopped by and yelled, "Hey, Kitty, let's go bike riding." I was ashamed of my blue second-hand bike which Mom had bought during the war and "fixed up" which meant mostly painting it. But I was eager for an adventure.

My house was next to the last house on the street. One house away the pavement ended and the red clay road began. When it rained for three weeks, the word clay had special significance. We rode about a half mile and passed Grindstaff's Dairy farm where many an afternoon, we would get extra milk and make home-made ice cream for four or five families.

Then on to the lowest point of our journey which was the creek. About sixty feet from the narrow wooden bridge, we could slam on our brakes. About half an inch under the red clay were huge soap stones… very slippery soap stones. When we hit a slab of soap stone, we had to hold on to our bikes for dear life because our bike would slip and slide and try its best to throw us into the creek. I certainly didn't want to land in the creek, the playground of many a copperhead.

When we were across the bridge, it was uphill until we reached Laffon's Orchard. Mr. Laffon had apple trees, peach trees, plums, pecans, giant oaks with rope swings, and a barn with pet black snakes. He loved for the kids in the town to stop by and pick an apple or two and swing a while to rest up.

Our destination was Old Saint Paul's Lutheran Church, the second oldest church in the state. The cemetery around the church was filled with some of the oldest graves in North Carolina. Some of the pine box caskets were just a few feet under ground. Some graves were on top of the ground. A piece of marble was laid on top of the grave site. The body would be laid on top of this marble; then stones were built up around the body using the very same kind of red clay that we walked on or gardened in. On top of the stones another large marble slab was laid. We could find graves where the rain had washed the clay from between the stones, leaving the stones free to fall to the ground. We could lay on our stomachs beside these graves and peek at the skeleton inside. By then I was reading "Premature Burials" by Edgar Allen Poe, so I always tried to determine if the person was buried dead or alive.

The church door was always unlocked. Inside, the downstairs pews were for the whites, and the upstairs benches were for the blacks. Upstairs there were two enclosed seats for the slave masters in the two corners near the back of the church. They could sit with their whip and swing at slaves who didn't behave in church. There were actually blood stains on some of the benches – the blood beaten out of slaves in the days when such things were legal and maybe after it was illegal. There was a pump organ which I loved playing. We would play church. One of the boys would preach from the high lectern, and I would play the organ. All of us would sing.

On this particular day we didn't notice that one of the boys had slipped out of the church. When we had had our fill of playing church, we all headed out the door. The boy had collected every pine cone he could find in the church yard. He threw them as fast as he could – one after another. Those cones really hurt. He was considered to be a real tough guy. Of course, the good thing about six or so kids being hit with cones was that eventually the kids had the cones, and the boy was empty-handed. When we began returning all the cones, he backed up. He stepped on a grave which must have had an old pine box. The box collapsed. He fell into the grave. What happened next cannot be explained in words. It happened so fast that it made us all dizzy. He jumped out of the grave, grabbed his bike, and was off toward home before we could figure out what happened. We all laughed so hard that we could hardly ride our bikes. This rebel grew up to become mayor of a small town a few miles from Newton. He has obviously been a man of integrity in adulthood. It's very good that we all taught him a good lesson that day way back in history.

When I was nine, I noticed a boy at church. I had never seen him before, so he must have been new or lived out in a rural area. After all, I knew everyone in town. He was three years older than I and cute beyond words. I began to look for him every Sunday. I didn't know his name until years later. When I was twelve, I was walking home from school one afternoon when I saw that this boy and his family were moving into a house a few doors from our house. I became very excited. He had a younger sister. His family became my second family. His sister became my best friend. The only way I could describe my relationship with this boy was that he treated me like a sister that he was ashamed of. At home his sister was always late getting dressed, so I often cooked his breakfast. We all usually rode the school bus to school and walked home. As soon as we reached school, Mr. Cute and Cool ignored me like he didn't know me. The same thing at church. This went on for five years. This treatment did not help my ego. I knew that I was lower than dirt. Did he not understand that I was not his sister?

During my teen years my second family would drive to Charlotte many Saturday nights to Gospel Concerts. All of the great singing groups showed up there. I was especially excited to be able to go to these concerts. The Oakridge Boys, the Carter Family Singers (June Carter Cash was getting ready to leave her teen years then), and many, many other groups sang for us. This was a great opportunity for me. On the way home I would sit in the back seat beside my friend and dream of playing the piano for some famous group of singers. Any group would do!

Mom just couldn't plow the red clay for a garden. This was the first time that I knew of something Mom couldn't do. By now a neighbor, the cute boy's dad up the street, farmed several backyards, so he farmed our garden. He allowed Mom to harvest all we wanted out of the garden. She could can everything he didn't want.

The cute boy's sister began cooking at a very early age. Like me, her mom worked in the mills and required supper to be on the table when she arrived home. Toward the end of one season, she and I made up a recipe which we still use today. It's yummy! Of course, then we didn't care about fat or grease. We were just using what was left in the garden. We named it vegetable goulash. We didn't know then what goulash meant. Many, many years later we renamed our creation, Vegetable Medley.

Vegetable Medley
Chop into bite size pieces and flour:
Green tomato
Onion
Yellow squash
White potato
Okra
Green, red, or yellow pepper
Fry in hot oil, flipping frequently.
Serve with a piece of ham and creamed style corn

Where the CCC Camp had been during and immediately following World War II, some of the buildings had been razed, but the concrete foundations were left with huge stone fireplaces on each foundation. The slabs of concrete were huge. We loved to roller skate on them. The boys, of course, loved to shove my friend and me off the skating surface. I didn't know it at the time, but now I know that this was definitely sexual harassment – abuse toward females. Then it was just attention I didn't really want. I knew that what made them happy was not the same thing that made me happy.

Mother knew psychology very well. She didn't know the word; she knew the subject. Any time I wanted to do something and needed her permission, she wouldn't answer until the last minute. So I was never sure if I could or if I couldn't. One day when I was fourteen, I asked to go play ball up the street with a gang of kids. They played baseball every evening. Mom didn't think I should play with boys or play boys' games. She gave me a long list of things to accomplish before she would give me a definite answer. (Her psychology!) She made a mistake in the number of things she wanted done. I accomplished the whole list and was allowed to go. I ran up the hill to the ball field hoping to get there before they picked teams.

About half way up the hill I was breathing hard. I looked up. There was the brightest cloud I had ever seen. I stopped and put my hands over my eyes. There was a figure in the cloud. It looked exactly like the picture of Jesus that Grandma Hendrix had over her bed. I stood there a few minutes trying to look at the figure. I could feel its presence drawing me toward it. I felt like I was lifting off the ground. Very strange, but not scary. I didn't know much about angels at that point in my life. Finally he dulled, and I proceeded to the field. But I never forgot the figure. Many, many years later I knew that it was my guardian angel. He was happy with me. It was the first time I had seen him. He was unforgettable! But I told no one about seeing him. This was a very special and private incident in my young life. Many, many times since that day I have found comfort in remembering this incident from my childhood.

We made homemade ice cream often that summer. My friend would make the mixture. She always surprised us. Jimmy Stokes turned the churn. He would tell me to sit on top, so he wouldn't have to hold it down and turn. One day toward the end of the summer, Jimmy (a very, very shy red head) said, "Kitty, what's happened to your butt. You're getting too big to fit on the top here." Both of us turned beet red. I liked for the boys to treat me like one of the boys. This was beginning to change.

The eighth grade was exciting. We were located in the upstairs south end of the high school building away from the high school students. We changed classes. We had three different teachers.

Mr. Robert Walker was new to Newton and taught history, my favorite subject, and physical education. He was the son of Rev. Alvin Walker, a Baptist Missionary. He was handsome and my first male teacher.

Miss Betsy Rawls, who was petite and scared of the students, was my English teacher. Rumor was that she had been let go from her prior school because she couldn't control her students. She was extremely hard on the students. Every day we did nothing but diagram sentences at the black board and read. Although this was monotonous, it suited me fine because I could handle both of these activities nicely. I loved writing on the board.

Mrs. Irma Long was our Math and Science teacher. She was the first married teacher I had. It was obvious to me that she was intelligent, confident, and capable. I admired her. Her lessons were interesting, but not my cup of tea.

We had lockers for the first time that year. This was an important part of beginning to feel "grown-up". Eighth grade was a wonderful year.

Mother had surgery when I was in the eighth grade. She was in the hospital for several weeks. She was home a few days and then had to go back for another week. My second family up the street (the family of my best friend and the so cute boy) took me in while Mother was hospitalized. I don't know why my own family didn't keep me.

Later in high school mom beat me so badly that the father of my second family who worked in the sheriff's department came and removed me from her house. I lived with his family up the street for several months til Mom calmed down.

Mother never missed work. We only had her salary to live on. Grandmother Hendrix had sold cosmetics for the California Perfume Company for years. The California Perfume Company later became Avon. When Grandma died, Uncle Carl's wife, Aunt Gert took Grandma's territory. Aunt Gert did not like to work. So at age fourteen I took the territory which included five long streets stretching across the whole town and three large factories. I convinced the mill owners to allow me to send Avon catalogs around. I would go after school to pick up the orders. Two weeks later I would take the products to the mills at the end of the day. I was allowed to set up a table and issue the packages and receive the payment as the ladies left the mill at the end of the day. This was very profitable. Mother loved the fact that I had cash for her every Saturday.

Now I was attending school, ironing Elam Cook's seven white shirts a week because his wife hated ironing, baby sitting Howard Workman's children for him and his wife to run a restaurant, working at Belks, selling Avon, and being very active at church. Plus I was responsible for the cooking and cleaning in my own home.

The summer between the eighth and ninth grade was important in my life. Mother always said that I couldn't date until I was sixteen, if then. I had the feeling that she meant eighteen. But a fast-talking seventeen-year old guy at my church asked me to a birthday party being given for our pastor's daughter. I wasn't interested in boys. They did pretty stupid things in my mind. I had too much going on in my life. Why would a seventeen year old want to hang around with a fourteen year old? I told the boy I couldn't go, but at home I told Mother about his asking. She said, "Oh, I trust him. You can go with him." This boy took me somewhere most weekends for fourteen months. He was fun and popular, very musically talented, a fantastic dancer, and active at our church. He played several instruments and had a wonderful singing voice. But Mother's trust was misplaced. I did not know how to handle dating. This boy was not what he appeared to be, but he was greatly admired for his personality and talent. At the end of fourteen months, I gathered the strength to break up with him. Mother was disappointed in me. I didn't understand that. I was the bad one for a week before he hit on a girl younger than I. He had wasted no time in replacing me. I felt sorry for her. She also attended the same church.

Part III

Chapter 8

On To The Big Time – High School

Ninth grade was the beginning of high school. We were already in the building, so the change wasn't difficult. Now we could go all over the building instead of staying on the eighth grade hall. We could use every restroom.

There was a warning going around that Miss Getty, our female coach, was very demanding (we called it mean, a word seldom used today). The rumor spread that she would embarrass you, making fun of you in front of the whole class in a very loud voice which would resonate around the walls and ceilings of the gym. The warning concerned the first day of school mostly. I was told that she made each girl stand in front of the class where she instructed them to do various things. One was to touch your toes with your fingers. I couldn't do that. My fingers barely reached mid-way of my lower leg. I practiced all summer.

When school started, my fingers were down to my ankles. I was embarrassed in those required little gym shorts. Very embarrassed! Of course, Mother was adamantly opposed to girls showing off their body. Now looking back at pictures of those days, I had gorgeous legs. But back then I had no confidence and didn't know that my legs were fine. When she called me, I felt like I was going to vomit. Horrors! Standing there in those shorts, I felt naked. It was a good thing that I could respond to her demands without speaking because if I had tried to speak I surely would have barfed all over her. She shouted directions at me. I could feel her breath on my face, but I was able to obey. When she said, "Touch your toes" I reached down knowing that she would be screaming at me within the minute. I wondered how her voice could possibly get any louder. I heard an audible gasp from the girls watching behind me. Suddenly I realized that the palms of my hands were lying on the floor. All sickness evaporated. A smile hit my face. I know those around me wondered what I was smiling about because for days I walked around with a huge smile on my lips. Now this was nothing but a "God-thing". Only I knew how close He was to me that day. He can actually make a teen lay her palms on the floor. Yes, He can. But He took His own good time to help me. Through many times of waiting I have learned the lesson that we humans have a hard time accepting. It is not in our time, but His.

The girls had the gym two days a week, and the boys had the gym two days a week. On Fridays we square danced. Bill Britain was usually my partner. He was good looking and sweet. But, for a fact, he played too much. One day on a do-si-do, he was busy shooting a water gun at other couples. He was tall, so when he came around me, his shoulder hit my nose. The next thing I knew Miss Gettys was shaking me. I completely passed out and scared Bill Britain half to death. There was blood everywhere. It took me a while, but I eventually thought it was funny.

I had Miss Williams, the Home Ec teacher, for homeroom. She wanted me to take Home Ec, but Mother wouldn't allow it. She said that I could cook and sew and clean as well as Miss Williams already, so Home Ec would be a waste of time. Miss Williams was a beautiful woman. She would allow me to grade the projects the other girls made in Home Ec. I guess I had found a real voice by ninth grade. One morning Miss Williams yelled at me, "Kitty Dean Hester, if you don't shut that mouth, I'm going to knock you into the middle of next week." I had never heard that expression. The picture of me sailing into next week tickled me. I laughed, so she marched over to my desk, her dark eyes popping, and said, "Oh, so you think that's funny, eh?" When I answered, "Yes, Ma'am", she began to laugh and said, "I do too."

I had Mr. Schuessler for English, Mr. Havnaer for General Science, Coach Broome for World History, and , of course, Miss Gettys for Physical Education. For the life of me, I can't remember who I had for Math. Math was my hardest subject, so I suppose I tucked it in the far recesses of my brain. All of the teachers in my ninth grade year were good people and fine teachers.

By tenth grade I began to feel more comfortable at school.

I was dating a school athlete. We were in most classes together, and we shared a locker although it was against the rules. He was on the football team and the tennis team, but he was outstanding in basketball. He also went to my church. His grandmother had been one of my Sunday School teachers. After about a year, one day I went to the locker to find his things gone. I learned several years later from one of his friends that his father told him that he couldn't play sports if he was going to go steady with me. What this really meant was that he couldn't date a mill kid. I wasn't good enough for him. The boy was never unpleasant to me, but he never spoke to me again. This was tough because he sat in four classes beside me. It was at the beginning of basketball season, so we had a long way to go before the end of the year. When the annuals came out, his friend asked me if the boy could sign mine. He wrote a whole page of sweet and good things. This was very puzzling. When we were dating, we only had cross words once. We were hanging college pennants on the wall of the Youth Center. We started about a foot from the floor, went to the center ceiling, and back to the floor on the other side. He loved Duke and wanted to go there. He wanted the Duke pennant to be at the highest peak, and I didn't. We argued. He won because he could reach higher and because I didn't know how to argue. Most people in my little town would say, "Those pukes from Duke." Actually Duke had a lot of rich students from the North. He did get a sports scholarship to Duke, but he came home after football season. The class work at Duke is hard. I thought of this boy everyday that I attended Duke years later to get my Masters. I became "a puke from Duke". The world is a funny place!

This relationship made me determined not to have feelings for another "upper class" boy. I had more important things to do than to pamper a painful slap down by some boy. In high school I never really cared for another boy enough for him to hurt me. That was a good decision. At that point it was simply a decision I made.

Later in my life the jobs I had in high school and my studies made sense to me. At the time they were just struggles to endure.

I had wonderful tenth grade teachers.

I especially remember Ms. Covert. She was an older lady. Her teaching gave me a lifelong love of the English language. She and her husband had been Baptist missionaries in Cuba. When they had to leave Cuba, they were then assigned to the Cherokee Indian Reservation. Her husband died, so she brought her teen-aged son to Newton, lived in the teacherage, and taught English and Spanish at our school. They could walk to school from the teacherage. Roger, her son, became my friend. He was the nicest boy I knew. Ms. Covert was one of the best teachers I ever had. She bought a car when she was in her sixties; then got her drivers' license. She then bought a house and drove to work. They attended my church. For a while, Ms. Covert was my mother's Sunday school teacher.

She and Roger invited us to go on vacation with them one summer. The four of us had a wonderful time. Roger did most of the driving. He would be driving down the road and yell at his mom, "Hey, Mom, there's a 'coudshe' house!" They would both laugh. After doing this many times, they told us that the broken-down houses along the roads in the mountains of North Carolina were called 'coudshe' houses because the measure of a woman was whether she could live in that mess and love him too. Ms. Covert knew the Reservation from the days she was a missionary to the Cherokees and was allowed into places regular tourists could not go.

Roger went to the new Air Force Academy in Colorado, and Ms. Covert stayed in Newton one more year. It was the year that I graduated. Ms. Covert came to the graduation and was sitting across the aisle from me. Our class gave her a trip to Jordan where her daughter Catherine lived with her diplomat husband. When it was presented to her for her retirement, they called her to the stage. She just sat there because she had fallen asleep. In cap and gown I rushed across the aisle to shake her awake.

Ms. Covert was one of the best examples of a Christian I've ever known personally, and her influence in my life was impossible to match.

Her fortitude inspired me. Her model as a teacher greatly influenced the way I later taught in my own classrooms. I often wished that my students could have known her.

Since my mom was forced by her father to quit school during her senior year, she carried a resentment against educated people her whole life. She never was able to return to get her high school diploma. The bitterness that overtook her thinking was like an addiction, and she resisted any rehab or help.

The time I had dreaded finally arrived. The February I turned sixteen, she decided that I had enough education. This was a sad time. No happy sixteen anything for me. The law was that a child had to stay in school until they were sixteen. Now was the time for me to go to work in the mill. She allowed me to finish tenth grade. I was sixteen and three months at the end of the year. She knew the value of an education better than I, so looking back I consider her thinking very strange. Even she almost finished eleventh grade. I hated the thought of spending my life in a factory. The only way to stay out of the mill was to work and make enough to give her the same amount every Saturday night that I would have made if I was working in the mill. From my dad I had learned to bargain. I bargained this deal with my mom. If she realized that I was using Dad's method on her, she did not let me know it. She didn't believe that I could go to school and handle all these jobs. For some reason I managed. Every Saturday night I gave Mom enough money to keep her off my back about quitting school. She thought I had a "high and mighty" attitude. One of the most serious factors in her attitude was her rule about homework. She told me that at home I would do chores assigned by her. If I continued in school, I was to do all school work at school. Fortunately I secretly used humor to help me through these times with my mom. I eventually got away from Mom, but the sense of humor was mine for life.

Never, and I mean never, did I sass my mom or speak to her with disrespect because I valued my life; however, my stance about working in the mills was a sure thing. No way! I didn't really think that I was too good to work in the mills. When I would occasionally venture into the mill to ask Mom a question, the vibration of the machines would send a shock through my teeth which was not only painful, but frightening. I wanted desperately to avoid sitting in that situation eight hours a day; it would have been a life sentence. There were times when I felt guilty wondering if I thought that I was too good to work in a factory. I wrestled with these feelings, but I always reached the conclusion that it was not a matter of worth. It was a matter of desire.

It was many years before I figured out that Mom really wanted me to stay near her to take care of her; I had spoiled my own mom. She also had a fear that I would outgrow her. There's no doubt in my mind that if I had stayed in Newton, I would have had to live under Mother's roof and rules for my whole life.

Adjusting to this new responsibility of giving Mom a certain amount of money each Saturday night was very demanding. I hardly remember anything about my junior year in high school.

In eleventh grade I had Miss Covington for English and French and Homeroom, Coach Broome for US History, Miss Morton for Math, Mr. Tyler for Chorus, no science.

As far as I knew, none of these teachers nor my classmates or even my relatives knew how hard I was trying to stay in school. The last thing I wanted was for anyone to feel sorry for me. Most of the kids who struggled in school or in their life situation had already dropped out of school and married or started to work in a factory. I realized this and felt lucky every day.

This was the year that I began to wonder about the system. The state required every student to take Biology which I had taken in tenth grade. I took General Science in ninth grade where the class was all boys except me and an eleventh grade girl. I didn't even wonder about this then. But in eleventh grade when I tried to take Chemistry, I was told that I couldn't because I was a girl. I also signed up for Drafting, but I was told that girls couldn't take Drafting because it was taught outside the main building. I wanted to take band, but Mother would not allow it. I was angry. I wondered what these people were doing messing in my education. I realized early that education was the most important thing a person like me could have. I somehow knew that education would keep me out of the mills. How I knew this at such an early age can not be explained. There was no reading or talk of poverty or the importance of education. Before I had a really close relationship with God, I knew that this knowledge and love of learning was a "God thing".

I got up enough nerve to try out for cheer leading. This meant that

I had to stand alone on the stage and do some cheers in front of the whole student body. This was a very big thing for me. I set aside the embarrassment to try something new. The whole student body voted. I won a place and was so excited. Mom stopped it as soon as she heard. She said, "No daughter of mine is jumping around in front of a crowd in those skimpy little outfits." I had to go to the coach the next morning and explain this to her. She yelled at me, but she went on to the next girl. No one seemed to notice my disappointment. Maybe they didn't know I was disappointed. Maybe they didn't care. Maybe they didn't know what to say.

I also tried out for the basketball team. The coach asked me to try out. I knew that Mother did not believe in any kind of sports for girls. I really don't know what I was thinking when I tried out. Every thing I did during the trials was right. When Mom found out, she announced that I must be crazy. She cited why girls shouldn't play sports. None of her reasons made sense to me, but to her they were legitimate. The short uniforms were a big reason I couldn't play, but the great No-No was the out of town trips on the school bus shared by the boys' team. When I told coach the next morning that Mom wouldn't allow me to play, she didn't yell at me. I guess that she expected it.

I thought that I would get into the Beta Club. My grades were good enough, but I didn't make it. I think that they thought I wouldn't need the honor because I wouldn't ever amount to anything anyway. By then I began to understand and accept my place in this town. Miss Shivers was the sponsor of the Beta Club. Maybe it was good that she overlooked me.

All of these disappointments could have driven me out of school had I not been so determined. It was like – I don't care what the world dishes out, I'll deal with it.

I was a hall monitor in the eleventh grade. Members of the Student Council had to stand up and down the hallways at the change of class to keep the student body moving. This was the year that I first remember doing something purposely wrong. There were a few snobby girls in our class. Their behavior indicated that they felt that they were better than me and all of the lower class kids. When you dealt with one of them at a time, they seemed pretty normal. But when they bunched together, they were real snobs. One particular girl carried her nose in the air to the point that I wondered how she could walk. All of her clothes were store-boughten. She lived in a beautiful house, and she didn't talk Newtonian. My position in the hall was outside the girls' restroom. She came out and walked down the hall. She had on a quilted circle skirt. She had accidentally tucked the hem of her skirt in the waist of her panties. I should have said something to her, but after all I was not supposed to leave my post. And she had on pretty panties. So she walked the whole hallway with her rear exposed for all to see before one of her snobby buddies jerked the skirt in place.

Math became harder every year. I had good teachers, but my brain was not wired for math. The only math that mattered to me was to count that money and turn it over to my mom.

In eleventh grade, I took one semester of typing with Miss Raymer. Before the end of the semester, I was typing more than sixty words a minute. I thought that my success was connected to playing the piano. Just a theory. Miss Raymer praised me. She will never know how beneficial this skill has been for me. I made extra money frequently in my life typing papers and books for those who couldn't type. Of course, it has helped me tremendously in my own work.

I took a semester of Driver Training which was funny since I had no access to a car. It was six years before I finally bought a car and started to actually drive. I remember distinctly that the man teaching me didn't find any thing funny about my driving skills. I got my license anyway.

Miss Covington had me for homeroom and two other hours during every day. She was a good English teacher, and she made French class interesting. By the end of each day, she was pretty tired of Kitty Hester.

One day she sent me to the office for swats. We were sitting quietly writing a book report. Our classroom was crowded. The desks were screwed into the floor, so that the desk seat in front of you was connected to the top of your desk. The desks were so close together that one had to turn sideways to slide into the seat. Each desk had an empty ink well. Probably because of the many spills in the past, Miss Covington kept a bottle of ink on her desk. We were not allowed to have ink of our own in the classroom. Gerald Whisenant sat in front of me. He was very good looking, very shy, and very quiet. Shortly after class started he went to fill up his pen at the teacher's desk. When he returned to his seat, he forgot to turn sideways, but rather he tried to sit down rear first. He was a football player, but he wasn't large at all. He was stuck. He wiggled and wiggled shaking my desk, so that I couldn't write. He couldn't move into his desk no matter how hard he tried. He had dark complexion, but I could see the red rise up his neck and into his face. I got tickled. I laughed and laughed. I couldn't stop. Miss Covington sent me to the principal. Mr. Rhyne listened to my story and gave me one flimsy swat. As I was leaving his office, I heard him cracking up. Mr. Rhyne was so stern that I had no idea he knew how to laugh.

Toward the end of the year Miss Covington's classes presented the play "An American in Paris". She chose me to be in the play. This was such a pleasant surprise to me. Mom whipped out her machine for another amazing outfit. Although drama was not easy for me, I enjoyed the fact that Miss Covington trusted me with the part. I didn't try out for the part; she just assigned the part to me. I had to trust her choice.

Richard Tyndall invited me to the prom that year. Richard lived at Sipes Orchard Home for Boys outside Conover. He went to elementary and junior high in another town. Shortly after I met him, he was run over by a school bus. He was in the hospital in Hickory for months. Most surely he would fail the grade. But he didn't fail. People pitched in taking him lessons and returning them to the teachers. The teachers considered the circumstances, and Richard had his own special brand of perseverance.

Richard was never more than a friend, but a very good friend. He had a crush on an "upper crust" girl all through high school. For prom we double-dated with a couple who had a car. Mother made a black organdy dress, and I had black lace shoes. Richard bought me a white carnation corsage; the flowers had red specks all over them. Richard had already been elected President of the Senior Class, so he had to go to the prom to lead a grand processional to begin the dance. Fact is, he had not planned to go to the prom until he was told he had to lead the processional. On Monday before the prom on Friday, he told me he had to have a date. I thought Mom would hit the ceiling, but she didn't. Instead she immediately set up the machine and started designing a dress on Monday night. I believe that Mom had so few joys in life that she relished dressing her daughter.

My mind was really not on school functions, but on making money to give to Mom. The summer of 1953 was a sad and long summer. There was a polio quarantine. In our little town anyone under eighteen had to stay in their own house and yard twenty-four hours a day. I couldn't work at Belks. I could sell Avon on the phone, but someone had to deliver it for me or the customer had to pick it up at my house. What would I do all summer? I was just seventeen. There was a substantial fine for the parents of children caught off their own property. For sure, I would not have to go to work in the mill that summer.

Polio was not unheard of. President Franklin Delano Roosevelt was diagnosed with polio at the age of 39. The disease was considered a child's disease, and it was rare to hear of an adult having it. The medical profession since his death has considered that he may not have had polio, but rather a rare disease that was not known when he was alive. He tried to set up Warm Springs, Georgia as a center for treating the disease. He was in a wheelchair while he was governor of New York and the four terms he served as President of the United States. He learned to stand with braces. Polio was his private hell. He died in 1943, not completing his fourth term.

A young couple on the next street had to take turns going to work because they had two pre-teen sons. I could reach their house by following a path between my back yard and their front yard. They convinced Mom to let me baby-sit for them. They paid well. Their sons, Steve and Ronnie, were real boys. Steve was a big football-type who was full of boyish pranks, and Ronnie was the little guy, the receiver of anything Steve wanted to dish out. My punishment for disobedience was to place a straight chair in the middle of a room and make the offender sit on the chair for ten minutes at a time. They couldn't reach anything worth playing with. If they talked or left the chair, they would be given additional ten minute segments of time. Some days Steve would sit on the chair for an hour or so trying to get a perfect ten minute time span. One day many, many years later I saw Steve in downtown Newton. As he approached me, he squatted as if he were sitting on a straight chair and said as I passed on the street, "See what you did to me!"

Many children in our town had polio. A few died. Dr. Jonas Salk found a vaccine for polio at the University of Pittsburgh in the early 1950's. The vaccine was in trial status till 1954 and was not approved by the government for used until 1955. It was very sad to hear that children I had baby-sat in the past were hit by this horrible, crippling disease.

My senior year was a joy only because I was near the end. I could hardly wait to get out of school and away from Newton. It was a great relief to have come this far. I kept wondering, "What will happen next?" I hoped to study at night at a business school until I was trained to be a secretary. Maybe I would move to Charlotte, forty miles away. I worried that I would not finish.

I had Miss Shivers for English, and Mrs. Bernice Cline for Sociology. The others I don't remember. These two alone balanced each other. The Bad and the Good of Education.

I had Miss Shivers for homeroom and English. She made me shiver. My mom and all of her siblings had had her. They were scared of her too. Three walls of her classroom were chalkboards. Everyday she wanted us to copy what she had on the board. I hated this. What was I supposed to do with these notebooks? By junior and senior year my mom would not let me do homework at home because her theory was that one should do school things at school and do home chores at home. So when was I to study all of these notes. I copied them just to keep Miss Shivers from yelling.

We studied Macbeth that year. We had no books, so Miss Shivers read the whole play to us out loud as we sat at attention in our desk. I thought that Macbeth was neat, so I listened carefully. She was on the part where two murderers rushed onto the road and murdered someone and ran into the woods. Miss Shivers stopped and said, "Kitty Dean, why didn't they go after these wicked men who were murderers?" I thought fast, and all of a sudden I blurted out, "Because they had no streetlights". The red-headed Miss Shivers jumped from her seat screaming in her scariest voice pointing her long red nails right in my face, "Out! Out, you insolent girl!" I left. I didn't know where to go, but I left. I made an A on the Macbeth test a couple of days later. I've always wondered what answer would have pleased her. A mill girl liking Macbeth? Come on. I knew that I was on to something good. Since then I have taught many Shakespearean plays, I still don't know the answer to her question.

I had Mrs. Cline for sociology, a new course in our high school. We were allowed to actually speak in this class. We had discussions of social issues. This was when I really found a voice; I actually had opinions on social issues and could explain them to my classmates. This was the class where one of the intelligent, haughty-taughty Lutheran students announced that Kitty Hester might be big at that Baptist church, but she was going to hell because she was not baptized as a baby. I was shocked. I have heard this girl's voice in my head many, many times through the years. It has caused me to search the scriptures and question theologians. She was intelligent and popular, but she was wrong. Thank God!

I had a date for the homecoming dance which was held in the gym. Right after the dance started someone told me that someone wanted to see me at the door. I went to the gym door wondering what had happened. There was "the cute guy" from up the street in his Air Force uniform. Wow! He took my hand and led me to his car. We didn't talk much. I had not seen him since he graduated and joined the Air Force. He drove and drove and drove and held my hand. An hour passed before I remembered that I had left a date at the dance. We were together for thirty days every minute I wasn't working or in school. At the end of thirty days, he didn't say good-bye or explain that he had to get back to base. He just disappeared. He didn't call or write. This was strange to me!

The summer after I graduated, he called one Saturday night and said that he was Cary Grant and was picking me up in a half hour. I had a date. I had no idea who was pretending to be Cary Grant. Maybe it was a joke being played by my date. I had never heard that voice on the phone before. "The cute guy" showed up at the door in just a few minutes. He took me to the drive in, bought me a bag of popcorn and coke, put his head in my lap and went to sleep. We were together thirty more days. At the end of his leave, he left without saying good-bye.

At the end of summer he left for France, and I left for college. I had only been at college a few weeks when I received a letter from France. He had decided to ask me to marry him. He wanted to fly me to France and live there with him. How sweet! But finishing college meant more to me than anything at that point. The answer was "I can't." Bad timing! He never wrote again.

The year I was a senior a miracle happened in January. At the time I didn't realize it. When it began, things happened so fast that it seemed that I was in a whirlwind. It was January of my senior year that I became aware of our first Guidance counselor, Miss Peeples, at our High School. Actually I would never have met her except that she began attending my church. She was considered an outsider because she was not born and raised in our county. She was pretty, but she was strange. Every Sunday she would walk down the aisle and sit on the second or third row. This was a Baptist church. Baptist people sit in the back of the church as far back as they can get. Our regular members would race into church to grab their back row seat as if they owned it. We had a rather large congregation, but still there were four or five empty rows between the congregation and Ms. Peeples up front. I felt really sorry for her way up there by herself, and my mother had stopped attending church again, so I began to go up front and sit with her. It was a very odd feeling sitting up front with the pretty new "foreigner" in town.

An amazing thing happened on the second Sunday that I sat down beside her...just the two of us up front together. Before the service began, she looked at me and asked the weirdest thing. She asked, "Kitty, where are you going to college?" I was dumbfounded. I had never thought of going to college. I responded with, "Well, Ms. Peeples, I'm a mill kid." She looked puzzled when she asked me what a mill kid was. I explained. She looked thoughtful and responded, "Oh, I see."

The next morning at school she called me to her office. We didn't have an intercom, so she sent a student to bring me to her office. I thought that maybe I could help her understand the rules. You know, that mill kids go to work in the mills when they are sixteen. But she fooled me. She gave me an application to Mars Hill Junior College. I tried to explain to her that I had no money for college. Excuses poured out of me. My mom wouldn't let me go. My grades were average. I was not smart. I didn't have nice clothes. Every thing I owned was homemade. Some dresses were made of flour sacks; some of remnants left over from the ends of bolts of fabric made at Burlington Industries, a factory in town. She said, "You get that application filled out and return it to me. Kitty, you need to go to college. Be sure to get your class rank from your homeroom teacher."

I could hardly believe what I was hearing. This college-educated woman was telling me that I should go to college. Could she be right? What if she were? How glorious!

I had entertained the idea that I would go to a business school and study a year. Then my chances of being a secretary would be good. I had even talked to Mom about this fantasy. Of course, she had booed it, such grandiose ideas in this girl's head.

The next morning I went up to Miss Shivers, my homeroom teacher. At present she was my mother's Sunday School teacher. Miss Shivers was generally considered by the townspeople to be the smartest and best teacher in the high school. Fact is, she was a real witch. I knew this because she wore open toed high heel sandals in the snow. She had bright red long finger nails and toe nails. She had bright orange hair. She was so old that I was sure that Methuselah had been her playmate. Her most outstanding trait was that she delighted in embarrassing students, especially mill kids, in class. When she started, she would go on for half the class period reaming out some student for some very minor infraction. Her sarcasm was always very dramatic as if she were on stage in some Shakespearean play.

This woman had to be not only my Senior English teacher, but my homeroom teacher as well. Before the bell rang to begin homeroom, I asked her what my class rank was. She had the list. Instead of telling me, she began screaming and laughing. It was a wicked laugh. Everyone in homeroom stopped talking. You could hear a pin drop. She yelled, "You in college? Kitty Dean Hester, you are not college material. I won't waste my time on such." I was not shocked. I had seen her act in a similar way with other students daily. But nothing could have prepared me for this tirade. I was very embarrassed. I shrank from her glare. I backed away from her. If she touched me, I might become a witch too. I only hoped that she would shut up then and not carry on as she usually did. I quickly sat down. In my heart I knew that she was right, and I hated that she was right. Who was I to think that I could go to college? My new dream faded fast. Thank goodness that homeroom was a short period, and when the bell rang to leave, I almost crawled out of the room. My face was burning hot.

It just so happened that Richard Gurley was in that homeroom. I would never say that we were running-around friends, but he knew that he could depend on me, and over the years, I grew to understand that he was there for me. Richard heard Miss Shivers' comment. His father was Superintendent of Schools. That night he must have told his father what had happened, for somehow Mr. Gurley heard the details of homeroom that day.

The next morning Mr. Gurley opened the door to our classroom during homeroom. He motioned for me and for Miss Shivers to come to the door. When we stood in the hall, he handed me a slip of paper and said, "Kitty, I looked up your class rank for you. You apply to that college. Miss Shivers, make sure you apologize to this girl." Mr. Gurley then turned and marched like a soldier down the hall, his back to us. This was the same Mr. Gurley who convinced Grandpa to let Uncle Joe go back to high school. The same Mr. Gurley who talked Grandpa into allowing Aunt Shirley to come back to school. Now Mr. Gurley was affecting my life in a positive way. My hero. Miss Shivers looked aghast, and she and I went back into the room. We never spoke of the incident again. She never apologized, but she never spoke to me harshly again.

From first grade to my senior year, I had the feeling that the third grade pest had turned into a mature grown up. Looking back, I can think of many instances which I didn't understand at the time. Times when things just went my way when I didn't think they would. Richard and his sister went to the Methodist Church with his dad, but his mom went to my Baptist Church across the street. I thought that this was strange, but it worked for them. Richard Gurley was not uppity like some of the "upper crust" kids. He was just Richard. Of course, it was that genuine love and support from his own mother and father which influenced his behavior. Some years he would be real flirty, but inside we both knew that we would always just be friends. In High School I learned to really appreciate his uniqueness. To this day, I have great respect for him. I wish there were more Richard Gurleys in this world. It would be a much better place.

Ms. Peeples looked over the application, and she mailed it for me. I was afraid to tell my mom. I didn't tell anyone. I didn't really have any expectation that I would be accepted. This was like a game at this point. Since I never had time to play games, I was not a good game player. Whatever happened would be what was supposed to happen. I didn't dare pray about this one. But I did trust God to handle the whole thing.

One afternoon in late May I walked home in a downpour of rain. The wind was whipping as if it had forgotten that it was now May, and

March had passed. I had suffered all day with cramps, so the wet clothes were not a good thing. I grabbed the mail from the front porch and rushed into the house. It was very cold. The pilot light had blown out in the laundry heater. I threw the mail down in a rocking chair near the stove. I had to soak up the oil which had accumulated in the pan in the stove with old rags and get them away from the stove. Then I had to light the pilot wick. It took a while. It would be an hour or so before the room would be warm. I had to change out of my wet clothes. Mom would be furious if she arrived home to no supper. So I also had to get supper on the stove in the kitchen.

By the time I did all this, I was exhausted and dropped into the rocker. I shuffled through the mail. Oh, golly, oh, golly, oh, golly, a letter from Mars Hill! I ripped the envelope open. The message was startling. They were giving me a two year work scholarship. I would work on campus. My books and meals and tuition and dorm room would be paid for IF I made the Dean's List each semester. Since I had no idea what the Dean's List was, I was excited. I hid the letter. I would have to find the right time to tell my mom.

I began to think that I might have fantasized that letter. Could this possibly be true? I would sneak a peek at the letter in its hiding place every once in a while for weeks just to reinforce the fact that this letter was real; it did exist; it did say exactly what was in my mind. No more daydreaming; no more fantasizing. I felt my posture change that day. I walked with an air of superiority, not that I thought I was superior. But for sure I was right. A mill kid could go to college.

Days passed while I carried the letter in my pocket. I would rub the letter when something came up to discourage me. I would rub the letter when I was scared of the idea of change. Carrying this secret letter was a charm. How could a piece of paper change my perspective on the whole world?! It did. My life seemed like a story in a book. Little did I know that this wonderful life was just beginning – that God had a plan for me. As long as I followed His direction, He would give me riches untold. Yes, it was true. It was not just words in a thick, black book.

In a few weeks Ms. Peeples told me that she had written an article for the town's newspaper about my scholarship. I wished that she hadn't done that. I was forced to tell Mom. Mom was unhappy; extremely unhappy. She told me that I was wasting my time, that I would never make it, and that she forbade me to take the idea further. She explained that my failure would reflect on her. It was the end of May, and she didn't speak to me again until the second week in August. Since we were the only two living in the house, it was horrible. When my mother was mad, our world trembled. I played the piano a lot during these months; it was my therapy.

It was just a few weeks before graduation. I wasn't sure that she would come to graduation, but she came.

Also I had my senior piano recital. I hoped she would come. She had made a beautiful dress for me. It was so beautiful I could hardly believe it was mine. The slip was a sky blue taffeta, and there was a double layer of mauve tulle over the blue slip. A month ago we had taken the bus all the way to Charlotte to buy the material. When I walked onlookers couldn't tell if the dress was blue or pink. Mother ruined my delight in the dress when she allowed my cousin to wear my dress to a dance the week before my recital. I had worked so hard on the pieces I was to play. This was the end of twelve years of much practice. Dad had bought a piano when I was six and insisted that I have piano lessons. Of course, he paid for the lessons until he left. The piano was one of the few pieces of furniture he ever bought. Of course, Mom didn't want me to have lessons to start with, so when Dad left, she was ready for me to stop this foolishness. But I earned the money and paid for two lessons a week from the time I was ten till I was eighteen. I wasn't talented, but I loved my piano teacher, Ms. Rowe. She was one of the greatest mentors a girl could have. She was a great positive influence in my life.

The second week in August Mom came home from work early. She never missed work. I thought she might be sick. Her sickness would keep me home was a thought which attacked my brain. I was in shorts and an old shirt. She said, "Get dressed. If you're going to that college, we have to get you some new clothes." We went shopping at the mill end stores. We didn't have a car, so we walked miles. We came home with new shoes and yards of fabric. I was shocked at how she went about dressing her daughter for college. She borrowed magazines. She would find a picture of a dress she liked. Then she would show it to me and ask if I liked it. If I said, "Yes", she would go to the kitchen table and begin to cut the pattern. She dragged the sewing machine into our large kitchen and sat up shop. She sewed for a week. Her staying out of work was unheard of. By the end of the week she had made slips, skirts, blouses, and dresses. She would send me to town with a scrap of fabric to buy a sweater to match a skirt. Mr. Brumley even got excited for me. He let me purchase anything at Belk's at cost. This was a wonderful opportunity. Mom worked like a mad woman from six in the morning till midnight. I worked very quietly cooking and serving her food and drink. I offered to help with the hems. All she would allow me to do was to clean up after her and to press the finished product. "Keep things in order, Kitty," she would say.

Strangely my Avon customers wanted to stock up, since I would be going to college. I made enough on Avon that August to pay Mom her salary for the week she took off to get her daughter ready for college. How strange was this? An unexpected encouragement! Mom was constantly surprised at the things "coming my way".

Aunt Rose had given me luggage for graduation. I considered this a vote for me to go to college although we never discussed it. She was afraid to cross Mother. All summer I would stare at the luggage pretending that it had a message from Aunt Rose. The message was, "You go, Girl!" I packed carefully. I was beside myself with excitement, but for Mother's sake I held it in. Aunt Rose showed up a day or so before I was to leave for college. Strangely, she had purchased two beautiful dresses at Taylors, a shop I had never even entered. The dresses just didn't fit her properly. Aunt Rose could sew even better than my mom. But here she was with two beautiful store-boughten dresses for me to take to college. They fit me perfectly. I never expected such a thing. How could I possibly deserve such nice things? Aunt Rose was one of my major mentors.

One day right before I left, Lucy Lou sent for Mom to bring me to her store. We went. There was a gorgeous winter coat hanging there for me to try on. Lucy Lou sold that coat to Mom for cost. It would be colder in the mountains before it got cold in our little town. Lucy Lou thought of me. This was so very overwhelming for me. I was so proud of that coat. I wore it for years and years.

Edna McGee, a loving woman from my church, drove me to Mars Hill Junior College which was about three hours away up in the beautiful Smoky Mountains. Mother was invited to go with us, but she refused. She didn't cry, but she got very quiet. I thought that she couldn't make up her mind whether to be angry or happy or sad or afraid. For some reason, I really wanted my mom to ride with us that day. I was sad that she refused to go.

Part IV

Chapter 9

Mars Hill Junior College

I had never seen the campus. It was beyond beautiful. I had always loved the mountains. We lived close enough that it was the usual thing to go for a ride on a Sunday afternoon in the mountains. To think that I would now live here was astonishing, but I was afraid. Afraid in many respects too numerous to write about.

The first year Mother sent me an envelope which I received every Monday. Inside I would find a one dollar bill wrapped in a sheet of paper. Never a word. One dollar was not enough to buy my personal needs, pencils, pens, and notebooks. I worried that I shouldn't be here. I had no confidence. I felt dumb and unworthy. Why was I here? What girl ever wore homemade dresses to college? What girl did not have the money to buy a cake of soap when she needed one? I truly did not realize at the time that God had opened a door and given me the willingness to go through. It was the middle of my first year when I accepted the fact that God had opened the door for me to be here. With my lack of confidence, shyness, and immaturity in spiritual matters, I wondered for years how I had nerve enough to think that I could do this. I was retired from a long teaching career before it struck me one day that God had also given me the willingness to try. God is so very good and wise.

Ms. Shivers' words rang in my ears when I became scared. I really didn't know how to study. I had no idea how to take notes. I knew how to copy notes from the board. I watched and learned from other students.

All of the faculty was amazing. Even the President of the college who was called Daddy Blackwell walked through the cafeteria and popped up in the dorm. He always gave a warm handshake and asked how you were doing in such a sincere way that you knew he wanted to know.

Pop Stringfield was my psychology professor. I loved learning about ideas which helped me understand other people and myself. I couldn't learn enough, fast enough. Mr. Jolly was the history teacher and the best of all. He was a great teacher with concern for all his students. For some reason I felt like his favorite. Mr. Howe was amazing. I scored low in math on my entrance exams, so I had to attend class five hours a week instead of the normal three. I only got three credit hours for the five hours. He would often show up in the dorm and ask the dorm mother to call me and two other girls to the parlor where he tutored us for an hour or so in the evening.

Dr. Ella Jane Pierce, recognized as one of the top ten smartest women in the United States at the time, lived in the dorm at the end of hall where I lived. She was ancient. I was assigned to go to her room at nine o'clock every night and give her the daily dose of several medications. She loved to hear that knock on the door because that meant a contact with another human being.

All of my professors were outstanding in their teaching and in their concern for the students. Each class had about twenty-five students, so by the end of the first class the professors knew each student's name. No student could have been luckier. For such a wonderful, talented group of professors to be in this small college was a "God-thing". There's no doubt about it. I know that I keep mentioning "God-things", but I really believe it.

We had to sign up for Physical Education. I held through the years that Daddy couldn't make me an athlete, so no one could. Fact is, I was a klutz. I signed up first semester for Archery. I had never held a bow or an arrow. Coach Hart was so good at what she did. She made me a star in the class within two weeks. I loved the course. I was glad that Mother was not there.

Two semesters of physical education were required. I carried a real shame that I couldn't swim. I had almost drowned twice and had a sincere fear of water. I knew that if I would ever learn to swim, Coach Hart was the person I could trust to teach me. I signed up for swimming. We had the first class where we sat on the side of the pool and heard the class requirements. I knew immediately that I had made a mistake. I would fail and lose my scholarship. I was horrified.

She emphasized that teachers in North Carolina were required to know how to swim. So. I didn't know what I wanted to do, but I certainly did not want to teach school. Before the second class a boy sneaked into the locked indoor pool and drowned. It was thought that he committed suicide. The whole campus was very upset. The pool was drained, and no swimming classes could be taught. Those students who had signed up for swimming played softball the rest of the semester. Whew! I made an A which was a miracle. Daddy would be proud. The boys up the street in my neighborhood would be proud and surprised. On the grade report, the class had not been changed. I had an A in swimming. Now who could have handled that amazing mix-up?

After a few weeks, it seemed that every professor I had made me feel special. Was I really the teachers' pet as a couple of the guys teased me? Was it possible? Looking back, I think that possibly I had an aura about me that drew people to me, especially the professors. I was dying to learn. I studied and asked intelligent questions. I was thirsty for knowledge. I was truly my daddy's daughter. It was fifty years before I discovered that KNOWLEDGE is one of my spiritual gifts. Who would have thought that, back in 1955? I didn't even know what spiritual gifts were. Maybe my professors who knew more about spiritual gifts recognized my gifts.

Nevertheless, I grew in this marvelous environment with encouraging faculty and concerned students. I grew spiritually and intellectually. This was good. These were the best years of my life. These years directed the whole rest of my life. The two years at Mars Hill made me what I have become.

We had to sign a promise that we would never buy, sell, or use alcohol, or dance as long as we were students at Mars Hill. I had no problem with that. I had never bought, sold, or used alcohol. I figured that I wouldn't have time to dance or anyone to dance with even if I had wanted to.

I frequently thought of what Daddy could have accomplished if he had had the opportunity to attend Mars Hill. He would have been a dynamo!

At Mars Hill no one was allowed to smoke or drink or shoot pool or gamble – unthinkable. It was like a convent on the girls' side of the mountain. On the side of reality, maybe Daddy would not have been able to adjust.

I was told that my job would be to clean tables after dinner in the cafeteria. Surely not! How embarrassing! I would be a maid. I quickly decided that I could be a good maid. After all, that's exactly what I had been at home. But here, couldn't I please do something hidden like shelf library books? These feelings made me feel guilty, so I hid them and forced myself to find joy in my job cleaning tables in the cafeteria.

My guilt only lasted a few days. Then I realized that cleaning tables was turning out to be the very best job a girl could have. The football team came in late every day in the fall. Most of these guys were ministerial students. The captain was a very good looking sophomore with dark complexion (maybe a Cherokee Indian, I thought), and he ate like a horse. He was the last to leave every night. While I was waiting to clean his table, we would talk. One day he asked, "Kitty, do you ever get scared?" I responded with a laugh. He said, " I'm serious. Sometimes I think that maybe I'll get a church way out in the country. I see them having a piano that no one can play. They'll expect me to lead the singing. I can't do that."

I thought about his fear. The next night I told him that I thought that he needed to learn to play hymns on the piano. He was delighted with the idea. I agreed to teach him. We found an empty room in the music building. He began taking two lessons a week and paid me $.50. No, not $.50 each. $.50 for two. It wasn't long till his football teammates who were ministerial students wanted lessons. I taught as much as I could. Most of them learned twenty or so hymns. I had plenty of money for everything I needed. When I look back on that situation, I now realize how bizarre it was that my piano lessons led me to teach many football players something they thought they needed, and I got what I needed. That really was a "God thing". No way it wasn't. I learned that when you become a blessing to someone else, you almost always receive a blessing from the experience. This has been true for me my entire life.

Being an only child who was raised in a small town, I had never known anyone like my roommate. She never studied. She was beautiful and had a wardrobe of beautiful clothes. She never closed the door to the bathroom when she showered or used the toilet. She would step out of the shower and stand naked in front of the mirror and say, "Hello, you beautiful thing." No one I knew at home ever acted like that. Being her roommate was a challenge I was not ready for. She would lie in bed skipping breakfast. When I would see her on campus, she sometimes was wearing my best skirt and sweater. I would seethe with anger. This really rattled my cage. Mom had taught me that anger was an instrument of the devil, so I rarely felt anger. When I did, I played the piano. Now I had to confront another student for wearing my clothes. It occurred to me that I should explain that my clothes were mostly home-made; some out of flour sacks. That would have solved the whole problem, but I couldn't bring myself to admit this. I was not familiar with confrontation. I would calmly tell her when she returned to the dorm not to use my things. She would smile and say, "They're in my closet, so they must belong to me." We only had one small closet to share. In the spring she would still be caught wearing my clothes. The worst part was that she never hung anything up; she would just throw my hard-earned clothes on a chair or on my bed or worse, on the floor of the closet. This was very frustrating to me because we had weekly room checks. We didn't know which day the dorm mother would pop in, so we had to keep a clean room all the time. I was the only one keeping the room clean. If our room did not pass inspection, we would not be allowed library privileges. I needed to go frequently to the library. That's where I did a lot of studying. Since she never studied, this didn't bother her at all. She had all kinds of money and a boyfriend who showered her with gifts. But she used my shampoo and soap. These things were major frustrations in my freshman year. I made sure that she was not my roommate my sophomore year. In my sophomore year, my roommate was perfect. This made up for the first year.

The campus was beautiful. My love for the mountains had been a life long love affair. Now that I was living in them, I felt exhilarated.

The boy's dorms and a huge, beautiful home where Daddy Blackwell lived were on one side of the campus on a small mountain top. I've never learned to tell the difference in a small mountain and a big hill, so Daddy Blackwell may have lived on a big hill. The classroom buildings and the Dining Hall, Student Union, football field, theater, and such were in a valley. Behind the football field was Faculty Row. The girl's dorms were on the opposite side of the campus also on a small mountain top. We had to walk to class, of course. Our leg muscles were in great shape. I loved this walk down the hill in the mornings and back up in the evening. Sometimes I prayed as I walked. It was a good feeling. Silly, but I felt closer to God in these high mountains than I had ever felt at home. I had a strong sense that He was there with me smiling every day. A small town was on the opposite side of the valley from Faculty Row. I mean small. A huge church, a service station, a grocery store, and a general store. I rarely saw any of the townspeople. Everyone seemed to be connected to the college.

One night about nine o'clock I was headed up the hill to the dorm, coming from the library. I was all alone. The night was beautiful with a full moon. All of a sudden I began singing to the top of my voice and dancing round and round kicking up my legs. I had a great time. Such joy! Every time I paused to get a breath, I heard ribbit, ribbit. I thought the frogs are enjoying the night also. I reached my room and took off my clothes to put on my pajamas. All of a sudden a boy threw the door open and rushed into our room. He threw clothes out of the chest looking for panties. I had never heard of a Panty Raid. I ran to the window. There were hundreds of hooded boys in the courtyard. I saw a housemother with a broom beating a vandal over the head till she could finally pull the hood off his head. He was a ministerial student and an honor student. His parents were missionaries. Because one of the hooded rascals yelled, "Hello, Kitty" as he ran through the parlor, I was called into the housemother's room and questioned. I actually had no idea who the boy was. I don't think she believed me. The next morning the cafeteria was very quiet. A popular boy walked up to me as I stood in line waiting to be served. He had never spoken to me before. He was very tall, and now he leaned down and whispered in my ear, "Ribbit! Ribbit!" I jumped so high that I almost caused the boy to fall. Too bad I didn't.

I would go out behind the dorm on warm afternoons and pray and study. I would sit down on the hillside and lean against a tree to try to figure out how to outline a chapter of the history book. Fortunately I had good penmanship. Many times other students would want to copy my notes because they looked like they had been typed. The more other students asked to see my notes the more I tried to be sure that they included everything and that they were neat. I learned that you can remember better if you write it down. I did not dare to write in my books because at the end of the quarter I needed to trade these books in on the books for next quarter.

The dorm lights were to be off at eleven every night. We were required to study every night from seven till ten. From ten till eleven we had to bathe, shampoo our hair, socialize, and do our laundry. If you couldn't do all you needed to do between ten and eleven at night then you would have to figure out another way to take care of your business. We lived in suites of two bedrooms and one bathroom, so there were four girls trying to bathe and take care of business in an hour. I had to give Dr. Pierce her medications.

These times in the woods behind the dorm, and times I would get up at four or five in the morning and sit shivering in the room were the methods I used to study. This was a good decision, for I was a success. Yes, the first semester I made the Dean's List. I was very happy to know what a Dean's List was. This list was A-B students. I had all A's except a B in math. These first semester grades let me know that I could do it. Now I would be sure to keep it up. I became more confident, but my near panic going into every test never ended.

By the end of second semester, I had devised another method of doing well on tests. I would pretend that I was the professor, and before a test, I would develop a test. When I would go into the classroom for the real test, I would have very few surprises. I just wrote the answers to the same questions I had written to study. This method worked extremely well during all of my college years. I kept this method to myself. It was my secret.

The second semester I made the Dean's List again. This seemed remarkable to me. My professors were so proud of me. Was this really me? I was changing so fast that I hardly recognized myself. I thirsted for knowledge and respect. By the end of the year I knew that I was no longer a mill kid. I would be no more. I also knew that this scholarship was mine for two years of an education because now I knew that I could do it. This was not just an education but a fine education. It was the changing of my whole being. This was good.

At Thanksgiving that year I had no money for the bus ride home. Mother did not volunteer to purchase my ticket, so I stayed on campus with the foreign students who didn't get an invitation to someone's home. I still worked in the cafeteria during the holiday because we had many foreign students who needed to be fed. I loved the foreign students. Mingling with them and learning about their countries was very interesting to me. I would try to help them as much as I could.

On Thanksgiving evening after the dinner meal, I headed to the theater where we were allowed to watch a movie. To get to the theater I had to climb about thirty steps to get to the street where the theater was. When I reached the top of these steps, I was startled. About twelve high school students had made hundreds of snowballs. They started with a rock in the middle and rolled snow around it. They began throwing these missiles at me with vigor. I was knocked out. A Cuban boy was studying in a building beside this attack. He heard the noise and ran out. The high school boys fled. Jose picked me up and carried me to the infirmary which was fortunately near by. I awoke in the middle of the night with the nurse shining a flashlight in my eyes. I had concussions and had to stay in the infirmary for three days. What a holiday! Recently when I was in a Bible class at my church, there was a discussion of the how unimaginable stoning was in the Bible. I told the class that I had been stoned once. They laughed and laughed. Believe me, it wasn't funny.

Mother lent me the money to come home for Christmas. I gift wrapped at Belks to make money to pay her back.

Right after Christmas I met a good-looking football player in the cafeteria. We began eating together, and he would walk me up to the dorm. There really wasn't any dating at Mars Hill. Every day at lunch we would sit with four other students. It was the habit at Mars Hill to say grace before each meal as soon as six people sat down at the table. One day after we had been together for about two months, I said, "You never say the blessing. Today's the day." He said the blessing in another language. When he finished, I said, "I didn't understand a thing you said." He replied, "I wasn't talking to you." This response was surprising.

When he walked me to class, he said, "I think you need to know something about me." I knew that he was rich, cute, and sweet. What more did I need to know? He continued, "I'm studying to become a Catholic priest." I was in shock. This was a Baptist school full of ministerial students studying to be Baptist ministers. What was he doing here? I never found out. I surmised that he was a rather short, light weight type guy who wanted to play football. Shortly after this, we stopped seeing each other, except to say, "Hi".

During my two years at Mars Hill, the only visitor from my hometown was my older cousin Naomi. She and her husband drove up several times. She always brought me huge boxes of supplies and junk food. The cokes she brought could be set on the window ledge to turn cold. It was better than a refrigerator. The coke would be cold within an hour and icy within an hour and a half. These trips were such a joy for Naomi. She and her husband were mill people. They married very young. I've been told fourteen and fifteen. She had her oldest child at age fifteen. They had three children. They must have lived on what her husband made in the tape mill because Naomi was always giving to everyone. She was a very quiet woman with always a smile on her face. She seemed to believe that her mission in life was to make others' lives easier. She was so proud of me for pushing forward. Naomi even cut my hair for years. She was a hands-on kind of person!

There was a girl on the third floor of my dorm whose hobby was photograph. The girl across the hall was a really cute red-head and a preacher's daughter. The photographer asked to take her picture. When the cute girl went to the photographer's room, she was asked to take off her clothes and put on a short fur jacket. She was to sit on a trash can turned upside down. A month or so later, she ran into my room screaming. She had a porn magazine in her hand. The photographer had sold the picture. She was horrified that her father would see it. Girls gathered from all over the hall. I stood there stupefied. I didn't know that such magazines existed. When one of the girls said that she was sure that the photographer was a lesbian, I had no earthly idea what she was talking about. I read the Bible through three times in High School, but I certainly did not get the gist of the Sodom and Gomorrah happenings.

When one of the older girls explained lesbianism, I could not believe it. I was sure that she was making it up. I didn't even want to think about it. I couldn't even understand how she could make up such trash.

The first year flew by. Besides the wonderful professors, I was surrounded by great friends. Life was good, clean fun and hard work. I thrived on all of this. Actually this year in 1955, I became me. The real me was okay. I have only realized this recently. The truth was that for eight years after Daddy left and Grandma died, I had no one to speak an encouraging word to me. Everyone seemed to be scared of my mother. Starting with Ms. Peeples my senior year and continuing the two years at Mars Hill, I was surrounded with people who encouraged me with words of hope. Every professor who wrote a "Great Job!" on a paper, every professor who asked, "What do you think, Miss Hester?" were speaking hope and success into my brain and soul. With every smile from a fellow student or every compliment they gave me, the pain and sadness within me inched its way out, and I began to have the confidence that I had never had before. I knew all of this, but didn't quite get the whole message until I listened to a taped message from Joel Osteen about speaking hope and vision into another person. I hope that I have been doing just that with the people, especially students, around me.

In the Mandarin Garden Club a few years ago, the board would be seeking ideas to make money. I would give an idea, and they would shoot it down. Months later in desperation, they would try my idea, and it proved to be a great fund raiser. Years later, one of those women said of me, "She's a real visionary." I remembered what one of our superintendents said, "Let the students know your expectations. They will live up to them." Actually in school and in other organizations, I have tried to speak "vision" into my listeners. This method actually works.

Chapter 10

Ridgecrest Baptist Assembly

I was on staff the summer of 1955 at Ridgecrest Baptist Assembly grounds in the mountains of North Carolina. I wore a uniform and made beds. A girl from Mississippi and I made a hundred beds a day. On every Thursday we changed the linens on these beds. Not once did I have a back ache. Neither did my partner Louise. For this we got $5.00 per week, our food, our room in a dorm to be shared by three other girls, a set of horrible green uniforms, and a spiritual experience of a life time.

I began dating a man on staff who had just come out of the Navy. He was manager of the gift shop for the summer and would begin Wake Forest College in the fall. He had a zeal for the Lord's work. He sang beautifully, played the piano by ear, and preached in the style of Billy Graham. He would work weekend revivals in small churches in the area. He had studied the Bible for the years he was on a ship in the Aleutias. Many weekends he and I and a small group of select staffers would be in revival meetings. I would play piano and maybe read the scripture. The group would sing special music and also lead the congregation in songs. Sammy would preach and shake the change in his pocket. After a few weeks of the change jingling in his pocket during his sermons, we made a plan. I would hold his change while he preached. Of course, we didn't get paid for these weekend revivals, but the love offering was divided among us. Sammy gave the singers and me the same amount he took. This was good.

Sammy had many fine qualities. He asked me to marry him, and I agreed. But I couldn't transfer to Wake Forest. I loved Mars Hill, and I had another year of a scholarship there. So at the end of the summer I returned to Mars Hill, and Sammy went to Wake Forest. It didn't make any sense for him to start at Mars Hill. We spent too much time writing letters and phoning each other. After a few months of this, we felt that we were not on the right path. So we ended our relationship. It was hard because Sammy was a "real catch". But the timing was wrong. I wondered if we had allowed inconvenience to ruin what God wanted in our lives. I have wondered the same many times over the years, as often as I think of all of our accomplishments. We would have been a powerhouse together working for our Lord. It didn't happen. Instead we served separately.

Dr. Samuel James went on to finish Wake Forest College and the seminary. He and his family went to Vietnam and opened a seminary to train Vietnamese pastors in Saigon. When the communists invaded Vietnam, he was one of the last to leave. He has continued to serve God on the mission field every day since he left Vietnam. He has been instrumental in opening mission work in many foreign countries. Now in his late seventies he is in Vietnam training pastors again. He'll stop only when our Father takes him to Heaven to be with Him. His life has been one of a servant. His choice. A good choice. I've never forgotten Sammy, and our time together. I knew for certain that he was too good for me. I was wrong. It wasn't a matter of too good or not good enough. It was a matter of following God's will.

Ridgecrest was a once in a lifetime opportunity. Every week we had a staff meeting. We had almost two thousand staffers who were college students from all over the world. Every staff meeting started with everyone standing and quoting I Corinthians 13 in their native language. It was awesome. One night Billy Graham, whose home was just two miles away, was to speak to us. He didn't show, so we had testimonies and sang and sang. About nine o'clock a long limousine pulled up to the meeting room. Billy Graham had arrived. He had been in the ER because Franklin, his then young son, had thrown a toy car at his head. He needed stitches on his forehead. Billy Graham had grown up not far from my mom's house. I had followed his remarkable career from the time I was a kid. It was wonderful being in his presence.

We had a different and marvelous speaker every week in the huge conference auditorium. I never missed a session. It was like learning at the feet of God's chosen every morning and every evening for twelve weeks. How fortunate was I!

Chapter 11

Back To Mars Hill

The second year at Mars Hill was more perfect than the first. I was more comfortable and more assured than I had been my whole life. I realized that I could make it. My professors accepted me like I was something special which puzzled me to no end.

I especially enjoyed Dr. Kendall's courses – a semester of Old Testament and a semester of New Testament. These courses were easy for me because my grandmother and the people at my church and my own studying in high school had prepared me well. I was in Logothia, the Bible Club. What a joy! In High School because Mom would not allow me to do school work at home, I had purchased Bible Courses from Moody Bible Institute. I studied and took the tests like I was going to be paid for the grade. I did well. I was paid because knowledge of the Bible increased my joy in living my life. It made me more aware. I was a serious student; therefore, I was blessed for my efforts.

I was promoted in the cafeteria to cashier where I learned to know everyone on campus. I also got to leave the cafeteria early. I tried to smile and say a word of encouragement to everyone coming through the line. Some of the boys goofed off so much that it was hard to keep working toward my goal. I refused to let the "goof-balls" foil my plan.

Almost from the beginning of the second year, Jack was everywhere I went. He showed up at my table at breakfast and lunch. We had absolutely nothing in common. He was handsome, well-dressed, and seemed smart. He stared at me in Botany. All of a sudden he was my lab partner in Zoology. This was fine with me because he was pre-med. He was also very artistic. I had no desire to cut open those frogs. I could actually look at Jack's lab drawings and make my drawings without looking at the frog itself. I made an A in the course, and he made a C. How could this be? He taught me most of what I learned in the course. He was an excellent teacher.

At Christmas he sent me a stuffed monkey to Mother's house. Okay, he sent me a monkey. I thought nothing of it, although the monkey was really cute. When I got back to school, he asked me if I was ever going to wear the ring he gave me. I answered, "Maybe". I wondered what he was talking about. Was I completely naïve? A week or so later I found the ring on the monkey's paw. It was my birthstone.

I was selected to represent Mars Hill at the state Baptist Student Convention. My roommate and I went with a bus load from Mars Hill. Jack showed up at the convention. He acted like he owned me. What was going on would be called stalking today. Everywhere I went, he showed up.

In the spring he ask me to be his girl. I emphatically said, " No way. You're not a Christian. I will never date anyone who is not a Christian." The next Sunday he proclaimed Christ as his Savior and was baptized that night. I knew for a fact that this was not God's plan for getting humans to accept Him. His parents had never taken him to church when he was a child. He had five younger siblings. I could not understand this. What did they do on Sunday? He began attending church. He didn't understand anything about the Bible stories. He would read them and ask questions. When I answered his questions, he would say, "No way." When I told him about the parting of the Red Sea, he explained to me that what I was saying was scientifically impossible. I explained that God is the greatest scientist of all.

Jack began waiting outside the cafeteria for me to get off from work. I had been promoted to cashier which meant I got off work earlier. He would walk me up the hill and talk. He was interesting enough, but I felt guilty that I suspected his sincerity as a Christian. He was playing with fire. I felt obligated to teach him everything I knew about God, so the walks up the hill were okay with me.

Toward the end of the year, Mother Caroline, the Dean of Girls, saw him holding my hand. She called me to her office, and told me that I had sinned. She said that if she ever saw me holding a boy's hand again, she would put a bus ticket home in my mailbox and that I must immediately pack and leave. She said, "Girl, what on earth are you saving for marriage?" I thought this was funny. I was smart enough not to laugh or to respond. My thought was, "The other hand." She made me get on my knees in front of her rocking chair, and she prayed for my soul till my knees were numb, and my back hurt.

Dr. Ella Jane Pierce was teaching Religious Drama. I still helped her with her medicine and felt privileged to have her for English Literature. Since I began college two years before, I had never chosen a course. I just took whatever was on my outline to get the AA degree. Now the last semester I attended Mars Hill I had a blank spot in my schedule. I dared to sign up for her Religious Drama class. At this point in my life I was very shy, but beginning to have some confidence to try new things.

At exam time I had no idea how to study for her exam. She kept assuring me that I would do fine. When we all settled into class the last day, she divided us into groups. My group was four girls. None of us had a Bible with us. She handed each group a slip of paper with the name of a Bible story. Ours was "Moses is found in the Bullrushes". Oh, my! Oh, my! I was to be a servant in the palace who runs to Jochebed, Moses's mother and says, "Oh, Jochebed! Oh, Jochebed! They have found your son in the river!" When my turn came, I flew across the stage with my hands in the air and a tremble in my voice and said, "Oh, Jochebed! Oh, Jochebed! They have found your river in the son!" Thoughts of a F on my grade slip kept haunting me, but when the grade slip came, I had an A. When I counted her pills that night, I asked her if she had made a mistake on my grade. She said, "No, Dear. You were the most perfect excited maid I could imagine." Oh, yes, our God is surely good!

In the spring, we were given applications to go to the mission field for the summer. I don't know if I wanted to go to the mission field more or if I just wanted to avoid going home. I bargained with God. I told Him I would go if He would arrange for me to go to some wonderful place like Alaska or Hawaii. I emphatically told Him, "Please do not send me to Mississippi or Alabama." Only two students from Mars Hill were selected to work with the Home Mission Board of the Southern Baptist Conference that summer although hundreds applied. I was sent to Alabama. Obviously, Daddy had not taught me enough to bargain with God. I learned a lesson I have never forgotten. That lesson is:

Do what God needs you to do, Girl.
When He wants you to do it, Girl.
Where He wants you to do it, Girl.
The way He wants you to do it, Girl.

Yes, I learned an important lesson about missions before I even got to Alabama.

I never wanted to leave Mars Hill. It was the most perfect place on earth.

Chapter 12

A Summer Mission Assignment

After graduation, I had to go home. I was scheduled a week later to be in Montgomery, Alabama, for a week of training. Getting my clothes ready, determining how I would get to Montgomery, and visiting all the people who had helped me during the past two years was my goal. Mother seemed to accept that I wouldn't be home for the summer. She was actually very helpful.

Larry Queen lived next door with his parents. He was a year older than I. All through school he had been a real pest. He followed me everywhere. He could recite every date I had in high school, what time they arrived, where we went, and what time they brought me home. This was very aggravating to me. He had dropped out of school as soon as the law would allow and seemed to have no direction in life. Surely he had something better to do with his life than to follow me around and to aggravate my dog. I really wanted him to get a life of his own. He had a car and frequently screeched to a stop to get attention. What a silly boy!

Mother arranged for Larry to drive me to Charlotte to catch a train to Montgomery. I was surprised that he actually drove like a sane person. He was very encouraging to me. He acted like a father sending his daughter to her death. He warned me not to talk to strangers. He handed me a five dollar bill for food. I almost cried when I realized that he cared about me. It was nice to have a brother.

I had never been on a train. I didn't eat because the food was outrageously expensive. I had to change trains in Atlanta and had a two-hour lay over. When I got to Atlanta, I was completely overwhelmed. The train came in underground. There I stood with two suitcases – one full of clothes and one empty. I had no idea where to go. All of a sudden a huge blond Adonis came toward me. He took both suitcases, so I followed him. I kept thinking, "Don't talk to him. This is the stranger everyone talks about." He didn't seem strange as I noticed his rippling muscles. He carried my luggage up a huge flight of stairs. At the top of the stairs he found a locker, put my suitcases in, put some coins in the slot, and turned to me as he handed me the keys. He smiled, but he never said a word. I smiled back. If he had asked me to stay in Atlanta, I would have considered it.

When I reached Montgomery in May, 1956, I was met by staff members of the Alabama State Home Mission Board. The prior December, 1955, Rosa Parks had refused to move when directed by a bus driver. Race relations in Montgomery were still boiling. Blacks had boycotted the bus system since her trial, and there were no buses running in the city for lack of customers and fear of violence. The staff members had to pick up the summer workers from their host homes and return them in the evening the whole week of training.

About fifteen summer workers were trained for a week. I was to go into churches where they had never had a Vacation Bible School. I would receive a bus ticket every Friday. This is how I would know where my assignment for the next week would be. I was shocked that they were sending us out alone. After all, in the Bible didn't they go in pairs or groups? Most of my assignments were in western and northwestern Alabama. When I arrived at the destination on Saturday, the host family would meet me at the bus stop. This was the plan, but actually this never happened once. I had Sunday to assess the situation, meet with the church leaders, find helpers, and decide on the time for the Vacation Bible School. By this time the empty suitcase had been packed with materials for each week. It was very heavy.

Most churches wanted me to teach a Bible Study for the adults also. I had been warned not to teach Revelations. I did ten Vacation Bible

Schools, and every church wanted me to teach Revelations. I followed the rules and guided them to any other book of the Bible. I leaned toward the Miracles of Jesus or The Relationship between Jesus and the Apostles. Every church seemed to be satisfied.

These country Alabamians whose homes I lived in and the ones I met in the churches were the "salt of the earth". I was treated like a drop from heaven most days. They were eager to learn and to have their children learn. This was good. I felt God's presence this whole summer. There was never a doubt about this.

I received my first bus ticket. I was beyond excited. When I arrived at the church, the pastor asked me to say a few words. Everyone was looking at me strangely. I had no idea why. After I spoke, there was a discussion. Many people had their say. I couldn't understand what the problem was. Most of the people in the church were staring at me as if I were an alien,especially an old woman across the aisle. She actually set an angry glare on me as if she was studying my soul. Although it was June, she was dressed as if it were in the middle of winter. She had on a old, lop-sided felt hat. When the discussion calmed down, she stood and said with authority, "Now, folks, this here fur'en gal has been sent by the Lord to help us this week, and we're gonna treat her with respect. Do ye hear?" After church the pastor explained what had happened. I had light brown hair streaked blond by the sun around my face. The tradition was to wear a hat to church. I didn't have a hat with me. And the folks thought that I bleached my hair. Who would have dreamed that my hair would have been a problem? I recently learned that a streak in your hair is supposed to be where an angel kissed you. How about that?

On Sunday afternoon I introduced three volunteers to the VBS material. Then we used homemade curtains (flour sacks pieced together like quilts) and rope to divide the one room church into four rooms. This was a community of farmers. They needed their children in the fields, so we decided to have VBS at night. I taught the teens, and the pastor taught a Bible class to the adults. Two of the women volunteers worked with the younger age groups. The third mother was in charge of refreshment. The little church would not hold all of the kids who showed up. There was no air-conditioning, so every window was open. The first night a teen-age boy standing in the churchyard yelled at me,

"Come near the window." I had twice the number of teens outside as I had in the stuffed church. I was so happy to see so many teens who wanted to know more about the Lord. The pastor and other adults in the church were surprised and happy. On Friday night we held commencement.

On Friday I received my bus ticket for my next church. I would take the bus on Saturday to my next assignment.

The second week I was picked up at the bus stop and taken to a rural area outside Rogersville, a small town in the northwest part of the state. The church was a store front. I stayed with a lovely family who had two sons and a young daughter. There were no screens on the windows and no air-conditioning. The first morning I awoke to the loud crow of a rooster. I thought that he must be right outside my window. I jumped out of bed to see how close he was. As I hit the floor, I realized that he was sitting on the foot of the bed. This was the first male I ever slept with.

I quickly dressed and found my way to the kitchen. The mother was making breakfast. As I reached the kitchen, I heard the younger son asked the mother, "Mom, do you think that Miss Kitty is a real princess." I was so shocked, but I didn't laugh. The mother responded, "I don't think so. I think she's an angel." I had to return to my room because I didn't want them to see me cry. I don't know if I thought this conversation was funny or sweet. But I know that it was touching!

Each week I had to do chores to earn my keep. This week I was supposed to go out into the cotton fields and pick cotton. I thought that I might be able to get a suntan. Every young woman wanted to be tan. By the time the mother had dressed me for the fields, I had on more clothes than I wore during winter. Apparently they had never heard of a suntan. I had to wear a huge straw hat and long pants and long sleeve shirt to protect me FROM the sun. I never dreamed that picking cotton was so hard. I tore my hands up on the dry pod as I reached for each ball of cotton. The youngest child picked more than I did. I was embarrassed. At the end of the day, I had no suntan, but I had a very bad backache and bloody finger tips.

I couldn't pull my weight in the fields, but in the Vacation Bible School, I had great success. The pastor worked in a factory to feed his family of nine children. He and his whole family were very supportive.

This was a week to remember. This pastor and his family became life-long friends.

The last night I was with this family after VBS commencement, their sixteen year old son ran away. They were very upset. I had a theory, so I found a flashlight and walked toward the barn. By the time I reached the barn, he rode up on his horse. We talked. Nothing special. Just teenage fever! I thought that a horseback ride under the moon sounded wonderful. His parents were forever grateful that I was there.

Friday brought another ticket for another exciting week.

This week began with adventure. The bus driver put the suitcase containing my clothes under the bus. When we arrived in Ethelsville, he asked, "Where do you want off, Ma'am?" Of course, I answered, "At the bus station, Sir." He replied, "Ain't got no bus station here." That didn't bother me. I said, "Okay. At the service station then." He replied, "Ain't got no service station here neither." He stopped the bus and put me off on the side of the road. He refused to give me my suitcase from under the bus. This wasn't funny. He told me that I could pick the suitcase up at the next bus station in Jackson, Mississippi. I was in Alabama, so Mississippi sounded like a far away place. There I stood in the red clay on the side of the road in a brown linen suit and white high heels holding a very heavy bag of VBS materials. I looked all four directions. All I saw was corn fields taller than I. I decided which way to walk by saying "Eeeny, Meeny, Minny, Moe." After walking about an hour on the side of the road, I came to the first house where a man and a woman were sitting in the front yard. I yelled from the roadside, "I'm looking for Miss Sarah Manning!" The man yelled back, "Well, you've found her!" Although I had not remembered to ask God for help in picking the direction I was to go, I remembered now to thank Him for guiding my way because there was no doubt in my mind that He led me in the right direction, right into the hands of my host family. I thought, "How Great Is Our God! He's so attentive!"

We sat in the yard until it was about dark. I was exhausted, so I said, "Well, I think I'll hit the hay." Since there were no screens at the windows in this house either, I undressed in the dark so as not to draw insects into the bedroom.

When I went to breakfast the next morning, Mr. Manning said,

"When you said you were gonna hit the hay last night, you didn't know you were telling the truth, did you?" All of a sudden I realized what the crunch – crunch sound was every time I turned over during the night. I had never slept on a stuffed hay mattress before.

I had to wear the same clothes to church the next day to meet my new church family. They didn't know, but I did. In the afternoon Miss Sarah's grown daughter came to visit. We talked her into driving me to Jackson to get my clothes.

Miss Sarah would cook all morning and all afternoon. At supper we would sit down in the dining room. Maybe she would have cornbread and cantaloupe on the table. For three days, I wondered how she spent so much time cooking and had so little on the table. On Thursday, Mr. Manning said, "I thought you were cooking them limas I picked." She jumped up, ran to the kitchen, and brought bowls and bowls of food to the dining room table. She was so absent-minded that she would forget to bring the food from the kitchen to the table.

A couple at the church took me out fishing in a boat that week in the hot sun. A huge bug sat down on top of my foot. I started to slap it, but the lady screamed at me to sit still. Within minutes the bug flew away leaving a gigantic blister on top of my foot. I was told that it had to dry up by itself because the liquid would cause more blisters every where it touched. I had to be very cautious not to break the blister. I had never heard of a blister bug. I wondered if God had sent me to Alabama to learn about blister bugs. Why did I need to know about blister bugs?

July 4 was during this week. Most of the people worked in a nearby mill. The mill gave a huge picnic for the employees. At noon when it was time for the parents to pick up their children, they didn't show. The children were hungry. I was left about three hours at the church alone with about eighty hungry boys and girls. I used the snacks for the rest of the week to feed these children the most unhealthy lunch they had ever had.

On Saturday morning my next host family showed up to drive me to their house. It was a family of Hesters. I was so surprised. I wondered if they were kin.

This family had a son and a daughter. They were chicken farmers. I shared a bed with the sixteen year old daughter. Although he was relatively young, the father had had a stroke earlier in the spring. About the time we fell to sleep on the second night the father ran into the room and said, "Hurry! Get up! Run for the car!" I thought perhaps he was sick again. I began to take off my blue silk pajamas, a gift from Aunt Rose, to put on my dress. He yelled, "You don't have time to dress. Let's go!" I jerked my pink and green plaid flour sack dress over those blue pajamas thinking, "This is tacky!"

We ran for the car the daughter holding my hand and shoving me in. Mailboxes and chickens and window panes were flying through the air. In the car I realized that I had pulled my dress on wrong side out. It didn't seem to matter. I was too scared to think straight. We drove about a mile down the road where men pulled us from the car and threw us into what I thought was a cave. It was a community storm pit. The men would take us each periodically to the mouth of the pit to get fresh air. One time the man helping me to the air had his watch ripped off his arm by the strong wind. Another time as we reached the air, I saw someone's roof flying through the air like a low flying plane. We stayed in the pit until mid-day the following day.

This was my second tornado. When I was a young teen, Mom was across the field visiting our next door neighbor. I was practicing the piano, when the lights began to flash on and off. I ran to the back porch and screamed for mom. She yelled back to turn off all electrical things and stay inside. Once during the hour or so that followed I walked to the kitchen windows. I saw shingles and pieces of tin flying off the roofs of the four houses on the next street. I was horrified. We were told later that it was a tornado.

All of the horrible weather conditions (tornadoes, hurricanes, tsunamis, floods, typhoons) create within me fear and a feeling of puzzlement with helplessness. I don't understand them. Are they natural happenings? Is it God warning us? Warning us about what? Is it God's anger? To this day, I still do not understand. It took years for me to realize that I don't have to understand every thing. I just have to deal with situations in my own life and trust God. It's really not about what happens to you; it's about how you respond to what happens to you. When I think of the house falling in on me during a hurricane, how can I rejoice? I'm still working on this concept.

When we reached home, the house was full of water. The chickens had been blown away to no one knew where. This was truly a disaster.

On Friday night we had a commencement. I was happy to see familiar faces in the congregation. The pastor from Rogersville and his son came to drive me to outside Talladega to a summer camp called Shocco Springs. We took a couple of teen girls from Ethelsville who had never been to camp.

I was supposed to help with the classes at Shocco Springs, a Baptist retreat, for a week. That didn't happen. My first morning on the way to class I was walking across the playground. There was a small group of four-five year olds on the playground playing on a piece of equipment. It was a huge wooden contraption. The children stood on the flat, round wood with one foot using the other foot to push round and round on the ground. A little boy was on the wheel with two little girls watching and laughing. I looked around. No other adult was around. I had an eerie feeling. All of a sudden a rope near the center reached out and grabbed the little boy's leg. He fell and was being dragged around and around on the ground. I had to stop the fast moving devise. I grabbed the boy who was heavier than I had thought he would be. I jumped onto the wheel and tried to stop it. In so doing, the fast moving wheel ground into the front of my leg down to the bone. They took me, the heroine, to the infirmary. I was there the rest of the week elevating my leg. I was very disappointed that I didn't get to teach.

Later that summer I had my most exciting week of my adventurous summer. I was sent the bus ticket. I took the bus. This time I was turned off the bus right in the middle of a very small town – maybe twelve small businesses. As soon as I stepped off the bus, a man from the nearest store ran out and showed me a car and handed me a set of keys and a hand drawn map. Remember that I took drivers' education in High School four years earlier. Since I got my license, I had never driven a car. I looked at the keys, and I looked at the car. It was an ancient car. When I finally got my bags into the car, I sat there in a state of disbelief for a long while. Finally I turned on the key and backed out. At that time I had never heard the saying, "God will never take you to a place that He won't take you through." But that day I prayed harder than I have ever prayed for God to remember that He had brought me here. I reminded Him that I needed Him. As I stepped on the clutch and moved into second gear, I wondered if God drives.

As soon as I passed the last store the paved road ended. Boiling dust followed me as I sought to find the host house. Finally which may have been thirty minutes which seemed three hours, I found the house. The little house had never seen a drop of paint. The porch ran along the front and down the middle of the house. I later learned that this type porch is called a dog trot. There was a bedroom and kitchen on one side of the porch and a bedroom on the other side of the porch.

This couple was very old (both in their nineties) and very sweet and excited to have me. They had horses, mules, and cows. I helped feed them all week. This was the kind of work that I enjoyed. I learned that the car was to be used one day. It belonged to their granddaughter.

The church was three miles away down the dirt roads with no street lights. I was hoping that this community would have their school during the morning. No such luck! They did provide me with a flashlight.

The ladies of the church wanted to meet one morning to just pray and sing. They had a piano with one of those round stools that would spin. The piano had not been used in years because no one knew how to play. They didn't have a preacher either. So we met. I sat down at the piano and struck the first chord. At least ten mice ran from under the piano, and I jumped on the nearest bench. I thought of my piano student at Mars Hill and wondered if his piano would have mice. The ladies laughed until I thought they would not be able to get back on task. One lady went over to the piano and hit a couple of keys. No more mice. The meeting continued with some of the most off-key piano and singing I've ever heard. They seemed to think it was beautiful. I have never heard such beautiful prayers before or after. I knew that God was pleased with this meeting.

The first night of VBS I immediately noticed something new. A number of the students were in their twenties and thirties. They were huge mentally handicapped men whose folks wanted them in class. They would sit and ogle me as I talked. It was very scary to me, especially when I walked along that dark road going home.

When I would arrive at the host house, I wouldn't turn on the oil lamp because, of course, they had no screens. The old couple would be in bed by the time I arrived home each night. Their bedroom and my bedroom were separated by a porch. One night I heard a noise on the porch. I slipped out of bed and picked up the huge stone used to hold my door closed. My door began to open. I raised the stone over my head fully expecting to see one of the huge retarded men coming through my door. I barely stopped the landing of the stone, when the little old lady said, "Kitty, are you okay? I heard a noise on the porch." We never knew what caused the noise that both of us heard. A tall, handsome son of one of the church members showed up the next night and every night until I left to walk me home. How great was that!

Every church I went to that summer was a separate adventure. If I could receive any more love, I don't know where I would have found it. These wonderful poor people, trying to scrape a living out of the land, were better than gold in my sight. I was very fortunate to have spent time with them. They thought that I blessed them. Contrary! I was the one who received the blessing. This was proof to me that God knew what was good for me more than I knew myself.

Larry picked me up in Charlotte. I saw him differently now.

I knew that God had provided a fantastic opportunity for me that summer. I would never forget these wonderful church people. I thought that Mars Hill had been the life-changing opportunity of my life, but I was beginning to understand that it was only a beginning. Where would all of this lead?

All I could think of when I returned to Mother's home was, "But, God, I need money." I had enough money to enter Appalachian State for one quarter. After that, what? I worried that I would be home and working in a factory in three more months. I wondered if I should just forget a college education. I knew that I had to have faith, and I pushed forward.

Chapter 13

Appalachian State University

Appalachian was also in my beautiful mountains. If I could manage to live in those mountains just two more years, it would be a wonderful thing for my spirit.

But Appalachian State was a big shock for me. It was the story at Mars Hill that attending Mars Hill would make you or break you. It made me. At Appalachian I was put with three girls who had been students at Mars Hill. Mars Hill broke them. When they hit Appalachian State, they went wild. I had to study, but there was no studying with them around. They would become so irritated with me that I wouldn't play cards with them. I certainly did not have time to play cards all night. Name it. Everything I did rubbed them the wrong way. I couldn't share any of my joys with them because my joy would cause trouble. They kept up with every test score I had and became extremely angry when I would make A's. They went through my books. They showed up at the door of my classroom to check on my test scores. As soon as a professor graded the tests the scores were posted by student number.

Jack transferred to Appalachian State also. I wondered why he did that. He was premed; Appalachian did not have premed. I didn't know at the time, but he almost passed out when he saw blood. He changed his major to science and PE. He was everywhere I went. I really did not have time for him either.

I wondered why I was at Appalachian. Everyone graduating from there had to get a teachers' certificate. To get a teaching certificate, one had to pass the National Teachers' Exam. I had no thought of teaching school. I was here because I could afford one quarter. I didn't know what I wanted to be "when I grew up". But I did know that I did not want to work in a factory or teach school.

Fortunately, enough good things happened which gave me the strength to handle my obstacles.

The first day in class Miss Helen Burch, my geography professor asked,"I need someone to help me grade papers and keep my grade book. Anyone interested?" I immediately raised my hand. I could do that. Miss Burch took me to her office after class and introduced me to her fellow professors. Five of them immediately offered me a job. A couple teaching in the same department asked me if I was available to baby-sit their elementary age daughter. The answer to all of this was, "Yes."

At the end of the second week, Dr. Eggers, the registrar, called me to his office. I was horrified. Had my check bounced? Would I be sent home? I sat down upon invitation. He said, "Miss Hester, how would you like to have a free ride at Appalachian State for two whole years?" I said, "I don't really play football." When I had investigated getting a scholarship to Appalachian the prior spring, I was told that they only gave scholarships to football players. I had applied for a football scholarship. I immediately began to think that he was talking to me to tell me that I was a smart-aleck. He laughed and responded, "Well. I have a COTE scholarship from the state organization which I have to give to some student. But there's a catch. You have to sign a paper that you will teach in North Carolina for two years after you finish school." Teach school? Two years? I could do that. I agreed. I later learned that COTE was Council on Teacher Education. I walked out of his office light-headed wondering what I would do when God stopped showering me with blessings from on High. As of now, He was on a roll. Thank you, God! I was definitely in His favor. This was a good place to be.

One of the telling things which interfered with my privacy was that fifteen students had been selected for an experiment. We were supposed to be the fifteen smartest students in the college. We had the same professor, Dr. Hargrove, for our education and psychology courses. We had to meet ten hours per week. But we only got six hours credit. I was suspicious of this, but after the first class I wanted to be a guinea pig. We went on many field trips to places of interest like the Mental Institution in Morganton. The bad thing was that every student on campus knew the fifteen and watched us like hawks.

I was really in tune with Dr. Hargrove. He was young and married to my music teacher who was incredibly smart and talented. I made the highest grade on every test he wrote. My method of writing a test to study for a test worked especially well with him. He was amazed, and so was I. It happened quite by accident that I learned that this aggravated and amused him. One day in a test I wrote the page number a couple of times without realizing that I had done it. The more I did this, the more I learned. He would question me unmercifully about my test taking skills. Toward the end of the year, I explained to the class how I handled studying for a test. I wondered why they had not figured this out on their own.

I understood from the beginning of my college years that having test taking skills was as important as knowing the material. I knew many students who understood the material better than I; however, their lack of test taking skills prevented them from having those high scores.

Strangely, I am one of two students in that class still living. Most of them died within ten years after we graduated. I have always wondered why. You know, smart people do not have to be corrupt. These smart students were good, hard-working, struggling students. Many of them came from very poor, farming families.

Shortly after the year began, a student in my Geography class asked me to not put my name on my test paper, fill in the answers and give the paper to him. Then he would put his name on the paper and get an A. He would hand me his blank paper when Miss Burch was not watching, so that I could fill in the answers and put my name on it. He was across from the cafeteria when he approached me with his brain storm. I didn't have to think twice to give him a, "No way!" First of all, it was cheating. I didn't cheat. Second, what if I didn't have time to fill in the second paper. I would fail. Third, my handwriting was so distinctive that I knew Miss Burch would catch us and be disappointed in me. I tried to reason with him offering to give him a copy of my notes to study. I offered to study in the library with him. Nothing I suggested tempted him. He had just returned from a military tour. He threw the three books in his arms at me and began screaming over and over, "I spent three years of my life protecting you while you were here living in luxury. And you won't help me!" I was shocked. A couple of guys ran over and held him till he calmed down. I was frightened. I wondered how he knew about all that luxury I had. Why didn't I know about it?

In the spring, the registrar called for me again. This was always a surprise to me and rather frightening. He said, "I need a favor from you. I want you to represent Appalachian State at the Student Mock Legislature next week in Raleigh." Raleigh was the capital, and I had never been there. He explained that all of my expenses would be paid by the university. I would just attend meetings and listen and interact with the other students. I could do that.

As soon as I arrived at the hotel, I was approached and told that I was to present a bill to the Senate the following afternoon. I could choose the topic, but they wanted it to be something pertinent in our society at the time. I panicked! What could I present? How could I stand in front of all these brilliant students and say anything. I immediately thought of Moses who claimed that he stuttered. And of Thomas who was a doubter. Would either of these "outs" work for me? Probably not. I began to think of issues. What bothered me most was how we were still treating blacks in 1957 almost a hundred years after they should have by law been freed. I thought of the fountains in the back of the Belks Store where I worked during High School – one labeled WHITES ONLY; the other labeled BLACKS. We didn't have a hand full of blacks in my hometown. I rarely saw one. Why would any store pay for separate fountains? Not cost effective. I thought of Rosa Parks just two years earlier who was arrested for refusing to obey a bus driver who told her to move to the back of the bus where there were no empty seats. Wasn't her fare the same for the bus company as any white fare? I composed a bill to allow everyone to use any public water fountain and to sit where there was an empty seat on a any bus. Did I dare to propose this? After all, it was only a student MOCK legislature. Sure I could. And I did.

The bill passed. When I first stood up, I was trembling on the inside, but as soon as I heard my very calm voice, I settled into a mind-set of convincing the listeners. The bill passed with no arguments. All of a sudden, I was a celebrity. My picture and my bill were all over the newspapers. I was proud, but also scared. My mom, a racist from the soles of her feet to the crown of her head, was going to kill me. Would she try to beat me? I was horrified. How many times could I stand still for a beating?

When the real legislature met a few weeks later, they passed my bill as written. Again I hit the newspapers. I was embarrassed, but proud. Progress! I relish progress. But did I have to go overboard with accomplishment? Could I not just sit back and observe accomplishment? Dr. Eggers was so proud of me. All of the Social Studies professors treated me like I was something special. My art professor even invited me to her house for dinner. My education/psychology professor bragged about me in class. My roommates made fun of me. Jack did not say a word.

I couldn't understand why I had to take so much PE. I had had a whole year at Mars Hill. Now there was more required. You would have thought that I was studying to be a coach. I had enough that PE was on my first teaching certificate. I was horrified that some principal would try to make me teach PE. That didn't happen for twelve years.

I had a football coach for Playground Supervision. Jack and I sat side by side in the required course. My roommate was a PE major and in that class also. The rest of the class was football players. These guys were nothing like the ministerial students on the football team at Mars Hill. The professor never mentioned the playground, the text, or grades. He came in every day telling "Matilda Muckinfuss" jokes. Everyone decided that the people who laughed the loudest at his vulgar jokes would get the best grades. I couldn't laugh. I buried my head in the text. Come the day of finals, I was shocked to get a test that had not one question which related to anything in the text. I was fit to be tied. Everyone in the class made a C. This was my only C.

The next quarter I had to take First Aid, a required course. Jack, my roommate, and I had no choice but to sign up. An older coach was scheduled to teach it, and I was looking forward to really learning some good stuff. The first day of class, we met in the gym. Someone from the registrar's office came in and told us that the class would be split because too many students needed the course. I was placed in the new class down the hall. It was the "Matilda Muckinfuss" professor. All quarter he told the same nasty, inappropriate jokes, and everyone in class laughed till they seemed like cartoon characters. I refused to laugh. I began taking a huge box of tissues to class. Every time he told a joke, everyone laughed but me. I cried. I sobbed out loud. Jack begged me to drop the class. It was required. I had no time to wait to take it again.

Two days before the final exam, I went to visit the class I would be interning with the next quarter. The professor's daughter was in the class. When he gave out the final exam, I refused to write an answer of any kind because again, the test had nothing to do with the material we should have covered. I finally was the last student in the room. I wrote my name at the top of the blank exam. Across the top I printed in large letters, NEXT TERM YOUR DAUGHTER WILL BE IN MY CLASS AT THE MIDDLE SCHOOL. When grades were posted, I had an A. Everyone else had a C. I felt so guilty. I tried to earn an A, but he just wouldn't teach. So in the end I laughed also. Jack didn't laugh. Neither did any of the football players. Of course, none of them knew how I got the A.

At the end of the year right before finals, I got food poisoning. No one else had food poisoning. Just me. I was very sick. I was near to not taking my finals because I was just too sick to study. A senior girl down the hall had no roommate. She came to me and asked me to move in with her for the last two weeks. I did. She helped me move, cajoled me to study for my exams, and fed me broth. I passed everything. She was such a blessing when I needed it most and right down the hall. I had really never noticed her before. She was from a poor family and understood what struggling meant. She was older, very smart, and beautiful. She kept to herself mostly. She had noticed me. When I look back, I wonder if she was an angel.

The registrar's brother, Dr. Eggers, taught Advanced Grammar. The students had petitioned the trustees to not require this course for certain majors. At the time of the petition just some students had to pass the course. So many failed. This would keep them from graduating. Many of the guys would be drafted when they lost their student status. The Vietnam War had just begun. These guys were furious when they were taken into the military and not allowed to graduate. The professor was furious. The rule changed that everyone had to take Advanced Grammar. He was out for blood. I decided to go to summer school to take the course. If I failed it, I could take it again in my regular senior year.

One of the many problems with the course was that he took the roll by asking each person present a question. If they gave a logical answer, they were counted present. If they gave an illogical answer, they were counted absent. His questions took most of the class time and were stupid. One day he asked me the score of a major league baseball game the night before. I didn't know the answer. He told me never to come to his class again without reading the morning paper. He counted me absent. The class was at 7:00 AM. Read the paper to learn the baseball scores before coming to class? He had to be kidding. He was the joke. In four years of undergraduate work, I never looked at a newspaper. So although I was in class every morning, I had one absence. How ridiculous!

Another time he asked me to name the hill where Jesus was crucified. I answered, "Golgatha" (first a as in father and accent on second syllable). He snapped, "No, no, no. The hill was Golgatha." (first a as e in let and accent on first syllable). So I had two absences. You had three absences; then you were put out of the class. If I hadn't been so scared, I would have been angry. Fortunately, for me, I could answer all of the other questions he asked me the whole summer. I was horrified of this man.

I was so very happy when the course was over. After the exam was administered early one morning, he called the dorm and had the housemother to send me to his office. He was angry. He asked, "You made a perfect score on my exam. How did you do that? No one has ever made a perfect score on MY exam!" His face was red, and he was screaming. I made a mistake when I answered, "I don't know." He told me not to leave that chair until I could give him a logical answer. He returned to question me every hour for five hours. I was getting very hungry. But finally I had an answer. I told him about Miss Rawls in the eighth grade. She made us diagram sentences at the board everyday. Then we could read. I learned to diagram, so that I could leave the board and read. He laughed and said, "Now that's an answer." I was so glad to leave that office. I hoped that no one would find out that I made an A in his course.

Jack had offered me a diamond ring everyday that year. I just wanted to finish college. Concentrating on getting through each course was as much as I could handle. But now I dreaded living in the dorm another year. He pulled out that ring again at my lowest point. I accepted. We had actually never dated. Before the next day passed, he had rented an apartment near the campus. I went home and hesitantly told my mother. She pitched a fit to top all fits. But she began planning a dress. It was a beautiful dress. Mother found magazines and kept asking, "Do you like this? Do you want it to look like this?" I really didn't care. I was tired; so very tired.

Jack and I were married August, 1957. We moved into the furnished basement apartment on the side of a mountain within walking distance of the college. We had no car. Jack worked at Winn-Dixie. On Saturday night he would bring home all of the produce and meat which wouldn't last till Monday and $11.43 in cash. Of course, I would cook all of Saturday night. I worked for the Social Studies Department another year. The longer I worked there the more they used me. This was good. Amazingly we survived!

Sometimes I would get fed up with cooking and washing dishes. We had no money to buy a hamburger, but I suspected that Jack had money I didn't know about . I learned by accident to manipulate Jack into going out. Ordinarily I would avoid manipulating people because I thought that it was a form of disrespect. But when I saw how easy this was it became my tool. One night he came to the counter and saw a can of sauer kraut. He asked what we were having. I said, "Hot dogs and sauer kraut." He said, "Let's go get a burger." Every time I got fed up with cooking which was about once a month, I just sat the can of sauer kraut on the counter. This worked for years. Really!

I would do the laundry in the bath tub and hang it on the line out back. Often the sheets would freeze into cakes of ice. Then Jack would bring them into the furnace room which connected to our apartment to let them dry. Too much of my time was taken up with ironing clothes. Jack worked as hard as I did.

It was evident that I needed to study more than he did. He would go through the material, and that was it. I would go over and over and over every word of the text and my notes. He was confident. I would almost have a nervous fit every time I went into a test. If I failed a test, it would make for the biggest "funny" on campus. So I didn't fail.

My senior year was a lark. My Economics professor was very flirty. There was a rumor that if you were a female, you should sit of the front row and move your legs a lot while he was teaching. I was appalled by such thoughts. Most of the girls made a B-line for the front seats. I sat in the very back and never looked up. Not only because of this rumor, but because Economics was foreign to me. He might just as well have been lecturing in Greek. I understood nothing. Jack was in the same class. For a whole quarter, he tried to teach me. I just was not interested. I studied the text and went to class. My notes were puzzles. The test time came. The professor asked me to type his test. I couldn't believe that he asked me to type a test which I would be taking. I told him I was too busy. Yes, I was too busy because I was studying the text. I made an A on the course. Don't ask me how. I don't know. I knew nothing. Most students, including my at-home tutor, made a C. Again my test taking ability proved to be a real gift.

In November I got pregnant. I was student teaching at the Middle School near our apartment. It snowed and iced so much that February that schools were closed most days. It was so cold that the pavement on the roads bubbled making them dangerous. We didn't have a television, but we had a small, red Zenith radio. I would roll over early every morning and turn on the radio only to hear, "There will be no school in Watauga County today." I would pull up the covers and sleep the rest of the day. I never experienced morning sickness, but I slept like a hibernating bear.

The university could not keep the classrooms warm enough to have class, so frequently Jack would return home. We were stuck in two rooms for most of the winter.

I graduated Magna Cum Laude. I didn't know what that meant, but I felt sure that it was a good thing. When I learned of an honor that I didn't even know existed, I felt really dumb. Although I was not impressed with Appalachian State University, I cherished the good people there who made it possible for me to get a Bachelors Degree. I also felt confident that there was a very good reason for me to be at that particular place at that particular time although I did not realize the significance of all of it at the time I was there. I just wanted to get a job teaching to pay the promise to COTE. After two years, I could get on with my real life.

I was happy to leave this heathen place. Little did I know that this was just a small picture of the world I was to enter.

Part V

Chapter 14

Entering The Real World

We got an apartment in Pikeville, North Carolina, next door to Jack's family for the summer. Jack would be working with his dad at the Mt. Olive cucumber auction in a near by town. The first morning I was there, I was unpacking towels when Dr. Pate, a family friend and neighbor, walked in. He looked at me and said, "Kitty, lie down. I'm going to get my bag." How strange!

Within a couple of hours I was in the hospital in Goldsboro. I had preeclampsia/toxemia. I didn't know what that was, so I didn't know how scared to be. It was serious. Dr. Pate asked another doctor who was in a group studying the illness to join him. Dr. Pate told Jack that he would try to save one of us, but one would surely die. I shuddered at the thought that I had finally got a degree, and it seemed now that I wouldn't be using it. I was allowed no visitors and could not read or watch television or listen to the radio. I couldn't even receive cards. Jack could visit twice a day for twenty minutes each time. But he was working from 6:00AM till 10:00PM, so he could only visit on Sunday. Mother came. It was a four hour drive. The doctors talked to her. Because she was so emotional, they would not let her see me. They asked her how old I was when I had Bright's disease, a kidney disease. She insisted that I had never had Bright's disease. She was insulted that

139

they were sure that I had. Mother did not tell me that Grandma Hester had died of Bright's disease.

For ten weeks I lay there filled with valium hardly noticing the nurses as they went in and out. I was on a salt free diet, so I didn't want to eat. Finally, I went into labor. It was a Sunday night, and Dr. Pate stayed with me. He told me that the baby would probably come about five in the morning. They moved me to a labor room. He kept asking me if I wanted anything for the pain. I tried to imagine how bad the pain would be by five the next morning. I kept telling him, "Not yet. I'll wait!" About nine o'clock, he checked me and said, "Kitty, bare down." I did. The little girl's head popped out. As I was being moved to the delivery room, the baby was delivered in the hallway. No pain killer! It was unbelievably painful. Plus I was extremely weak.

As soon as we reached the delivery room, the nurses and doctors began working on the baby. I knew for sure that they would make her live. Four hours later, Dr. Pate told me that the baby was perfectly formed, but they would not allow me to see her. He said, "Kitty, I'm sorry to say we lost her." It took me a few minutes before I realized that "they had lost her" meant she was gone; she was dead. How could this happen? There were no answers for me. I felt so alone that I couldn't imagine anyone on earth being more miserable. Where was God? Was he busy with more needy people? But, God, I need you. Please fix this. You can do anything. Touch her. She will surely come to life. This can't be happening! I was convinced that if the doctors would have let me touch her, she would have lived. Jack was not there.

The next day Jack's mother and aunt came to pick me up. My blood pressure was normal. My kidneys checked out fine. They seemed so cheerful. Now I realize that neither of them knew how to comfort me. I couldn't eat. I cried so much that my eye balls were sore. Dr. Pate would walk across the street to check me every morning, and say, "It's okay, Kitty. Let it all out." Jack didn't talk. I had no idea what he was thinking. We had decided to name the little girl Kimberly Lynn Scott. I asked about a funeral and a burial. No one would respond to me. Since no one in the family attended church, they didn't seem to understand funeral...memorial service...burial. And, of course, money was a factor. We had no insurance.

The following Sunday Jack and his three brothers drove me to

Wilson to see a movie, "The Bridge over the River Kwai". They made sure that I ate plenty of salty popcorn and drank a gallon of coke. None of them mentioned my illness, the baby, or the hospital. It was an afternoon of all laughs. How sweet for them to understand when I couldn't understand myself! Yes, I needed to laugh. Laughter is a wonderful medicine.

For years I could make my lips smile, but inside I was dead. The organs in my body felt like rocks. My soul (where ever it might be) was heavy. I had no one to grieve with me. Jack never asked questions. He never mentioned the baby once.

Dr. Pate told me that I should just rest for a few months. He told Jack that I could go to work the following January. It was July. Rest? I had been resting for months. Who needed for me to rest? Jack had one more year in school. He needed to finish. I needed to serve two years teaching.

We did not have medical insurance. I didn't even know anyone who had health insurance at the time. I don't know if it existed. In the thirties and forties people who got sick, just died. As science progressed and developed cures for some of the major illnesses in the fifties, the cures cost so much that people couldn't afford them. Companies began to write health insurance policies on a broad basis in the sixties.

Jack spent everything he made all summer working sixteen hour days, six days a week, on doctor and hospital bills. There was no money for him to return to college. I was afraid that he would never finish if he didn't return that fall.

Fortunately, I received a call from my home county. My own first grade teacher had had a nervous breakdown. They wanted me to come within three days to take her second grade class. I didn't ask anyone. I said, "Sure thing!" When Jack got home from work, I announced that he would be going back to school for his senior year in three days. Appalachian was about an hour's drive from Mom's house.

The next morning we headed for Newton. That afternoon we shopped for a car. We purchased a 1954 Ford for $600.00 cash. Jack took me out into the countryside and taught me to drive once again. I was twenty-two and had driven a car only one day in Alabama since I passed Drivers' Ed in high school four years earlier. The next morning I drove on the winding road into the mountains to take my husband for his senior year in college. He begged me to stay a while. As it turned out, I drove back down the mountains on the winding roads in the dark alone. Today there are super highways in the mountains. Then the roads were scary.

The next day I began what I thought would be two years teaching but turned out to be a long career. I was supposed to be teaching twenty-eight second graders at a little school in the town of Catawba about ten miles from Newton. I never dreamed that I would teach little ones. My certificate covered first through twelfth grades. I had thought more of teaching "Macbeth" to high school seniors – my way. That was to come much later.

The first day of school the principal/eighth grade teacher marched ten first graders into my room and explained, "The law says that we can only have thirty first graders in a room." The first grade teacher had forty first graders. So he gave me ten first graders to add to my twenty-eight second graders. I was sure that this should be illegal.

The school did not have a copy machine. School supplies? Very few. I purchased crayons and begged sheets of unused paper from the local newspaper. When the principal found my love of reading, he appointed me school librarian.

The first week of school, one of the students from the fifth grade across the hall came over and said, "Would you come check on Ms. Moore?" I told her to stay with my students, and I rushed across the hall to check on Ms. Moore. She was sitting at her desk with her eyes closed. She looked like a marble statue. She had a red pen in her hand. I touched her. She wasn't breathing. I sent the student nearest the door upstairs to get the principal. I lined up the fifth graders in the hall and took them to the library, and then rushed back to my room. Ms. Moore's long fight with cancer had ended. She was a seasoned teacher and would have been a great help during the year. But it wasn't meant to be.

I truly learned more from the students that year than I taught them.

We studied many different community helpers that year. I demonstrated how to use a tooth brush properly when we studied the dentist. I was horrified that only four of the thirty-eight students had ever been to a dentist. When I discovered a sweet little girl who did not own a toothbrush, I had to fix this situation. That very afternoon

I purchased paste and a brush. At the end of school the next day I gave this secret little gift to this poor child who had twelve brothers and sisters and lived with both parents. I warned her to remember how I had demonstrated the use of the brush. The next day while I was working in a reading group, I would look out over the other children. This sweet little girl would be staring at me with a big smile on her face. Finally, she slipped out of her chair, came up behind me, and whispered, "I love it. I let all my brothers and sisters use it too." She rushed back to her seat smiling from ear to ear. I sat stunned in a reading group who wondered what had happened to their teacher. That very afternoon I rushed to the store to buy toothbrushes for the whole family of fourteen. Never before or since have I bought so many toothbrushes at one time. I had thought that Mom and I were poor. Now I was meeting real poverty face to face. It hurt.

One boy in the class had failed the second grade the year before. He was so smart. I began to wonder why he would have failed. He was extremely artistic. He was already two years older than the first graders in the room. He was born on my birthday. We took to each other like ducks take to water. I had four large bulletin boards in the room. He was the hardest to keep busy because he did every assignment perfectly and speedily. I went to the principal about putting him in the third grade. My lack of experience caused me to fail in this endeavor. So unfair. I let him design new bulletin boards. There was an art exhibit in Newton in February, our birthday. I got permission from his single mom to take him to the show. It's always said that teachers don't have pets. Which teachers are those?

Another girl in the class lived with her grandparents. Her mother had died of cancer the summer before. Now her dad was dying with cancer. She was one of the sweetest children I've ever taught. She gave me a Christmas pin which I still wear every Christmas and think of her every time I wear it.

One little second grader came in late everyday. He was so worn out that he would immediately put his head on his desk and go to sleep. He was sweet and smart, but he was just tired and dirty. I visited his home. He had seven siblings and both parents who all lived in a small three room house. When I entered, I was not asked to sit down because there was not a chair in the house. There was a stove for heating and cooking and a shelf for plates and pots and silverware and glasses. There was a high pile of bedding in the corner of one of the rooms. The mother told me that they didn't have a clock, so she just let the kids walk to school, about five miles along the side of the highway, when they woke up. I left the house and headed to the store. I took an alarm clock back to the mother and taught her how to set the alarm. The little student was never late again.

Strangely I remember every child in that class. They were very special to me. I can see their faces. I even remember where they sat in the classroom.

One child I remember with sadness and love was a first grader from the other class. He was a problem child. He ran away every chance he got. He would often be found in my cloak closet, a separate room connected to my room where the students left their coats and book bags. One day about an hour after school ended, I began my drive home. Our day was from 7:30 AM till 4:00 PM. About a mile from school, the boy jumped up from where he was hiding on the floorboard in the back seat. He scared me so badly that I almost wrecked the car. He said, "I'm going home with you because now I'm your little boy." His parents were in prison, and he lived with his grandmother. I immediately drove to her house. No one was home. I sat with the boy in the car until after 6:00 PM. No grandmother. I didn't know what to do. We had no cell phones in those days. I drove to a service station a mile away. They knew the boy and agreed to keep him till his grandmother showed up. He grabbed my legs and held tight until the man pulled him from me. I jumped into the car and locked the door.

About the end of the first month of school, I realized that I was on the mission field. No, not in Peru or Japan or Angola. Right here in my own home county. I felt privileged to serve. Teaching thrilled me.

My schedule that whole first year teaching was difficult. I would leave very early from Mom's house to drive the ten miles to my school. Every morning I would have the car loaded with teaching materials. So many that I would have to make several trips into the school. Teach till four. Drive to Grandpa Hendrix house to cook supper for him and Uncle Allen. Clean. Rush home to cook supper for myself and Mom. Clean. Get my clothes ready for the next day. And prepare lessons and grade papers. It was hard, but I was young and energetic and excited about my students. I still had the idea that I would teach two years to keep the bargain with COTE. I was so grateful for the scholarship that I would never have dreamed of not keeping the bargain.

That year my bring home pay was $251.00 per month. It seems so little now, but I feel confident that God stretched that check beyond my capacity to buy for the children when there was a need, to help my mother and Grandfather and Uncle Allen, and to send my husband to college. No matter how much of my salary I spent on these students, I always had enough for my bills...God's Divine Multiplication.

Things became easier for me in the spring when Jack became an intern in the same school under the direction of the principal/eighth grade teacher. He then did the driving. He bathed my grandfather and shaved him. He was an excellent teacher and coach.

Almost every parent had a huge garden, if not a farm. The cafeteria food was donated by the parents. It was good. These were mostly poor, but good people who wanted better for their children. They appreciated the teachers and the school.

I learned more about teaching that year than I learned in all the years in college. Every child and every parent had a lesson to teach me. I was eager to learn. I was just serving the two years I owed North Carolina. Little did I dream at this point that I was being turned into a career teacher.

Jack graduated at the end of the year. This was an accomplishment. I like accomplishment. Jack was an excellent teacher.

Part VI

Chapter 15

Living In Raleigh

We applied to teach in Raleigh City Schools because that was what Jack wanted to do. Both of us got jobs, but neither of us were in the grade level that we wanted. He was at a large middle school near NC State Campus, and I took a position next door to his school in an elementary school because we had only one car. Eighteen years passed before I finally was placed in a high school. Six years passed before I finally had the opportunity to teach history, my preferred subject. Because my certificate covered so many grade levels and so many subjects, I was mostly put in positions where other teachers were not available.

The teachers in the elementary school were the best you could find anywhere. They were career teachers. They wanted to teach. They cared about their students. Those who have not spent their days inside the school system can not imagine how many teachers hate teaching. No doubt that these fine teachers taught me by example more than I had learned in college. It seems like I am knocking my college education, but I'm not. I learned so much in college. Now I was learning reality.

The principal was another matter. I thought that she didn't like me. It took a year of observation to learn that she "picked on" one teacher every year. She had red hair and a temper to match. Today people rarely use the word mean. Back then, it was a popular word. This lady was mean. In 1960 I was her target. Actually she reminded me of Miss Shivers back in high school.

Coming from my first school where we had no materials and most of the children were so poor, I was stunned by the students. One boy from a very rich family came up to the door where I was standing the first day of school and said, "You better not swat me. My grandfather will have you fired." This was when the form of punishment was to take students in the hall, get the teacher next door to witness, and swat a bad kid a couple of times. Every teacher I knew the first nine years I taught was provided a paddle. I knew as soon as I saw him that there would be many days when he would deserve a swat or more. He was as tall as I was, and he had a mouth that I never saw shut the whole year. He was a bully and always right. This boy committed suicide his senior year a few weeks before graduation.

Some of my fourth graders attended NC State for math or science and my fourth grade for the rest of their classes. Early in the year at Show and Tell, a boy whose father was a NC State professor told about flying in the family plane to Mexico for the weekend. I listened with great attention thinking, "Oh, yeah, yeah, yeah!" Later I told the story in the teachers' lounge and was told that he was telling the truth.

Every fourth grader learned to write cursive in North Carolina. I was adamant that they must hold their pen/pencil properly. It was the first year they used ink also. It was very hard for left-handed students not to smear the ink if they didn't hold the pen properly. I was good in penmanship myself. As a challenge, I taught myself to write left-handed in order to help my left-handed students. The principal was very impressed. She began to move every left-handed student in the whole school to my class for forty minutes every day. This was an honor, but it was a pain also.

Every fourth grader had to learn to play a tonette or flutaphone also. In the spring we would attend the Symphony and play with the orchestra. My knowledge of the piano helped me. My students were outstanding. Even the parents were amazed. So was I.

We had to teach a piece of state selected art each week. I loved this also. Around 1970 the North Carolina state legislature granted a million dollars to build an art museum in Raleigh near the capital building. I was very excited about this. I took classes to become a docent. I created a summer curriculum for elementary students and another for older students to study the art in the new museum. The museum would be the classroom. During the summer, there was a half page news article in the local paper about my art classes. The principal of my school was pictured as the creator of the summer school. I was in shock. This was just the beginning of such things happening to me. Later professors would publish my papers using their name as the author. They expected me to thank them for getting my work published. I thought this was stealing. Jack was seething over this. I had to talk fast to keep him from going to the superintendent about this incident.

Fourth grade teachers had a very strict regimen of things to accomplish. Besides what the state and the city required, we had a list of things the principal required.

Jack was called to her office one afternoon early in the year, our first year, from his school next door. She told both of us that the Teachers Organization dinner was that night. She insisted that we arrive at this dinner with the yearly dues in hand. She explained that her school always had perfect attendance at this event and perfect membership in the organization. We left her office in a dither, and for the first time we rushed to a loan company to borrow a hundred dollars. We attended the dinner. Our school had one-hundred percent attendance and membership. What shiny young, devoted teachers we were! Oh, yes, and obedient!

I had twenty-eight bulletin boards and display shelves in my classroom. She wanted each of these changed monthly. Not only was this time consuming, but expensive. She kept the school open two nights at the end of every month, so that teachers could change these displays. Sometimes Jack, the artist, would help me.

One month I was teaching the children to read maps, so I put a map of Raleigh on one of the bulletin boards. Each student got to put a star where they lived. A radio announcer woke the city every morning with a loud, "This is WNNC Rawleigh, North Carolina." I placed large red letters at the top of the map saying, "RAWLEIGH". Teachers, janitors, parents, and children praised the bulletin board. It was up several days before the principal came in and saw the glaring W. She raised Cain, Abel, Adam, and Eve in front of the students and one parent, the Presbyterian pastor's wife. The parent was shocked, not at my error, but at the principal's temper. Although I tried very hard, I certainly was not perfect. No where near.

Another of her rules was that every child in the class had to have a perfect piece of work on display at all times. This was not an easy accomplishment.

Our plan books were checked regularly. We had to write plans for every subject including PE. Every "i" had to be dotted and every "t" crossed. She would often make teachers do their weekly plans over to include her suggestions. Here my typewriter-like penmanship was an advantage.

At the end of my second year in this school, I was called to the Superintendent's office. He asked me if I would accept a scholarship to Duke University to get my Masters. Duke gave a scholarship to the school system each year to award to a teacher. I was overwhelmed. Of course, I would. I was so excited that I could hardly drive back to my neighborhood. I never dreamed that there would be people who were not pleased that I got this scholarship. After all, I didn't take it from another person. I didn't apply for it. It just fell into my lap. Driving home, I was overjoyed as I sang "Thank you, Lord". Several days later my picture was in the paper reporting the good news. The principal was openly furious about my news. She called the Superintendent to complain that he should have asked for her in-put. Two years later I found out that she did not even have a Masters Degree, but got her job because of her husband's position. The other person who was greatly upset was my husband. He wanted to go to Duke, but was not accepted.

Chapter 16

Doing What I Did Best —
Going To School

My first day in class was amazing. Duke allowed only twenty-five in each class. The professors knew your name as soon as you sat down.

My first class was Modern Math with Dr. Petty who was head of the Education Department. At the end of the class he asked me to follow him to his office. He turned after we entered and said, "We would like to give you a full scholarship to Duke University." When I told him that I had a full-scholarship through the Raleigh City School System, he said that didn't matter.

I rushed home to tell Jack that he could get his Masters at the University of North Carolina at Chapel Hill. We immediately left for Chapel Hill to get him enrolled.

So for two summers we left Raleigh around 6:15 AM. He dropped me at Duke in Durham and then drove to UNC at Chapel Hill. He would pick me up at Duke around noon. We would eat lunch in the Oak Room at Duke, and then drive home to Raleigh. I would drop him at home to study. Then I would go to my new job at the library at UNC (State) in Raleigh. I would work till ten at night. I had little or no time to study except Saturday and Sunday. Usually I was writing papers for myself and him on weekends.

I had to take two classes on the weekends during the school year.

We had a bad accident three days before exams my second year. An elderly man pulled out in front of us from a parking place on the left side of the narrow road.. Jack was driving on a wet road going about 15 mph. He swerved to keep from hitting the old man. On the right side of the road was a deep ravine. The front of the car wrapped around a huge tree trunk. I went through the windshield onto the hood with the radio knob lodged in my chin. The lids of both eyes were almost torn off. Jack fainted and was not hurt. I was fortunately pulled out and rushed to the hospital. Bandages were placed on both eyes. Jack and my neighbor who was a nurse fed me. I was told that the eye is the fastest part of the body to heal. How wonderful! Exams were just days away.

Jack was so upset he couldn't think. He didn't go to class. He didn't go to his exams. An up-grade in pay down the drain.

I went to my exams. My Russian History exam was very interesting. It was scheduled for 6:00 PM one day. The professor who was Russian gave us a list of song titles and poem titles. We had to choose four and write a lecture for any period of Russian History using the song/poem titles as the theme. I wrote two legal pads full. I finished about 11:30 PM. When I got home, Jack was so upset because he was worried about me.

I called one of Jack's professors and told him about the accident. He waited for a few days. Then he called Jack and convinced him that he should come take his exams. He did and passed everything.

A coach at Jack's school was married with five children. Even with his coaching supplement, he couldn't make ends meet. One day his brother who owned a car dealership came to our door. He asked me to write a paper for the coach to finish his Masters at UNC at Chapel Hill. Having a Masters would increase his salary substantially. I told him I didn't know enough about PE to write any kind of important paper. The next day the coach came over to bring me a stack of papers and begged me to write the paper on Nutrition. I did write the paper. He got his Masters. I felt guilty. This was cheating. But for the good of his family I felt like my sin would be quickly forgiven. But I had already learned that sin is sin.

About a week after his grade was posted, his brother drove up to my house in a station wagon. He gave me the station wagon as payment for the paper. I was shocked. We really needed a car since ours wrapped around a tree and was totaled. Jack was happy; I was guilty. I began to think that I would go to hell for my good deeds. Was that possible?

I didn't go to my graduation from Duke. My face was a mess. I had no money to pay for a cap and gown. My marching would upset Jack. So I didn't even mention it. A very intelligent man who had taught with Jack for a year and was now a principal at another school talked to Jack the week after graduation. He told Jack that he had graduated first in class from Duke. He asked Jack why I didn't come to graduation. He told Jack I was second in class. Jack came home wanting to know why I didn't go to graduation. I told him because my face was all cut up. I lied. I was becoming a bad person.

Chapter 17

Assessing My Life

Here I was an educated, thankful woman. I had the assurance that I would never have to work in a factory. Many days I wondered at the marvel of being educated. Now what was I to do with all of this education? By now I had four years of teaching to my credit. Although I had not wanted to be a teacher, I was beginning to realize the classroom was my home. My education had actually been given to me. I would pass this gift on to my students. I would make them love learning and help them to see that education could lift them out of poverty, abuse, and many other things which they did not want in their own lives. That was my mission. I was grateful that God helped me see this while I was young. This was about the time that the government began putting pressure on large companies to bring women into their executive level jobs. Through the years I had several enticing offers to make more money and to have more prestige, but I stuck to my mission. Therefore, I have been truly blessed.

After four years at the elementary school, I was transferred to a High School on the other side of Raleigh. This was not a pleasant move because the principal wanted to be rid of me. But it turned out to be a good thing because we were building a house in the neighborhood where the new school stood. I was placed on the eighth grade hall teaching two blocks of North Carolina History and English. I enjoyed this curriculum. It was my cup of tea. Would I never get to teach Macbeth in High School?

At my new school I met the best principal I ever had. Mr. George Kahdy was perfect. He later became Superintendent of Public Schools for the state of North Carolina. He was very good to me. He inspired me. He appreciated me. He was a blessing in my life!

By the seventh year of the marriage, I was totally disenchanted with my mate. I didn't believe in divorce, so I was stuck. Jack couldn't be pleased. He didn't like the color of my hair. He didn't like my hair, period. He wanted me blond with a particular body type. He wanted to pick my clothes and dress me like a child would dress a doll. I was 5'5" weighing 118 lbs. at the time he was showing such displeasure. I got the message. He was as disenchanted as I was. My hair and body were the same as they were when he carried a diamond for two years asking me daily to marry him. What happened? The challenge of the conquest had ended.

One day we were shopping at Cameron Village, a mall near our house. He saw a full length red suede, double-breasted coat in the window at Burton's. He immediately wanted to buy the coat for me. We went into the store where he demanded that the coat be taken off the mannequin. He purchased the coat. He was so excited about the coat that he charged it on the charge card AND paid cash for it. He didn't know that he had done that until we received the bill with a credit of $300.00. I liked the coat, but I felt guilty about paying so much for a coat. This was about a month's pay at the time. But Jack had to control. The coat was really a way to pamper his desires. This was what he wanted.

He would go to the beauty parlor with me to give the hairdresser instructions. Finally he had had enough of my mousy brown hair; he wanted a blond wife. He demanded that the girl make me blond – the shade of blond he picked from a chart. He was so satisfied with the work that he gave the girl a huge tip. I didn't look like me at all. "Is this what you want?" I thought. Maybe so. This was not me.

We rented a huge house every year at Carolina Beach for two weeks. At some point during the two week period, everyone in his family would come down to spend a few days. We went to the beach the afternoon that I became a blond. The sun turned my hair bright orange. Jack was horrified. He had a big nose. When he was upset which was often, the veins on the side of his nostrils would expand, and his nostrils would flap in and out as he ranted. When this happened, I always laughed which made the situation worse. He huffed and puffed that whole vacation.

As soon as we returned to Raleigh, he took me to the shop and demanded that the girl do something with my hair. I had no say whatsoever. The two of them decided that she should turn me back to my original color which was an indescribable brown. She set to work. When she finished, my hair was black. Jack really showed himself. He wouldn't pay her and threatened that he would sue her. She explained that only time, air, sun, and water would fade the black to the dull brown again.

When we arrived home, he rushed upstairs as I began to prepare dinner. Food always seemed to calm him. He could eat tremendous amounts of food without gaining weight – one of those people to envy. He yelled at me to turn the stove off and get upstairs. He had hooked up a sun lamp and a fan in the shower. He turned on the shower and turned to undress me. He explained that I would stay in the shower until my hair was its original color. I tried to argue, but he was too upset to listen. With these electrical appliances, I thought that he may be trying to electrocute me. In two days school would start. He tried to keep me in the shower most of those two days. It didn't work. To me, this whole matter of my hair was ridiculous. Fortunately my hair grows exceptionally fast. By Thanksgiving I was the brown mouse again. Mother had wanted to change Daddy; now Jack wanted to change me, but it wasn't habits which I could stop. It was me.

Jack was a very talented artist. He wanted to take a portrait painting class at State (UNC at Raleigh). He signed up, but wouldn't attend the class unless I went with him. I wondered why he wanted me there. I was an observer for one semester one night a week. He painted my portrait. As I sat, it occurred to me that maybe he wanted my hair blond because it would be easier to paint than the nondescript brown. The portrait was very nice. He used a photograph of my mother to paint a portrait of her. I could never figure out why. He had such a big family. Why not his mother?

He taught science and coached basketball in the Middle School next door to the Elementary School where I taught, but he did not want me at the games. I had private time while he coached. I decided that for Christmas I would do a portrait of him to match mine. We could hang them in the entrance of our new home. I sat up an easel near the front window of the den. I would work on this portrait when he was coaching. Once the neighbor across the street warned me that I was going to get caught with the man who kept visiting me while Jack was away. They thought Jack's picture was a real man. I got a big laugh out of this. I used an 8" by 10" photograph of Jack to do the portrait. I'm not really artistic, but I laid wax paper over the photo. I divided the wax paper into one inch squares. I did the portrait one inch at a time. It turned out wonderfully.

Surprise! When I gave it to him all framed to match mine, he first of all did not believe that I did it. When he found out that I surely did do it, he was mad. Strange man!

I think that Jack wanted to build a house because he was trying to save a sick marriage. A year after we had moved in, he announced that we should have another baby. So we got pregnant. I was twenty-eight, and we often talked of wanting a big family. Now was the time.

I had a wonderful team of doctors. One month when I was more than half way into the pregnancy, I went in for my monthly checkup. Dr. Greer turned pale. He wrapped the sheets on the examining table around me, lifted me into his own car, and drove me just down the street to Rex Hospital. I had pre-eclapsia/toxemia again. How could this be? Every doctor I had been to for six years had told me that I would have no problem carrying another baby. I was sure that the result would be different this time.

But it was the same. This time Jack did visit every day for months. Otherwise I only saw doctors and nurses. I could not watch television or read books or receive cards. I was knocked out on valium twenty-four hours a day. The doctors were trying to save my life and the life of our unborn daughter. The doctors seemed to feel optimistic, especially so because a doctor from the prestigious Duke University Hospital had taken an interest in the case and drove from Durham to check us daily.

One night when I had been in the hospital for months, Jack visited.

When he left, I reached to turn out the light. The cord was attached to the top of my bed. I felt a wetness and rang for the nurse. In all the months in the hospital, I had never called for a nurse because they were in and out so often. Three nurses rushed into the room. Immediately every piece of furniture was moved to the hall, except the bed. It was pulled to the middle of the room. I was hemorrhaging. Blood was everywhere. When I saw all the blood, I knew we were in trouble. Dr. Greer was there within ten minutes. He explained that he needed to get the baby out immediately. He said that I was in labor.

Jack arrived home, got a call, and drove the half hour drive back to the hospital in ten minutes. As they pushed me to the delivery room, Jack got off the elevator. He fainted when he saw me. I didn't get to speak to him.

I was prepared for delivery in the labor room. I heard Dr. Greer yell, "We're losing her. Oh, God, give her oxygen." They were trying to locate a vein to administer some medication to bring me back although I had IV's and tubes everywhere. My circulatory system had collapsed. I heard Dr. Greer say, "We've lost her." He was crying, and his voice sounded really far away although he was standing right beside me.

The whole room turned to bright light. I had never seen such light. There are no human words to describe it. From the far right ceiling area the light consumed the whole room. There were colors glistening in the light...like hundreds of rainbows sparkling. It was unearthly and inviting. I actually felt peaceful and extremely happy. I heard what seemed like every hymn I had ever learned all at once being sung by the most beautiful voices. There was a marvelous voice in the midst of this whole vision repeating all of my favorite scripture verses. The voice was resonant and comforting. I felt drawn to the voice and had no thought of my doctor's anguish or my husband's sorrow. I just lifted off the table. I saw my baby coming with me. I felt no pain or discomfort. I had no regrets. Leaving was fine with me.

The nurse finally put a large needle into the back of my left hand. She injected the horrible medicine which returned me to this cruel world. It's a very good thing that she injected my left hand because I could barely use that hand for several years. I had no grip.

Seven years before I had lost a daughter under the identical circumstances, and I was angry and hurt. This time it didn't seem to bother me. I accepted that the baby would live if it was God's will, and if not, so be it. There was a gentle peace surrounding me. Today I am confident that the voice reciting the scriptures for me was my guardian angel. Again visible there to comfort me, and comfort me he did. I didn't share this experience for years because I didn't know anyone who would believe me. Jack could not grow as a Christian because with each child, he couldn't accept that God would allow his babies to die. Jack was not in control.

I awoke in my room several hours later to find Dr. Kimbrell sitting beside my bed. I said, "Dr. Kimbrell, what are you doing here?" It was about five o'clock in the morning. He replied that he was there for me. I sent him away assuring him that I was fine. We named the little girl who lived four hours Lisa Beth Scott. I asked about a funeral and a service. Jack never answered me. I wasn't a very demanding person at that point in my life. Strangely, I trusted Jack to do the right thing. Misplaced trust, but sincere nevertheless. He was my husband – the same man who had begged me for more than two years to marry him because he loved me so much.

Jack had an application to adopt a child when he visited the next morning. He explained that Governor Sanford had two adopted children and had advised him that he shouldn't put me through this again. I signed the papers. Dr. Greer had already told me that he and his wife had adopted children.

Dr. Kimbrell was in his thirties and brilliant. He was so very kind to me. He was dark and handsome, tall and thin. Several weeks after we lost Lisa Beth, he attended a medical convention in New York City. Knowing him, you would think that he had the world by its tail. At a workshop, he dropped dead of a heart attack. I was sad, but I was so thankful that God left him here long enough to take care of me.

The waiting for an adoption was even harder than waiting for a child to be born. We applied at Children's Home Society in Greensboro, North Carolina. We were given a tentative date. About six months later we received a letter that our case worker had had a serious surgery. This would throw our adoption from three to six months later than the date we had been given. Jack took this hard. After all, Jack was a man who had to have his way. Not later, but now.

I was home for several months. Then I received a call from the superintendent asking me to come back to teach. There was a group of children who had had a different substitute every day for two months. The next morning I gladly returned to teaching. I was horrified when I found that the block was ninth grade Algebra and Biology. I rushed to call the superintendent as soon as school ended that day to tell him of the mistake. He told me that I was a teacher who could teach anything. I taught these courses satisfactorily for one and a half years. It was hard. I think he was right. A teacher is a teacher. When you teach something you don't want to teach, it takes more time. When the students do well, it's more satisfaction for the teacher who has worked so hard. This is what I needed at this point in my life, a challenge.

Part VII

Chapter 18

The Beginning Of A Real Family

One cold, snowy night in January, 1967, we received the call. They had a baby boy for us. We could pick him up in Greensboro the following morning. I rushed to school, found the night custodian who let me in, and wrote four boards of assignments for my students. Then I went home and washed nine dozen diapers given to us at showers over the years. The nursery was ready – decorated in pale turquoise and white. We had a white crib, chest, and rocking chair. We were ready.

The next morning we drove to Greensboro to Children Home Society through the snow. We were excited beyond description. We were quizzed about many details. Jack was becoming impatient. Finally we were walking into the room to see the child when Jack said, "What if they call my son Chrissy, the Sissy?" We had decided the first year of our marriage on names to name our five children. Christopher was the name for this child. I responded to his surprising question with, "You better think fast if you're going to change the name."

The child had bright orange hair about four inches long standing wildly on his little head. Jack accepted the orange hair because he had a wonderful brother Lindsay who had red hair. The child was seven weeks old. They had difficulty finding a formula for him. He would break out in a bright red rash with every formula, until at last they found a suitable one. When the case worker asked for the name, Jack blurted out, "His name will be Jonathan Sterling." I was surprised, but pleased.

As we drove home, I didn't know how to hold the baby. I did not feel comfortable with him. I kept thinking I was going to break him. When we arrived home, there was a banner thirty feet long and four feet high across our front lawn. The banner read, "WELCOME HOME, JONATHAN STERLING!" Jack's family had all driven to Raleigh and were there. I was so glad to see his mother because she knew everything about babies.

The first four months Jonathan lived with us I sat in the rocker beside his crib every night watching him breathe. I lost more than twenty pounds. I would stand at the window every morning and cry as the school bus passed because I couldn't go to school, my comfort zone. Gradually I became acclimated to the baby. He was the prettiest baby I've ever seen. He was so agreeable. Rarely did he demand something I didn't agree with. God had truly blessed our home. What had I ever done to deserve such joy? Much later I realized that God never takes something from us leaving us empty-handed. He empties our hand, so that He can put something else there. Our part in this scenario is to trust and show patience. Without a doubt, the adoption of this baby was the greatest thing which had ever happened to me. I loved him and still do with a love I had never felt before.

Jack had been promised that as soon as he finished his Masters he would become an administrator. It didn't happen. So he left the school system to work with Governor Terry Sanford. I think that the realization that he was responsible for a family worked on him. It gave him the courage to leave the comfort of the classroom/gym. Jack was the best teacher. It was the year that community colleges were being developed in North Carolina, and the governor gave Jack an important part of that effort. Jack taught both of Governor Sanford's children, so he knew first hand how dedicated Jack could be to any project which interested him. For the two years Jack worked for the state, he was constantly harassed about getting a doctorate. He was not a good student and wasn't interested in going back to school. He was interested in making money.

He purchased a book called *Executive Jobs Unlimited*. He studied it like he had never studied a text book. He flew out of Raleigh-Durham airport eight times that summer to be interviewed for a new career.

His best offer was working at the main office in personnel for Winn-Dixie in Jacksonville, Florida. We had lived only three years in our beautiful new home. Each piece of furniture fit a specific place in the house. The yard was perfect. We both had worked so hard on that yard. We had thousands of rare plants. It was so beautiful that cars would park in front of our house and snap pictures. We had over fifty white and pink dogwoods on the back of the property going down hill to a creek. Now we were to leave this house which had been our home for only three years.

My disenchantment with the marriage increased. He became my friend. He seemed to love Jon, but he became extremely aggravated when Jon was old enough to chose a hand. He was left-handed. Jack claimed that this was a major flaw. What was wrong with this man? When we moved to Jacksonville his energy and attention were on his job. Jonathan and I were on our own. When he was home, his mind was somewhere else.

He bragged on my cooking and never interfered in the kitchen. Except to eat, of course. He ate tremendous amounts of food, so I was cooking a lot. He wanted a quart of tea, ten biscuits, two vegetables, a meat, and a salad at every meal. He never gained an ounce. We had had a dinner club with three other couples in Raleigh. We all ate once a month together at one of our homes. He was always happy with my dinners and expressed his feelings in front of our guests.

He bragged on my intelligence to our friends; however, when we were alone, he would make remarks like "You think you're so damn smart." This puzzled me. He used "damn" as much in his speaking as an ordinary person would use "the". He seemed angry when I accomplished some difficult feat. Then the curse words would fly.

Once back in college he waited till I reached home about 10:30 PM from the library where I was working. It had been another long day. He told me that for his class the next morning, he had to administer an IQ test. He wanted me to take the test right then. I just wanted to get a shower and go to bed. But I took the test to help him out. I knew for sure that he would not have done the same for me. When he saw my score, he was very angry. He wouldn't tell me the score. To this day, I don't know my IQ and could care less. He was angry until he needed help on another paper.

In Raleigh he came home every evening right after work. We were together all the time. But he wasn't faithful. He was always receiving calls from women he worked with. One Saturday as I was walking through the kitchen where he was talking on the phone, I overheard a few words which lit a light in my brain. It suddenly dawned on me that day that he was active at lunch with something besides a sandwich. I couldn't blame the women. Jack was very charismatic. He looked like a male model. He knew how to dress and wore his clothes well. When we went out to a big party, every head would turn when we walked in. They weren't looking at me. He was very energetic and always into some project around the house. Later when I became aware of his conquests or his giving in to women's conquests, I laughed to myself. I knew all of them. They were mostly plain Janes. One was quite overweight. I began to realize that I was married to a major player. This was a problem. When I tried to discuss it, he would just begin a new project. He denied everything and pretended that I was stupid to ask questions. He loved to find a way to diminish my intelligence. He was unsuccessful in the long run.

Both of us were horrified that I might become pregnant again. He had already heard from several doctors that another pregnancy would kill me.

I withdrew more into myself. I began to sleep. Sometimes I would go to sleep on Friday night around nine and sleep soundly until four the next afternoon. No doctor diagnosed me as depressed which obviously I was. I didn't want to participate in Jack's many projects. I didn't want to share my creativity or thoughts with him. I didn't want to share with him because he would run with my ideas and get tons of admiration never mentioning to anyone that I gave the idea to him.

When I was unhappy with him, I would try to find something really good about him. He had many good qualities. Most of all, he was fun to travel with.

Once we drove to New York City with two of his friends after school on Wednesday before Thanksgiving. For Thanksgiving lunch we all ate at Mama Leone's Italian Restaurant ... a seven course meal.....so good. Then we all went to see the original "My Fair Lady" with Julie

Andrews. This was our first Broadway play. Afterward we went to a place where movie stars go for dessert. The dessert for two cost $40.00, half of what the whole seven course dinner had cost. Of course, we saw the Macy's Christmas Parade and shopped at all of the big stores.

He was great at surprises. One Friday he came in the front door saying, "Pack and pack warm. We're going to Washington to see the Mona Lisa." The Mona Lisa was on loan from the Louvre to the National Art Gallery. We left by five with a bag of sandwiches. We drove through snow, and the next morning we stood in line three hours to see the painting. She was placed in a semi-circle of navy velvet curtains with Marines standing guard on either side. The audience passed before her as if she were the pope. You could hear a pin drop. No one even whispered. We stood in awe of the beautiful painting. Years later I searched the Louvre for her. She was hanging in a hallway with forty to fifty other paintings with air from an open window wafting across her face. I was appalled.

Jack loved these little impromptu adventures, and so did I.

Part VIII

Chapter 19
Moving To Jacksonville, Florida

We arrived in Jacksonville on a Sunday morning ahead of all our furniture. We went out to breakfast, and then Jack told me something he had been withholding from me. He said, "Kitty, our house is five minutes from Regency Square, Jacksonville's largest mall." How could it be? He had never noticed that I didn't enjoy shopping. We had only been together thirteen years. As I stood at the end of Regency Square, I almost cried. The whole mall was about one-fourth of the size of the malls in Raleigh. Rinky – dink!

We joined Parkwood Baptist Church near our house. It was a wonderfully friendly church. I fit right in; Jack didn't. In Raleigh he had attended church and Sunday school with me, but he knew nothing of the Bible stories. When the teacher mentioned Noah's ark, Jack had no idea what he was talking about. But it was important for him to attend and be active because his new employers were active Christians who expected their employees to be church-goers. The nursery workers who handled my beautiful son Jon were well-trained and kind. I immediately was put on the finance committee, made director of VBS, and asked to teach classes here and there. The pastor showed appreciation for me.

In our whole marriage Jack and I attended church service regularly and Sunday School most of the time. But it seemed to mean nothing to Jack. We never actually became involved together with any church.

Jack was out of town a lot. At that time I was very shy. I never volunteered for anything, but people would ask me to help. The people at the church were my strength.

Chapter 20

Finally The End

One evening about three months after we moved, Jack asked me to play a new piece of music on the piano for him. He had purchased the sheet music that day. It was "Please Release Me". I thought that this was strange. When I finished, he said as if he were saying hello, "I want a divorce." I was very shocked. I knew that he changed a lot when we moved to Jacksonville. He had begun to smoke and drink alcohol which he had never done before. I didn't believe in divorce. He said that he was a CEO now and needed an attractive wife. Let's see. Stab the knife; then twist. How many times would he twist before I understood? His next words shocked me more. He said, "I want my own children." He continued to twist. He said, "I have rented an apartment. I want you to decorate it for me. Anything you think will be fine." I refused to decorate the apartment. He was surprised. He wanted me to keep filling the baby food jars with toll money for the bridge. He said that he would miss my cooking. He announced that he would eat dinner with us every evening. He would call me about two in the afternoon to tell me what to fix. He did say that I had served my purpose well – that I got him through college.

Divorce was so prevalent in my family on both sides. I had always been determined that when I married that would be it forever. I could not be a divorcee. I knew that if I became a divorcee, my image would forever be tainted. No, I couldn't do this! I searched through the medicine cabinet. I only had aspirin. Would that do it? I swallowed 100 aspirins. I showered, fixed my hair, and dressed in my nicest dress. When Jack found out what I had done, he pulled up a straight chair beside the bed where I was lying waiting to die. He seemed to think that the least he could do was chat with me till I died. We talked all night. Once I felt that I might vomit. I decided that if I threw up, I would throw up on him. But I didn't vomit, get nauseated, or go to sleep. Nothing happened. By eight the next morning, Jack suggested that we go out for breakfast. I was puzzled. Could I not do anything right?

Jack packed his things and moved into his apartment. He only took his paintings, the Grandfather clock, the stereo, and the oriental rugs. Taking these few items made the house feel empty. Every room had been decorated to show-off one of his paintings. Without the paintings the décor made no sense. I busied myself with doing paintings to replace the ones he took with similar colors to make sense of the décor. When he visited, he was shocked and questioned where I got the paintings. I never told him. I just responded that I knew talented people. I could live without the clock, the stereo, and the beautiful oriental rugs. I would make myself live without Jack. But I have never been the same, for in the Baptist Church divorce is frowned upon. I felt like a failure. I knew that every Christian I knew and God himself were disappointed with me. No one was more disappointed with me than I was disappointed in myself. That was in 1967. I felt like I had forever lost my Christian witness. The current attitude about divorce is very unlike the thoughts on divorce back then.

One morning during the early summer when I was feeling my lowest, I received a phone call from a student I had taught in Raleigh four years earlier. She felt that something was wrong and talked her parents into letting her ride the train to Jacksonville. Her uncle was a train engineer. She was at the train station in Jacksonville. I went to pick her up with joy in my heart. We had a peeping tom in the neighborhood that summer. When she saw my situation, she arranged with her parents to stay the whole summer. What a blessing she was! Not only had she been a student of mine at school, but she was a member of the church I attended in Raleigh. Sandy was one of the best friends I've ever had.

She was about seventeen that summer. We enjoyed wonderful times together. She knew more about taking care of a baby than I did. She became my teacher.

Jack's employers promised to help us adopt a little girl if we moved to Jacksonville. Two weeks after Jack moved out, Children's Home Society called to say that they had a blond baby girl for us. He had told me he would cancel the adoption, and I trusted him. I was so naïve. When would I stop trusting this man? I never lost my temper much. Mom always told me that anger was an instrument of the Devil. So when I felt anger, I would play the piano. When I heard the voice on the other end of the line, anger swelled into my throat so badly that I could hardly speak. I was shaking so badly that my fingers would not allow me to play the piano. I never called Jack at work. But that day was no ordinary day. It was the day I lost another child; it was the day Jon stayed an only child. It hurt me worse than anything Jack had ever done. All of the anger that I had felt for all our years together spilled out.

That evening Jack showed up for dinner. I stopped him at the back door explaining that he would never taste another thing that I cooked. I told him to stay away from us. I told him that he didn't deserve a faithful wife or wonderful son. I didn't want to be his friend. Anger is a deadly sin. I was already dead on the inside.

A few mornings later I received a call from Seattle, Washington. The woman was the mother of a flight attendant who had had an affair with Jack. Jack had asked her to marry him, telling her that his wife was at death's door and that he had a one-year old son. The girl had shipped her furniture to my address. Unbelievable! That night the girl herself called apologizing. She was devastated. Apparently the charming Jack had broken another heart.

Another very bad day that summer was when I was cleaning out the desk. I found papers showing that Jack had contributed our two girls to science research. No wonder he would not discuss a funeral.

Here I was far from home with no job, no Florida teaching certificate, a one-year old adopted son, and seven rooms of furniture. Why didn't he do this in North Carolina? It was years before I dealt with the truth. The truth was that in North Carolina a couple has to be separated a whole year before they can file for divorce. Florida has no such law. He had moved us to Florida for his convenience in getting a divorce. I had not wanted to move to Florida, but I never mentioned this fact to Jack. Now I was angry with myself that I had allowed him to move us here without saying a word of protest. What was wrong with me?

Before we went to court, Jack made an attempt to move back in. It was an effort to keep his job with Winn-Dixie. I wasn't happy with this temptation. I called my Baptist minister. He came right away and spent several hours talking to us on a Sunday afternoon. I walked him out. Standing on the porch, he told me not to allow Jack back into the house. This was surprising, but wise advise.

So I hired a lawyer, a good one. One problem was that I was afraid to drive across the bridge. People who know me today could never imagine how shy and quiet I was back then. The morning of the court appearance in November, I dressed just as the lawyer had instructed. Jack came to court looking used up (not the neat, well-pressed Jack I knew) and smelling of alcohol. It was 8:00 AM. I got everything .....the boy, the house and all contents, and the car plus alimony and child support.

That Jack in court was a stranger. I did not know this man. I felt angry and hurt that I had wasted thirteen years living with a man like he had become. How could this have happened? He hurt me badly. Worse, I felt that my life was in ruins. It was.

As I left the courthouse, I realized that I didn't have fifteen cents to get back across the bridge. I had never felt so alone. Then I remembered that I had a box of used books in the back seat. Suddenly I saw a Used Book Store and a parking place at the same time on Bay Street. I backed into the parallel parking space with no problem. I had not parallel parked since Drivers' Education sixteen years before. I drove across the bridge with no fear. As I dropped the fifteen cents into the container, I screamed "Thank you, Sweet Jesus! I know that you are here!" I could feel myself changing into the kind of woman who could handle anything. The problem was that I didn't want to be this kind of woman.

When I got back to the neighborhood, I stopped to pick up Jon from Martha's house. She was a very supportive neighbor. She told me that she would keep him the rest of the day.

I went home and changed to casual clothes. I rode my bike around the neighborhood. I wanted to teach. I dropped by Arlington Junior

High. It was November 11, 1967. I went in and argued to get a minute with the principal who laughed at me. He said, "You don't have a Florida teaching certificate, and it's November. We don't have any jobs available. Besides you have to apply through downtown." I wrote my number on a pad and said, "I'm just around the corner when you need me." He took my elbow and ushered me out. He was plain rude. That same night he called saying that a pregnant eighth grade teacher went in that day for a check up, and the doctor had put her to bed. She resigned. He wanted me to come in the next morning. As I stood the next afternoon staring out my classroom window over the sandy playground, I knew that teaching was my mission. I also knew that this was a foreign mission field. The swaying palms told me.

I taught at Arlington Junior High for eight years. My experiences with these students grew me beyond recognition. By the end of the first year, I wasn't afraid of anything. Where did my shyness go? Where did all the feelings of inadequacy go? I guess that Jack took that part of me with him. He lost his job in Jacksonville and left town.

I eventually realized that Jack's leaving was a great relief. But I also realized that I was devastated. I so wanted to be married to the same man my whole life and to have three boys and two girls and be happy ever after. Just a fairy tale! In my whole life, I never really enjoyed fairy tales. I've always thought that they seemed kind of silly. I have never even read comics. Reality is my style. Reality frequently hurts.

A month after I started teaching at Arlington, I got very sick with Hong Kong flu. I could hardly make it to the bathroom and back to the bed. Jon was not being cared for as he should have been because I was so sick. A male teacher at Arlington called when he noticed that I had missed two days of school. I broke down and explained that my child needed care. He came immediately to my house and took care of Jon. He fixed something for me to eat. He came every day after school for the whole week I was sick. We became friends. Eventually we began dating. He was very, very nice to me and to Jon.

Chapter 21

Evolving Into An Independent Woman

When school was out for the summer, I had three months to get a Florida teaching certificate. I had spoken to the head of personnel. In conference he told me that his first teaching assignment was in North Carolina. When I asked where, he responded, "You've never heard of the place." When he said, "Star Town", I almost fell out of my chair. Star Town is a crossroads just a few miles outside Newton, my hometown. He advised me on colleges nearby where I needed to take six credit hours of graduate work since I already had my Masters.

Nothing about this set well in my head. I was going to pay tuition for two courses, buy a minimum of two textbooks, pay someone to take care of Jon, use gas for transportation, and study every night. When my friend Helen, an English teacher next door, told me about a trip she was taking to Europe, I really felt like whining. She told me to contact Tallahassee to see if I could get college credit for traveling. Answer –Yes! The trip had to be out of the country, at least 31 days long, and be written up in detail. The trip Helen had planned was 31 days long.

Mother and Aunt Rose kept Jon, so I drove to Newton, and I flew out of Charlotte to Kennedy Airport. I arrived in late morning, but the Jacksonville people were arriving around nine that night. I was in the whole airport with just two other people all day. Four hours after I arrived, the two women walked over to me. As we began chatting, one of them said, "Are you Kitty Hester?" Then she told me that her sister Jewel Hildebrand went to school with me in high school. They were flying Air France on the same tour out of Atlanta that I was on. How could this be? Small world, eh?

We toured eight countries. I stayed by myself as much as I could because I needed to find the history of the places we visited for my report. Every country presented a new and wonderful treat better than the one before.

We arrived in London, England. There was a huge parlor across from the check-in desk in the hotel where we stayed three nights. The first night we mingled in this beautiful parlor. We met eight Russian engineers who were in England to study new methods for six months. They asked me how many rooms I occupied in my home in America. When I answered seven with two baths, they wanted to know how many people. All of them had two disconnected rooms – one to sit in and one to sleep in. They shared a bath and kitchen with three other families. They couldn't believe the true answers we gave them to their questions. They were shocked.

On Sunday morning I got up early to try to find a church. I just walked. One of the engineers was looking for a morning newspaper. He asked me there on the street, "What are you doing out so early this morning?" When I told him I was looking for a church, he asked if he could go with me. We found an Anglican church and sat down just as the service was beginning. He began crying at the very beginning of the service and cried the whole service. When we left, he asked if we could walk along the fence of a huge park where there was an art exhibit. I was delighted to see all of the beautiful handmade things. After we had walked an hour or so, we bought some food and sat on a park bench. I got up enough nerve to ask him why he had cried in church.

His story was so sad. It was 1968, and this man lived where he could not worship freely. His grandmother had read the Bible to him and talked to him about Jesus when he was a child. She died when he was young. He knew no other Christians. He didn't dare ask if his parents or his wife believed in God. He wanted to know, but he could not trust them not to turn him in to the government officials which meant he would lose his job and house. That day was the first time in his life that he had ever been in a church. He was in his mid-forties. We held hands and prayed for his country and his family that day. I never saw him after that, but I have prayed for him many, many times through the years. I believe that God put that man in my life that Sunday morning just as sure as I am that I believe we are privileged to live in America.

We flew next to Amsterdam, The Netherlands. We were held up at Heathrow Airport in London, so we were quite late arriving in Amsterdam. The hotel had a cold cut smorgasbord set up for us. I promised myself that I would not try all the foreign dishes. I was fearful of becoming ill. I was starved by the time we got to eat. Helen said, "Oh, Kitty, try this." I did. It was a wonderful sliced white meat. Finally a waiter came to me and said, "Please, Ma'am, do not eat anymore of this meat. It is very rich, and too much will make you sick." When I asked what it was, he said,"Eel!" What a beautiful country the Netherlands was! What strange things they ate!

We went on to Germany.

In Heidelberg I had an interesting experience. Being the strong-willed woman I was becoming, I had bought new shoes to wear on the trip although I had been advised to wear old shoes. Now six days into the trip, I had blisters all over my feet. When we entered the huge hotel, my roommate told me to find a place to sit down and that she would stand in line and register both of us. The entrance was long and narrow leading up to the desk. I told her "Okay, I will meet you at the red couch." I walked around the desk, down a long hallway, and into a huge parlor. There were many couches and stuffed chairs in groups in the room. All of them were covered with tapestry type material, except one. It was red. I sat down. When she found me, she said, "How did you know that this room was here? And how did you know that there was a red couch here?" Both of us wondered that I knew this. After resting, the group went to visit a castle. I considered castles something in fairy tales, and I was not a fairy tale type woman. I left the hotel to find a shoe store. When I left the hotel property, I went left, walked a block, turned right, walked a block, turned left, and went into a shoe store on the corner. Sizes are completely different in Germany, but I ordered the right size. I purchased a pair of sandals that barely touched my feet. I've always wondered how these things could have happened.

The second day in Germany we went down the Rhine on a ship.

On the dock we went into a gift shop. I bought a few things and paid cash for them. As I walked out onto the dock to get onto the ship, the clerk from the shop ran out and yelled at me, "Kitty, I gave you the wrong change." He handed me the rest of my money. Helen looked at me strangely, and I shrugged. We never figured out how he knew to call me Kitty.

The trip down the Rhine was an all day trip. The banks of the Rhine were unbelievably beautiful. There was green, green grass on either side of the walled sides of the river. Then there was a paved road on both sides. On the other side of the road the landscape went straight up into steep hills (maybe they were mountains). Grape vines were growing on these hills. People with rags tied around their knees were crawling up the hills picking grapes. Probably these grapes were used to make wine. I thought of Grandma Hester. I was glad that she didn't have to crawl up these hills. Her life was hard enough.

At the end of the day the bus picked us up and took us to a long, wonderful dinner in Frankfurt. I felt so at home in Germany.

The ride from Germany into Switzerland was amazing. I thought I had seen mountains, but I had never seen anything like the Alps. There were seventeen hair-pin turns on the road to Bern. These were turns where the bus could not make the turn, but had to back up and move a little forward and sometimes more than once. We had lunch in a small village high in the Alps. I went for a walk alone while the others ate. I saw a woman sweeping her yard. She didn't speak English, but she took my hand and led me into her house. I stood looking at hundreds of hand made ski sweaters. I bought three and rushed to find the hotel where the tour group was eating. The bus was gone. I was sure that they had left me in this village where no one spoke English. I freaked. But the bus had gone to gas-up. After a long winding bus ride across the Alps, we were in the most beautiful country I had ever seen. We stayed in a hotel in Bern, and then moved on.

We had the best time in Lucerne. We took the ski lift to the top of a mountain and back down. I was amazed. Flowers were blooming on the side of the mountain where the sun shined, but snow covered the ground on the side of the mountain where the sun never shined, just refusing to melt. One of the most treasured books from my childhood was *Heidi,* given to me by our neighbor, Larry Queen, when I was in the fourth grade. The book was full of pictures. Now I was actually seeing the pictures I had so often enjoyed in my book. Looking at the pictures in the book, I knew that flowers could not possible bloom right beside a mound of snow. Now I understood.

We were invited to travel by boat down Lake Lucerne to a Swiss party. How wonderful! The Swiss people were so friendly and entertained us like we were royalty.

We walked many times across the Chapel Bridge which was a crooked, covered foot-bridge crossing the Reuss River where artists had painted beautiful pictures in the ceiling of the roof. I walked back and forth across the bridge studying the pictures. I was amazed. If I actually lived there, I was sure that I would walk the bridge frequently, maybe every day. The bridge was built in the 17th century. It was almost destroyed by a fire in 1993, many years after I was there. It has been rebuilt.

On to Italy. I knew that Italy would be my favorite. We crossed the mountains where Bo Bo and No No, the Waldensian couple from my childhood, were born. No No had told me stories of climbing out the attic window in the winter time and walking on snowshoes to a neighbor's house. The snow was almost as high as their house. I still have a hard time picturing that.

The first city we visited was Milan. I really wanted to see the Last Supper. It was painted on a church wall and was deteriorating. They were in the process of repairing it, and we were not allowed to see it. We toured the first Mall in the world. It was covered with a beautiful stained glass ceiling. We were told not to be surprised if some man pinched us on our behind. It was supposedly a friendly gesture. With my deflated ego still suffering from being divorced, I could not believe that no guy pinched my butt. What was wrong with my rear? This threw more water on my already dampened spirit which had been improving on this trip.

Fortunately, we reached Florence next. I considered missing the bus and just living in Florence the rest of my life. I had studied all of the beautiful art work when I took a correspondence course from the Metropolitan Art Museum in New York City and at Appalachian State in Art Appreciation class. Now I was looking at the real thing. I shopped along the stores on both sides of the Ponte Vecchio (Old Bridge) which crossed the Amo River in the middle of the city. This bridge was first mentioned in documents as early as 996 AD. The present bridge was constructed in 1345 when America existed only in the minds of dreamers. Through the years it has been damaged in storms and floods many times, but always repaired. Now dozens of merchants were selling jewelry and art objects from table tops. I felt like I was walking through a history book.

As I stood staring up at the statue of David, tears came to my eyes.....tears of joy. He was huge, carved from a seventeen foot high hunk of marble between 1501 – 1504. Here I stood gazing at him 464 years later. How on earth did Michelangelo accomplish this feat? What perseverance he must have had! How dedicated to the talent God had given him! I stood there in awe wondering how many hours he actually worked on this beautiful masterpiece. I thought of how he must have rejoiced when David was finished.

The whole city was filled with beautiful art work. Did I think of Jack? No. I wonder that I didn't grieve that he was not with me enjoying these pieces of real art. But the whole trip I didn't think of him once. This was good. Not only was I getting six hours college credit, but I was having a once in a life-time adventure. And I was recovering from a major disappointment.

My roommate was the teacher next door at Arlington. Her next door neighbor and her sister were with us, so she was not pressuring me to spend time with her. I quietly studied and thoroughly enjoyed all that I saw, taking my time to absorb every opportunity. I was pleased that I had studied for years before the trip, so now I knew exactly what I wanted to see in each city.

I was sad to leave Florence, but extremely excited to reach Assisi. We had lunch first and then walked up the narrow street to the Basilica. I wanted to shop in the little shops along the way up the mountain. The shops were filled with dinnerware made in the village. I wanted a set, but how could I carry it? The shop keepers were down-to-earth people and very friendly with the tourists. I appreciated this.

St. Francis was born here. Although he was born into a wealthy family and lived his young life in luxury, he visited Rome and joined the beggars begging for food. His life was forever changed. He became a friar and founded the Franciscan religious order in 1208. St. Clare, the founder of the Poor Sisters, and St. Gabriel of Our Lady of Sorrows were also born in Assisi. St. Francis became the patron saint of animals, nature, and the environment. He and St. Catherine are the patron saints of Italy. His tomb is in the crypt under the altar of the Basilica. As we visited his tomb, I couldn't speak. It was an overpowering feeling to stand in this place.

It was getting progressively harder to leave each town. I fell in love with each place and each group of natives.

On to Rome. I was looking forward to some really good Italian spaghetti. I didn't find it. We went to a fine eatery. When the plate of spaghetti was set in front of me, I saw white pasta barely cooked and some kind of orange water poured over it. How disappointing! The sights in Rome were wonderful, but so many of them were connected to the violent past of the city and their struggle to maintain their power. I was glad to leave Rome. We did visit the Sistine Chapel at the Vatican. I couldn't speak. There are no words in my vocabulary to say how touched I was.

We traveled by bus to Nice, France. It was blazing hot. No one wanted to do anything. I walked down to the Mediterranean Sea to walk in the water's edge. I was shocked. The water looked black and the bottom was all rock. I never got this picture by reading about it. I walked back to the hotel, into the bar, and ordered a lemonade. The bartender had never heard of lemonade. So I asked for a lemon, some sugar, and some water. The ice was a problem. Seems that everywhere we went they were stingy with the ice. I hope they have learned the joys of ice by now. The bartender tasted my lemonade and began making large pitchers full to serve everyone in the bar. All of the Europeans were amazed.

We drove up to Monaco. I had had my ears pierced before I left America...part of my liberation. I needed some alcohol to treat my new piercings, so I went into a pharmacy to buy the alcohol. The pharmacist told me to go across the street to the casino where they had lots of alcohol. Another training session was required as I tried to explain the kind of alcohol I was seeking. He was a slow learner.

As we left Monaco, we drove past the palace where Queen Grace Kelly was walking on the lawn. She waved to us and probably realized that we were American because of the wild manner we used to get her attention.

On our way from Nice to Paris, we stopped at a McDonald's. The building was out in the countryside with nothing else in sight. At the time (1968) one could purchase a coke and hamburger at McDonald's in America for less than two dollars. We were charged $6.00 for a small hamburger and a coke. I was never sure whether other customers in the joint were charged the same. We got the impression that they saw a bus load of Americans approaching and raised the prices. We complained to our courier Deena who was Belgian. She only laughed.

We arrived in Paris around noon. I immediately registered at the hotel and headed to the Louvre. I was very excited. The place was much larger than I had imagined. I looked everywhere for the Mona Lisa and for the Winged Victory. I walked miles. Finally I asked a guard. He responded with, "If you want to know something, you speak in French." I had had two years of French in High School, but the class was mostly reading. I went to another guard. He responded to my inquiry with, "Speak French, American Bitch." I was shocked. If I had known the French for what was in my mind at that point, I probably would not have held my tongue. When I finally found the Mona Lisa, she was hanging below eye level in a hallway. On the other side of the hallway were dozens of open windows. I remembered seeing her in Washington, D. C. and the reverence we gave her. Tears filled my eyes, but I swished them away quickly because I didn't want any guard to see that the American bitch had a heart. They would have been disappointed. When I found the Winged Victory, she was standing on a stair landing going to the basement. Again I was sad, so sad that I sat down on the stairs. Enough of this disrespect for these famous works of art. I had been there hours, so I took a cab back to the hotel. I could have stayed in the Louvre for days.

I placed a call to my mother. I had not called her since London. In London I had no problem. Now the operator called me back to say the lines were busy. The next day as we were boarding the bus, a policeman came to arrest me. I sat down on the sidewalk and refused to move. It seems that the operator had tried the call many times during the night. I never spoke with my mom. I had never told the operator to continue trying. I had no proof that the call had ever been attempted. I owed $400.00 for a call which never happened. The call had been $20.00 in London. The courier nor the bus driver were doing anything to help me. I yelled that I wanted someone from the American Embassy. I was shocked when I heard the screaming voice leave my mouth, but it was the magic word. I was amazed that I knew what to say. Some people would call this luck. I knew that it was the hand of God. I was allowed to board the bus, and we were on our way to Madrid.

Spain was full of welcoming attitudes and smiles. We checked into an American Hotel. Women were not allowed to go to see the Flamenco dancers or to many places unless accompanied by a man. None of us had a male companion. After an afternoon of shopping, we considered this a real dilemma. Four American business men stood talking in the lobby. I took the situation into my own hands. I needed this information for my report. Again I shocked myself. I simply walked up to them and asked the four men if they would consider escorting the four of us to a Flamenco show. What a brazen hussy! The answer was, "Of course." So easy. My friends were shocked and delighted. Who was this person I was turning into? Was it another personality which had been hiding inside the quiet, shy me? Or was it the smart, desperate woman who knew that she had a report to write? Going shopping and to get a haircut would not be a very interesting report.

The second day we traveled by bus into the hills to Toledo. As I sat on a wooden bench inside the small church and stared at the painting by El Greco on one whole side of the church, I felt a part of the history. I had studied this painter in Art Appreciation at Appalachian State. I wished that my sweet professor was there to discuss this work with me.

In those days I suffered from sinus trouble most of every year. I had taken a bottle of prescribed sinus medicine with me. But I never needed it and had, pill by pill, given it to the other members of our group who needed it. The road to Toledo was very dusty. By the time I reached Madrid in the evening, I was in bad need of the medicine I had given away. When the bus reached downtown Madrid, I got off to find a pharmacy. As I stepped down from the bus, the driver said, "You better hurry because the stores close in fifteen minutes." I panicked. I looked up and down the street. Then I began looking for an American. I suddenly saw a tall, blond young man leaning against a store front. I ran up to him and said, "I need a Pharmacy." He took my hand and started leading me to a side street. We chatted on the way, a matter of five minutes. I learned that he was visiting Madrid. He was a medical student in Barcelona. When I asked him where he was from, he assured me that I had never heard of his hometown. He told me that he was from Murray Hill in Florida. When I asked him if he meant Murray Hill, the suburb in Jacksonville, Florida., he was surprised. I barely got inside the door of the pharmacy as they were closing. The pharmacist didn't understand me. I sniffed and blew my nose and coughed. He just looked at me. Did he have a brain in his head? Finally his wife came from the back. I repeated my act for her. She immediately said to him, "Give her some Dristan." I was sure that God was in Spain.

We entered by bus into our final city, Lisbon, Spain. Everyone was tired. All I could think about was how beautiful the people of this city were. So attractive! Their coal black hair accentuated the gorgeous tone of their dark skin. Mainly I was thinking about getting home.

Finally on the thirty-second day, we landed at the Air France terminal at Kennedy. I had to find my flight to Charlotte in another building. My cousin picked me up in Charlotte and took me to my mother's house. I felt like a stranger now. I was forever changed. My mind was full of wonderful memories. I stayed two weeks in Newton which now seemed stranger than before. I held Jon for almost the first whole week. If he had been with me, I probably would not have come back to America. The second week I organized my report for the Department of Education in Tallahassee which would get me a Florida Teaching Certificate.

Chapter 22

Doing What Seemed Necessary

When I returned to Jacksonville I discovered that Fred, the teacher from the school where I had taught the year before who was supposed to be checking on my house, had moved in. I was shocked. In those days you rarely heard of couples living together if they were not married. Of course, I really wanted a father for Jon. Since I was single, I could not adopt a sister for him. Fred was really good with children. He adored Jon. So I made the worst mistake of my life. I did what seemed necessary. I married him. Since married couples could not teach in the same school at that time, he was transferred.

The three of us began a new journey. Fred adopted Jon. For the first year or so things went well. Then we adopted another son. The child had numerous problems. He cried constantly. He was in braces awaiting the beginning of a series of surgeries to straighten his legs. His digestive system simply did not work for his first three years. We were blessed with wonderful women who cared for the boys while I continued to teach. This was necessary, for the many doctor bills almost buried us. Our insurance would not cover his medical bills because we knew of the problems before we adopted him.

By the time the second son reached the age where he paused in all the crying to show his sweet little personality, Fred had begun showing favoritism. It was no subtle thing. He was verbally cruel to Jon. We had many, many discussions, but talking didn't fix the problem.

About three years into the marriage I discovered unbelievable things about this man who was my husband. My pastor sent me to a psychologist who recommended a psychiatrist for Fred. Fred agreed to go. He was embarrassed about his condition and begged me to not tell anyone. I didn't. I began teaching at the college two nights a week to pay for his bills because our insurance was connected to the school system. Of course, he was especially cautious about having anyone in the school system to know of his problems. With cash in hand from my second salary, he went weekly to the psychiatrist for more than two years. He never wanted to discuss his sessions. I honored this.

During this whole period of time we attended church regularly and had Bible studies in our home. After two years, I quite by accident found out that he had only been to the psychiatrist once. He was taking the money to get a room at a local hotel a few blocks away where he wore my clothes and entertained male friends. It was not in me to understand such behavior. For the first time in my life, I lost my temper. I screamed, I ranted, I cried, I threatened; I threw things. All to no avail. The psychiatrist suggested that I get away from my husband as quickly as possible. I didn't; I couldn't. He turned on the TV, sat down in a recliner, and sat there for over a year. He did not move from the chair while I was in the house. He didn't go to work. I had to make sure that he was never left alone with the boys. So I stopped teaching at the college. I was literally glued to my boys.

During this time I desperately needed funds. I saw a house in the neighborhood which was a mess. I had painted our house, so I knew I could do this. It took all the nerve I could muster to ask if I could paint their house. I didn't know the people. The man was delighted. He furnished all the paint, brushes, ladders, and everything else I needed. They moved to the lake for a week. The house was covered in vines which had to be pulled away. The house had to be scraped and scrubbed with chlorox. The boys played in the back yard as I worked. I finished in a week. On Sunday the man called me and asked me and the boys to a cook out. His boss was there. I was surprised to find out that the boss was a HUD supervisor. He asked me to paint sixteen apartments. I did. He liked my work and the fact that I didn't take fifteen minutes out of every hour to smoke. Then he asked me to paint two town houses. He allowed me to paint alone and keep my boys with me. He didn't want me to go back to school. I was making more painting than from teaching, but his offer did not tempt me. By then I was a tried and true teacher. Teaching was my mission.

When my husband came out of this stupor (I call it that because I don't really know what it was) almost a year later, he began to have spells of violence. The younger son nor I were never the target of his violence, but he was horrible to the older son who was about nine at the time. Finally after seven and one-half years, during a discussion we decided to separate. He separated his best friend and his wife and began living with the woman and her three daughters.

For a year he would faithfully pick up the boys every other weekend. He would say that he would return them on Sunday at 6 PM. I was scared to let him have the boys, but the courts ruled. Every Sunday he would call threatening to sell the boys. He had a cousin from Honduras who owned shrimp boats and frequently docked in Fernandina Beach. His route ran from Columbia, South America to Brunswick, Georgia. Fred said that his cousin could sell them in South America. I was horrified. With all the threats, he would put them out in front of the house around 11PM each time he took them. I braced myself for five hours of fear and praying every other Sunday, not knowing if I would ever see my sons again. The woman he was living with was very kind to the boys. After a year, I divorced him. There had been no child support during the year of separation, and this continued another year before the department through which he was to make payments dragged him into court. He lied to the judge saying that he had never missed a payment. Within two days of his court visit, we received two years back pay from his mother.

Soon the visits stopped all together. This was a good thing. He had married. She would call me crying that he was beating her because he was drunk all the time. I listened, but I had no sympathy. The man was pitiful. I prayed for him every day for twenty years until I heard that he had died. There was no doubt in my mind that he truly wanted to be a good man, but he was never strong enough to fight all the demons that lived in him. It was something that he had to do himself.

Both boys were relieved that their father was no longer in the house. In adulthood, they both have shared with me that the eight years after he left were the best years of our life together. We truly became a team.

During this period, I never questioned God or lost sight of His goodness, but many days I wondered how I could be so naïve. I really got down on myself. How could I be the single mother of two sons? How could I be divorced, not once but twice? In my heart I believed that I must be the scum of the earth. Yet I was proud of the fact that I got myself and my two little sons away from this man. I tried to stay busy. But at night when I was too tired to do another thing, I would lie in bed and think of all the wrong things I had done in my life. All of the good things seemed minor by comparison. I prayed and prayed, but God seemed to be busy with everyone else. Was He too ashamed of me? Was He ashamed, like I was? Was He angry? I was.

Professors from Florida State University had been coming to Jacksonvillle every Saturday and Monday nights to teach doctoral classes. I attended the classes. Then came the day that I could not move forward until I established residence for a year. I was given a sabbatical by the school system. So the boys and I moved to Tallahassee for a year. It was a wonderful year. When we returned to Jacksonville, the older son refused to visit his dad. Of course, if he didn't want to go, the younger son didn't want to go either. I had been careful never to speak of their father in a negative way. I learned this from my mother who caused me to idolize my "no good Daddy" (as she called him) with constantly down-grading him. My thinking was correct. I explained that if they didn't want to go, they had to call and explain why.

Many evidences of God's love were present. But they didn't dissolve the hurt and pain. I tried lying in bed and thanking God for every positive thing in my life. There were many blessings. But at the end of my prayers I still felt worthless. I wanted to avoid church. I didn't want people to know our situation.

One morning was a particularly rushed and hectic morning. The boys and I always joined hands and prayed before we went out the door heading for school. When we finished, I mumbled under my breathe, "God, please give me some evidence that you are hearing our prayers." We opened the door and rushed toward the car. I stopped dead in my tracks. There in the middle of our front yard in the grassy area was a large, bright yellow jonquil in full bloom. Just one! You must understand that the jonquil is one of my favorite flowers. We had beds of jonquils in North Carolina. This was the middle of the yard not near any flower bed. Jonquils do not grow in Florida. How could this be? I knew immediately that God had given me evidence of His presence as I had asked. This beautiful jonquil was my evidence.

We had many incidents in the next nine years where we felt God's presence. What a wonderfully comforting presence He has! Sometimes the boys saw these things happening, and sometimes they were just for me. It wasn't that I didn't believe that God was there with us. It was that I was so very lonely and, more often than not, had to meet challenges that the world dumped on me alone. When you teach school and raise two little sons, there's no time for friends. When I was not at school, I was preparing lesson plans or grading papers. I knew better than to let a stack of papers go a day. They could pile up and drown you. So every night when the boys went to bed, I worked on school work or some money making project to get funds for a needed repair on the house. Unbelievable opportunities to make the needed cash came my way from unexpected sources so often. The amount of money I could make seemed always to be just the amount I needed.

Looking back on those days I wonder how I ever had the strength to keep going. Actually the energy absorbed from my two sons was more energy than I could muster from myself. Both of my little sons were balls of energy, and they were always ready to help their mom. The three of us made a super team.

Money came to me in many surprising ways. This was good.

The pastor at my Baptist church asked me to decorate the dining hall for a dinner to begin a Family Life Seminar. The speaker had written seven books. I read each book, and made a mural. I just purchased two yards of cheap fabric at Walmart. Then I painted my impression of the book on these murals. They were hanging around the hall when the speaker rose to speak. He immediately asked who did the murals and asked to speak to me at the end of the evening. He told me that he wanted the murals. That was fine with me because I had no use for them. Several weeks later I received a check for $700.00. That was more than two months salary at that time.

A few weeks later on Wednesday night at church, a man walked up to me and told me that he had been promoted on his job that day. He explained that he had to have a promotional meeting the next morning, but didn't have time to get a commercial artist to make the graphs he needed. When he asked me to make the graphs, I declined. About 10 PM, his wife rang my doorbell. There she stood with poster board, markers, and the originals on notebook paper. She begged and begged. So I did three graphs. I was up half the night. The next morning at seven the man showed up and was amazed. Of course, he was not as amazed as I was. Actually I am not very artistic. Several days later I received a $300 check from his company. I can not explain how much I needed this money. This was a month of teaching salary.

I have always been amazed at the opportunities right in front of us. Our own problems and lack of awareness cause us to overlook these opportunities.

A few weeks later I went into a butcher shop one Thursday afternoon. The owner was talking to a man. He was very angry. The owner was a pastor. When the other man left, the pastor apologized to me for showing his anger. It was caused by a sign maker always bringing the huge sale signs into his shop a day late. The sale began each week on Thursday morning, and the guy delivered the signs Thursday afternoon week after week. I told the owner that I could do the signs for him. He gave me a try. He furnished all the materials. This worked for both of us. I lived two blocks away. He paid me $100.00 a week.

Starting in my teen years, I knew that I was not good at dating. One night I had a date ... a horrible date. He kept calling and calling. He was a business man who owned his own business. Finally I explained to him that I just didn't have time to date. When he learned of my struggle, he wanted to give me money. There was no way that I would accept a penny from him or any other man. He laughingly told me, "Well, why don't you just design greeting cards?" He explained how. I received $50.00 a design and $50.00 a verse. This was great. No pressure. When I decided to try, I would send in a verse or design or both. A week later I would receive a check. I would have a half hour and try to write a verse, but nothing would come to mind. I would get in a pinch for money, and verses would flow into my mind – even while I was driving.

Things eased as the boys grew older and could help more. Both boys did things that were not required of any of their classmates. They did

195

yard work, carried the garbage to the curb, gardened, cleaned, cooked, helped buy the groceries, helped shop for their clothes, and helped to plan vacations. They rarely complained. They accepted these things as just a sharing of family responsibilities.

However, their helping so much backfired at times. Once I promised them a surprise for the weekend if they weeded the 5' x 30' bed of chrysanthemums on the side of the front yard. They got to work, and I began cooking supper. It was dark when they came into the kitchen after washing up. They reported that they had finished. I was proud of them. They were about six and nine. The next morning as we climbed into the car for school, I got the shock of the month. Every weed stood straight and green in the flower bed. The boys had pulled all of my chrysanthemums. I rushed to the trash, pulled them all out, and pushed them into several pails of water to be replanted after school. I've never figured out if they were just "gardening dumb" or trying to teach me a lesson.

One day the only television we had began acting up. Jon wanted to fix it. I was always afraid that Jon was going to be electrocuted before he reached adulthood. I gave him a strong warning not to try to fix the television. He didn't listen. He tried to fix it, and the picture made a quarter turn. All the static was gone, but you had to lay down to even try to see the picture. I was angry enough to leave it exactly the way Jon fixed it for a month. I threatened to ground him the rest of his life if he touched the television again. His knowledge was helpful. His installing ceiling fans in the house was a blessing.

Both boys did their own laundry beginning around seven years of age.

We were careful to appreciate the talents of each person in our little family. We often played music together. We attended recitals and showed admiration for the one playing. We were there for Jon's games as he went through the Little League experience. We celebrated every success with ice cream, or McDonalds, or their favorite meal at home. We nurtured Charles through Scouts helping him dig up the back yard for his gardening badge. In adulthood we remain the same, always nurturing during each others' interests and trials.

The three of us planned vacations during the winter on Sunday afternoons. Then in the summer we followed our plans. We had several big vacations together; one to D.C. and one to Nashville. We went to Disney and Epcot and Universal Studios. We visited relatives who lived in interesting places.

Many times during these years of being a trio, we had serious setbacks. We had wonderful times and very troubling times. Many of the hard times were caused by lack of money and Charles's health issues.

At age three Charles had severe digestive problems and wore braces at night and as much of the daytime as possible. One morning as we were getting ready for church, a most wonderful miracle happened. Oral Roberts from Oklahoma was on TV. He said, "If anyone in your home needs a healing, put your hands on their head, and I will pray for their healing." Charles walked up to where I was dressing just as Oral Roberts spoke these words. I placed my hands on the wiggly little son's head. At three that afternoon there was evidence that Charles's intestinal problems were healed. The whole family rejoiced. A few weeks passed before we had to go to our quarterly check up to the orthopedic surgeon. Charles had been born with twisted legs. He was wearing the braces most of every day waiting for a series of surgeries to start. On this visit the surgeon said, "What happened? There's no need for the braces or the surgeries. His legs are healed."

We were in the car before I realized that, as with the intestinal problems, his legs were healed through Oral Roberts' prayer. I was so excited that I screamed, "Thank you, Sweet Jesus!" all the way home in the car. Charles was not sure what happened to his usually quiet Mom. I was so excited that I couldn't offer a proper prayer. I knew that God understood.

When Charles was seven, he began years of internal bleeding and many rounds of exploratory surgeries and visits to doctors. He could bleed from any opening in his little body. This bleeding happened about twice a year and continued into adulthood. He was treated at Shands, a research hospital in Gainesville, and Bethesda when he was in the army. We did have about a three year period in high school after I took him to Ken Hagin who had a healing service in the old Coliseum. He had no incidents of bleeding until he entered the Army.

When we returned from Tallahassee, we began attended First Baptist Church in Jacksonville. The sermons and studies there were very helpful. They most likely kept me from going insane. The boys were always very active. They both played in the orchestra from the time they could play an instrument in the sixth grade. The eight years that our family was fatherless were the best years of our life. I learned that every obstacle you overcome actually makes you stronger. I became a very strong woman with confidence that God is real and that He enjoys a real relationship with me. Me...nothing but a mill kid. Indeed!

I worried that my salary would not be enough to keep our family together. I read, "Fret not." When I would begin worrying, I would say, "Fret not" over and over. I would drive saying the command.

Each blessing I received made me want to push further. I desired and needed God's favor. I tithed, but I began to realize that tithing was what was expected. To give a gift to God, one must give more than a tithe. I began adding one percent to my tithe every four months. The more I gave the more I had. Years later I learned that this phenomenon is called Divine Multiplication. I wondered how much I could actually give and still have enough of my small nine month salary to survive. Over a year or so I reached twenty percent. We were living comfortably until the boys joined the band and ball teams. These activities ate up the money.

Because I had so many experiences where I was sure that God was directing my path, I became interested in experimenting.

I heard of FISH which was nothing but a number in the phone book. I began accepting their phone calls one week a month. I had many interesting experiences doing this.

One night after the boys were long asleep, I received a phone call from a girl crying. She was a prostitute who had been dumped out of a man's car way out at a remote area of the dunes at the end of Ft. Carolina Road. This was where the result of dredging the river was dumped. The man cursed her and dumped her to teach her a lesson. She begged a resident near by to let her use the phone. I drove way out there to pick her up and bring her back to civilization. I witnessed to her, and for years she would call me and talk. I like to think that I made a difference in her life. I know that I gave her something to think about.

One afternoon I received a call from a woman who needed help. Ironically she lived only a few miles away. She was bed-fast. Her adult children ignored her needs. When I arrived, she had soiled her bed, and she was hungry. I took care of her immediate needs and fed her. I found a service who would check on her daily. Finally she was put into assisted living.

I began to think that tithing meant ten percent of your time in addition to a tenth of your money. So I designed a plan to give specifically ten percent of my time to God's work. Jon was in seventh grade, so I felt comfortable leaving the boys home without me. I would get into my car in the parking lot of the school every Monday afternoon and sit there praying for direction. I had some wonderful experiences doing this.

One afternoon I thought that I should drive to "sin city", an area of the city known for drug dealing and crimes of all kinds. When I turned into the area, I had no idea what was happening. Finally just on a whelm I stopped the car in front of a huge fir tree. When I walked around the tree, I saw a tiny cottage. It was very cold. I knocked on the door several times before I heard someone coming. Finally a little lady wrapped in several blankets opened the door. She was blind. She had adult children who rarely visited her. She had run out of her medicines and gas for heat. I helped her dress. We went to the grocery store where we purchased groceries while the pharmacy refilled her prescriptions. Then we drove to the gas company to pay her bill and get the gas turned back on. She was so happy to have my help. I was amazed that I found her. I visited her weekly for years.

So many similar things happened the years that I was experimenting with this. I should have become used to the marvel of it all, but I never did. Every adventure was filled with wonder. When Jon began band, we had to change our schedule, and I had to drop this work. But I had had a taste of "doing God's bidding". I had lived in God's favor.

For three years a man in my Sunday School class and I took the boys to three nursing homes every Saturday afternoon. We would visit, chat, sing, and have scripture. The first home served dinner at four o'clock on Saturday. It was usually cereal. I worried that they would be hungry before the next morning. The second home served dinner at five. Most of the residents here were alert and enjoyed our visits. The last was the worst. It was located in "sin city". When one opened the door, the stench would almost knock you over. They would have just finished their dinner. These people were pitiful and rarely had visitors. Of course, they really enjoyed our visits. One evening an old man began to cry. Jon had taught himself to play the trumpet. He played "When We All Get to Heaven" for the old folks. The old man sat in his wheelchair and sobbed. When we began to leave, he rolled over to Jon and said, "I played trumpet for the Philadelphia Philharmonic Orchestra. I enjoyed that song so much." You never know how you can touch another person. Intermingling with these "forgotten" impressed me in ways I can't explain. Being used brought happiness.

In these situations I knew for a fact that God was happy with me because I was following His direction. This was a wonderful time in my life.

Chapter 23

Another Husband

I never thought of remarrying. It was apparent to me that I was not intended to have a normal life. I had stopped dating altogether. I certainly was not thinking about bringing a man into our family. I was teaching in the Singles' Sunday School Department at the big First Baptist Church downtown just across the bridge from our house. There was a man in the class who would follow me over to church and sit beside me during Sunday services and on Wednesday evenings. This continued for a couple of years. I thought nothing about it because many singles sat around me in church.

The Singles had a Bible study and covered dish supper at one of the members' home every Friday night. It grew and grew until this home was too small to hold all of us. We had to find a larger place. This man asked me if I would help him check his home to see if I thought he had everything needed to have the Friday meeting at his home. He picked me up and took me to his home. We checked the kitchen first. Then he asked me if I would like a tour of his home. I thought this was very strange. It was obvious that he wanted to impress me. The kitchen and den and master bedroom were furnished. The dining room, three bedrooms, and the living room were empty. The house was a colonial style on the St. Johns River. The screened in porch on the back of the house was huge. We began having the Friday meeting at his home.

Most of the women (all of them being single) began ridiculous moves to attract this man's attention. He had no idea how to handle this situation. He was a catch. He had never been married; therefore, he wasn't paying child support or alimony. He was a Christian. He had never done drugs or drank liquor or smoked. He really wanted a family. His older brother prepared for the ministry, but did not have a church. He had a wife and two adopted children. This man really wanted children. His parents were very nice to me and my boys.

The third year I knew him, he went to Alabama to be with his parents for Christmas day. He left the dinner table and drove back to Jacksonville. He showed up at my door with a new microwave and a pair of bedroom shoes for me. I was shocked. He had never been in my house. He had never given me anything before. He waited till very late that evening to say that he thought we should get married. This made no sense to me. We had never even been on a date. He could see that I was very surprised, so he asked me to think about it. The next day I discussed this proposal with the boys. Of course, they were thinking of the boats and the river and the big house. Most of all they really wanted a good dad.

We married in his home. His parents came to make sure that this was really happening. The boys were there. We didn't have a honeymoon, but stayed home from work for a week.

The day after we married, he announced the schedule we were to follow. He made out a schedule of who would wash the dishes and who would dry. He put himself into the mix. He said that we could not use the dishwasher. He had a schedule for cleaning, shopping for groceries, yard work (he left himself out of the mix here), and laundry. He had Charles doing laundry on Thursday, Jon on Tuesday, and I was to do his laundry and mine on Saturday. I had been very organized when I was the head of the family, so although I thought he was being a little overboard a little too quickly, I didn't say a word to stop him. He informed me that I needed to have my check deposited into his account because he would handle all of the money. When he told me this, he said it in a tone of voice that made me know that there would be no compromising. I couldn't believe what I was hearing. But I went along with - it because for fifteen years I had handled all of the money. Maybe this would work for all of us. Little did I know!

We furnished the rest of the house. He began asking his Sunday School class to our home. An example of this was one Thursday morning when he told me that I was preparing a sit down dinner for around seventy people that Friday night. I had to work on Thursday and Friday. I was a Dean of Girls in a large High School. If I missed a day, I would never find my desk under all the referrals the next day. I went by Winn-Dixie on the way home from school on Thursday. I began cooking and setting up the tables. I cooked all night. I went to school the next day. As soon as I got home Friday, I began decorating the tables and laying out china and silverware. Everyone seemed to enjoy my food. When they left, many of them made remarks like, "Oh, Kitty, you are so lucky to have Mike." This was the first, but certainly not the last time that he displayed this controlling nature. Mike not once ever thanked me. I learned to tolerate times like this. I filled the dishwasher, straightened up, and went to bed. I was exhausted. The next morning the kitchen was flooded. Without any warning, my husband had disconnected the dish washer, so that I couldn't use it. To say the least his communication skills were lacking. But for the first time he heard the tone of my school-teacher voice when I told him for sure that I would not be helping mop water and neither would the boys. He caused the problem; he could deal with it alone. He mopped as he explained that the dishwasher used too much water and electricity. I had no response.

It was hard to tolerate the way he handled my money. On planning days, the teachers would go out for lunch. He would give me two or three dollars.

When I picked up the boys from school one day, both of them begged to go to McDonalds. I thought that this was strange, so I asked if they didn't eat lunch at school. They were really hungry. Their father dropped them at school three days in a row. He didn't have the right change for their lunch, so he didn't give them anything. We had words about this. His excuse was that they would probably lose the change. I didn't understand this at all. There was a minute market near the school. He could have gotten change there. Or he could have given them a week's lunch payment on Monday. The boys and I went to McDonalds using Jon's allowance out of his savings jar. This man's brother and parents apologized to me every chance they got about his greediness. They knew him well.

In the evening he would sit at his desk figuring out our next move. While I was married to him, we bought many houses and rented them out. We purchased five time shares. We sold my house and used the money as a nice down payment on a beautiful home in my North Carolina mountains. After a period of studying, he would announce to me that we needed to buy a house for his set amount of money and have it rented out for his set amount by a specific date. The purchase had to be made and the house had to be cleaned and repaired by a certain time. Of course, he used me and the boys to do this work. Once he found out how handy Jon was, he wanted Jon with him every time we had cleaning and repairs to do. Jon's specialty was changing the locks on new property. We all learned to sand floors, lay carpet, lay tile, and landscape a yard. Of course, the boys and I did almost all of the painting.

We rarely ate out. When we did, he would not tip. If I tipped he would pick it up as we stood to leave. Of course, he picked the restaurant. Same-o, same-o!

It really shocked me that he wouldn't share devotions with us. When we were a trio, we studied the Bible together and prayed every meal and more. He would visit with a partner from church going from home to home every Tuesday night to present the plan of Salvation. But at home he wouldn't study the Bible or pray with us. I found this very strange. I decided that he was not Baptist, but he was a Homerite. Many people at First Baptist worshiped the pastor Homer Lindsay, Jr. I labeled those people Homerites. They were missing the point.

We did travel some. One wonderful vacation lasted almost a month. The boys and I had no part in the planning. We drove west to Arizona and turned south to spend a day in Mexico. Then we drove north from Arizona to Montana stopping many times to see just how wonderful our country is. We loved the Grand Canyon and the Grand Tetons.

It was a wonderful trip for the four of us. Charles had just finished the seventh grade, and Jon, the eleventh. We saw the Mormon Tabernacle, and driving home, we stopped at the Oral Roberts' church in Oklahoma. We drove east to Graceland remembering Elvis Presley's tragic death. It was good to get home.

Another time we also spent a week in Hollywood. We attended the beautiful Rose Parade. We visited Robert Schuller's Crystal Cathedral and walked in the gardens around it. We went on to visit Chuck Swindoll's Church in Fullerton, CA. I was disappointed that they didn't have a Wednesday night service that week because of Christmas holidays. We attended services at Dr. John MacArthur's Grace Community Church in Sun Valley, CA.

We ate at Sonny Bono's new Italian Restaurant. Mike was irritated that he had to use valet service. And, of course, the four course meals cost $7.00 each. This high price irritated him, so we ate many meals in the hotel room for the rest of the week. The whole trip was using up his frequent flier miles.

My younger son Charles and I went to a Dunkin' Donuts shop across the street from our hotel. We were to deliver breakfast to Jon and Mike. As we left the shop, a homeless lady stopped us and asked for food. We gave her two donuts and a coffee. Then we went back in to purchase two donuts and a coffee again. When we left the second time, the parking lot was full of the homeless. We gave out all we had, and then we returned to the shop the third time to refresh our supply. The manager asked us to stop feeding the homeless. I would have told him to mind his own business, but I was out of money anyway.

During the fourth year of our marriage, I was forced to take a stand. I never saw the check book. Mike told me that we did not have money for groceries when I needed to go to the store. After pushing for an answer, he told me that he had loaned my money to a colleague who was assigned to go out of town so suddenly that he didn't have time to get a voucher processed. He would replace my money in about ten days. I called that very day and stopped my check from being direct deposited into his account.This was an unpopular decision. I didn't care.

By the sixth Christmas, my expectation for this marriage had crumbled. His parents were visiting for the holidays. They were the loveliest people. They always gave Jon and Charles $2000.00 for their birthday and Christmas. They always gave Mike $5000.00 for Christmas. At the table at the end of the meal, his father asked me, "Kitty, the boys always tell me what they do with the money I give them, but you never tell me what you do with the money I give you." I sat silent and shocked. Finally I responded, "Dad, you've never given me any money". He abruptly stood and told Mike to come with him. After just a few minutes, Mike came back to the table with a check written to me for $5000.00 from his dad. Every Christmas (six of them equaled $30,000) and every birthday (six of them equaled $30,000) Dad had given me a check through Mike. Mike had never mentioned the checks to me. This was a big shock to me. It actually scared me.

I was present at the closing on each piece of property, but now I was apprehensive. I wanted us to have a will, but Mike would not agree to do one. Then I decided to get a will of my own. He did not want this to happen. The lawyer hearing my story immediately said, "Now, Kitty, you don't really believe that Mike doesn't have a will, do you?" I needed a copy of each deed for each house we had purchased since we married. He would not even let me see them. Why? Finally I went to the Court House for a copy of each deed. While I was there, just on a lark I asked if my name was on the title for the house we lived in. When I gave Mike the money to make the payment on our beautiful mountain house, he agreed that my name would go on his house on the river. Now I saw that he didn't follow through on his end of the agreement. On the way home from church that night, I asked if he had ever put my name on the title for his house. He replied, "Of course, I did. That was the agreement, wasn't it?" I was sick with disappointment. I told him that I knew for sure that he had not carried through on our agreement. I gave him an ultimatum. I told him that I was giving him twenty-four hours to get my name on his house. I resented having to give ultimatums, but I felt that it was necessary. The next day after school, I went back to the Court House although it was a very long way from my school. He had had my name added during his lunch period that day. I didn't feel comfortable in his house. This incident added to all the other evidences of greediness made me leery. I knew that I could not trust this man. I had never heard of wealth addiction until I began studying it at this point.

He would not allow us to have cable tv saying that having a couple of stations were enough. The boys could not understand this, nor could I.

Jon went to college at Samford in Birmingham near his grandparents' home. He was there two years. I could not believe how much Charles and I missed him. After two years, he transferred to the University of

North Florida. He went to college full-time and worked a full job. By now, Charles was gone.

When Charles finished high school, he went into the First U.S. Army band, I was sure that I would lose my mind. I missed them as much as I would have missed my right hand should I have lost it. Mike had traveled for CSX Railways most of his time the first six years. Now he was promoted and stayed in town all the time. His selfish ways continued even more now that I was the only one he could control.

During this time, I became aware of an organization called Christian Light Foundation. The men who founded and ran this organization had a prison ministry. They also handled donations to missionaries who were not sponsored by a specific denomination.

Judy Russell had married and had a child. She and her parents attended First Baptist Church. Judy had a small girl when her husband left her. She later felt a call to the Philippines. She sold her home, took her child, and flew to the Philippines. It was in the reign of Corazon Aquino. She got a small house. She rented a bedroom to a Filipino female doctor. She and the baby lived in a bedroom. The kitchen was the meeting room. The living room was a library and training center for training young ministers who would go out and plant a church. The location was near Quezon City, a disease infested cess pool with no running water, cardboard houses, and no bathroom facilities. Once during a storm over a hundred of these poverty stricken people camped out in Judy's yard because their houses had blown down. I would send large donations to Judy, and she would respond with news of her work. She was a real servant for God.

Once she got permission from President Aquino to hold a crusade in a major square in Manila. People from First Baptist flew over to help her. I was not one who went, but I was excited about this. Judy saved all year to buy Bibles to give out at the crusade. She gave out all she had the first night. I could not sleep that night. I called Judy to find out what was wrong. She was happy that the crusade was such a success the night before, but she needed Bibles. Through a tract company in Washington state which I often ordered from, they found a printer just outside Manila who printed the Book of John and delivered them to Judy daily the rest of that week.

When Judy was on furlough, I heard her say that the Filopinos were a visual people. I began buying two yards of cheap cloth at Walmarts. I painted a scripture and picture on each piece of cloth. Then I wrote a lesson for the teacher or preacher to use with the cloth. On the first one I painted a huge butterfly. I showed the caterpillar, the chrysalis and then the adult butterfly. Under it I printed, "If any man be in Christ, he is a new creature. Old things are passed away; behold, all things are become new." 2 Corinthians 5:17 I packaged the cloth and the lesson in a large envelope and sent it to Judy. She immediately reported back to me that a young pastor had checked the lesson out of her library, taught it in a village, and twenty people were saved. I was overwhelmed with thankfulness.

I made nine more lessons with visuals. There were reports that they were used with great success. How wonderful that God used me like this! The most amazing thing that I have learned about talents or skills is that you have them when you are doing God's work; then sometimes you lose them.

I had suggested several ways that we could try to improve our marriage. One was to sell this house and buy a smaller one which we would both plan. I did this because Mike was so prideful of owning this big house which we didn't really need. Another was to join a Baptist Church nearer our home. We were obviously not happy in any way. He ignored any thing I said. He was not willing to try. He didn't even know how to try. My efforts were getting me no where. After seven years, I told Mike that I was divorcing him. He responded, "No, you're not. You'll never get your hands on enough money to divorce me." I knew that that was true. I found out that he had a will. Everything on his part was a big secret. What was he trying to do?

The next morning I called a lawyer from school. He needed $1500 to begin divorce proceedings. Where on earth would I get $1500? About an hour after I called the lawyer, my friend called me. When I first moved to Jacksonville twenty three years earlier, I had one date with this man. We weren't really attracted to each other, but we became great friends. After I married Mike, he would call me at school about once a year. In the conversation, he asked how the marriage was going. I had always answered this question with "Fine" whether it was or not. But on that morning I answered with, "I want a divorce." When he found out that I needed $1500, he told me to meet him at a specific restaurant after school. I entered the restaurant and saw him at the bar. I had a coke, and we chatted a bit. Then we walked to my car. He put fifteen $100 bills into my hand as he opened the door to the car. He said, "Pay me back someday if you can. If you can't, forget it." I drove from the parking lot straight to the lawyer's office. Yes, I got a receipt. I knew that the divorce would go well because I didn't want anything.

A month later, I had to sit before a judge to get a court date for the divorce proceedings. Mike didn't show up. He didn't want to hire a lawyer. I told the judge that I didn't want his money. The lawyer and the judge tried to convince me to take half of everything. I couldn't. I was afraid that Mike would have a heart attack if I tried to take my legal share. The judge granted the divorce. I determined that this would be the last marriage and the last divorce. I knew that this was a big decision because both boys were grown and gone. I would be completely alone. To celebrate, I had my first manicure, had my hair fixed (a rarity), and flew to North Carolina for Christmas.

While I was packing to fly to North Carolina for Christmas, a truck pulled up to the apartment where I had moved. Mike's father had sent me a washer and dryer for Christmas. How wonderful!

Here I was! A true complete failure now! A proven fact! I threw myself into my work. I studied interesting topics where I felt that I knew too little. Charles was in the Army, and Jon was in his own condo not far away. My new apartment was near my job.

Five months later I was transferred to be Vice Principal of an elementary school. I was not wanted and was never assigned any specific tasks. I mainly did what no one else wanted to do. It was very boring. I was really a teacher. What was I doing in administration?

Part IX

Chapter 24

All By Myself

I had made a list of things I wanted to do before I died, so I got busy clearing the list. Long after I made my list, it became popular to make "a bucket list".

I began ballroom dance lessons. Being a Baptist, I knew that I shouldn't be dancing. I had wanted to ballroom dance since I was in my early twenties. Now I was fifty-two. When I began, I could see all of the benefits of dancing. It was only a matter of weeks before I became a dance addict. Since I never smoked or used alcohol or drugs, I didn't realize the addiction until I was really into it. I suppose when an addiction takes over one's life, it can be hard for the addict to accept that it's an addiction. When I realized that I was addicted, I was happy that it was with dancing instead of one of the deadly addictions. I was very thorough in all of the lessons. I would sit in the car in the parking lot after each lesson and draw diagrams of the dance patterns we had worked on that day. I spent hours at the studio. The big competitions were amazing for me. I danced at a studio for about seven years. I became certified to teach through Bronze. I passed tests in Silver American and International. Although dancing was wonderful and exactly what I needed at the time, I reached the point where I could go no higher without spending a tremendous amount of money. I had invested far too much already.

On one of my early lessons my instructor, while whirling me around the floor, said, "Kitty, do you know what being saved means?" When I answered with a yes, he sat me down at a corner table. He asked me to explain it. He said that every morning his mother talked to him about not being saved. I explained it. If being a Baptist taught me anything, it was to not shun witnessing using scripture. The lesson was over. On the way home I realized that I had just spent over $100.00 to explain the plan of salvation to a man I hardly knew. There was something wrong with this picture.

Dancing had benefits other than being fun and very good exercise. The people I met through dancing were gems. One of the most amazing people I've ever known was my dance partner's elderly mother. She was a real saint, and I had earthly contact with her.

My dance partner's mother lived in Fayetteville, NC. She was Pentecostal Holiness. Every day Earl called her, and every morning she told him he was going to hell because he danced. If she only knew of the way he conducted his life. She couldn't read or write a word, except the Bible. The city begged her to move to the suburbs, but she wanted to stay in her home which was right on the edge of the most dangerous part of the city. She was actually a real character.

From the porch she had a glass door, then a wooden door behind it. One morning she heard a noise at the door. She opened the wooden door and saw through the glass door that a robber was trying to break into her house. He had a gun. She unlatched the lock and said, "Come on in here, Son. I've been waiting for you. I'm going to put together a pan of biscuits, and we are going to talk." Three hours later this young robber accepted Jesus as his Savior.

You may asked how I know this. I attended her funeral. The young robber spoke. There were hundreds of people there. Person after person spoke. Her nine children were surprised because they had no idea that their mother was anything other than an ordinary, stubborn woman. The service was more than two hours long. Robbers, drug addicts, prostitutes, police officers, and many others told of this saint who helped them. The service seemed like a half hour.

She conducted a Bible lesson at the women's jail every Sunday morning before she went to church. They told me that she would drag her walking stick across the bars to wake them, yelling, "Get up, young ladies, I have to tell you important stuff you need to know." They loved her.

One night I was working at the studio. A very bad storm swept in. Earl asked me if I would leave and go to his house to be with his mother and father who were visiting. By the time I reached his house, the wind and rain were terrible, and the electricity was blinking on and off. The old lady and her husband both grabbed me as I entered the living room. By the time the three of us reached the couch and sat down, all electricity was dead. I couldn't think of what to do. No one spoke. There was complete silence except for rain and thunder and lightning. The house was one short block from the ocean, and we could hear the waves as they slammed the shore. I began singing "Amazing Grace" (the words to every verse poured out). They joined me. We sat there singing for three hours, holding hands on the couch. We could remember several verses of many of the hymns. We actually never spoke a word. Then Earl arrived home. When he realized that the singing was coming from the couch, he felt his way over and sat down on the other side of his mom and began singing with us. I had never heard Earl sing. Later I found out that he and his sister sang duets in the little Holiness church where they were raised. I consider this one of the sweetest memories in my life.

I stopped attending church because I felt tainted. I could no longer teach Sunday School at First Baptist. Mike was attending First Baptist. I knew for a fact that I could never serve God again because I had disappointed Him. How could God use a sinner like me. For sure, I believed that I was as disappointed in myself as He was in me. I began studying the Bible again by myself. I begged for forgiveness for being divorced. Many times I felt like God was not listening and wanted no part of me. I began to envy the sinners in the Bible who were shown mercy after they displeased God. I tried to figure out what they did to regain the favor of the Father. After studying the life of David and Peter and Thomas and Paul, I had my answer. Actually they did nothing, except obey. Finally, I accepted that God loved me, no matter what. Truth be known, my problem was that I didn't love me; I didn't even like me. I was shocked to realize that it was the ministers and the very religious people in the church who looked down on me and my kind. They would do anything to protect themselves and their families from my kind. I was a bad example.

I felt deep sympathy for all people who were divorced, and there were many. Recent divorcees began to seek me out. I really did not want to hear these sad stories. I began to think that all married people were just covering up their pain. I would go into a restaurant alone. The hostess seemed to always make a big deal. As I entered I would say, "Just one today.' Then they would say in a loud voice, " Are you eating alone? No one is coming to eat with you?" I have walked out of more than one restaurant embarrassed that many people were staring at me because a loud-mouthed hostess couldn't understand that a person can consume food alone. If I stayed, I would often be amazed with the people around me. The couple behind me would be arguing the whole meal. The couple across from me would be texting. The couple in front of me would not speak a word the whole meal. Although many times the hostess would make a loud, ridiculous issue about my eating alone, I would be happy to be alone.

Part X

Chapter 25

More Angels

Since I didn't own a house and since the school system seemed to be transferring me to every part of town, I moved five times in eight years to avoid the heavy traffic of getting to work. In the first apartment, I moved near my school where I had worked for twelve years. In this apartment I entertained myself by studying angels. When I began, there were only a few books out on angels.

One time I was asked by an acquaintance if I had any collections. Apparently women were expected to have collections. I needed to get busy. She probably expected me to say Hummels or porcelains or some such, but from out of the clear blue, I responded, "Oh, I collect angels." I actually had no angels. This lie was evidence that I wanted to be like other women. Why?

I learned years earlier that the way to have a collection is to tell people that you collect a certain thing. Students were not allowed to give teachers presents, but every teacher received gifts. It was rude not to take them. Since I worked at the beach, when I was asked what I collected, I randomly said that I collected shells. Over a two year period of time I had so many shells that I had no place to put them. They were beautiful shells from all over the world. I knew nothing about the shells, except that I collected them.

From that point on, no one has had a hard time finding a gift for me. I have shells and angels everywhere. They are not just displayed at Christmas. It was too much work to pack them away. They are in their place every day to remind me daily of my guardian angel's presence and the many people who want to give to me.

Only one memory comes to mind from that period in my life concerning the actual contact with an angel although I now realize that there could be many, many times when I was just so wrapped up in myself or too busy trying to solve someone else's problems to notice that an angel was present.

The incident many years ago came after weeks of studying every scripture and every book I could find on angels. It was Christmas, the first Christmas here in Florida that we ever had ice and power outages and no way to bring in supplies. I was extremely pleased that my younger son was on leave from the army and spending the holiday with me. I had had an ear infection during the two week vacation period from school. The medication seemed to make me sicker than the ear infection itself. My equilibrium was affected, so I spent my days on the couch and only moved to the bed at night. The two weeks passed too quickly.

My son returned to his base, and the next day I had to return to school. I was extremely anxious that I wouldn't wake up. During that period we couldn't depend on the electric clock because the electricity blinked on and off frequently. Icicles still draped from the telephone wires. After some agonizing hours, I decided to try something. I challenged what I had been reading. I prayed, "Dear God, I must depend on my guardian angel to get me to school on time tomorrow."

I went to sleep easily. Although I lived in a third floor walkup apartment, I awoke to the sound of a car horn which seemed to be right beside my bed. I jumped up and peeped through the blinds across the parking lot. The parking lot was asleep. I glanced at the clock to find that it was only 4 AM. I fell back into the cozy, warm bed thankful that I felt no dizziness from the ear infection when I had leaped from the bed. As I was almost back into a deep sleep, the horn blasted again. This time more persistently, louder and longer. I hit the floor in anger and looked out the blinds again. No car! No lights! What was going on? As I crawled back into bed, I noticed that the clock was blinking on 4 AM. The electricity had been off.

This time I remembered the prayer of the previous evening as I reached for the phone to call Time of Day. It was exactly 6 AM, the precise time I had set the alarm.

I asked several neighbors that evening if they had heard the horn in the parking lot that morning. No one had heard a peep. Each time as I walked away I was chuckling from within because I knew that my guardian angel was actually there. No story, no stable, no faraway hillside, but actually there with me. God was connected to me and my needs. I was assigned to a real angel.

For several years after that I didn't actually study angels. However, there came a day when I was looking for a gift in the book store that I realized that over a few years several new books were published about angels. As is so often the case, I bought myself gifts and resumed the study of angels.

Chapter 26

B eginning in the early months of 1993, I began to experience a series
of unpleasant events which I felt I could surely have lived without
– the death of a dear friend, a major financial loss, cutting the apron
strings from two close sons, watching the demise of a long dreamed-of
business, a job cut, a large salary cut, several moves, and a career choice
at a time I had wanted to concentrate on retiring. As so often happens
this series of events caused a reevaluation of my spiritual life. And as is
not so rare, my spiritual life took a new, exciting direction.

This new spiritual direction and the resumed study of angels caused
me to become more aware of my circumstances and surroundings than
ever before in my life. Being the self-made woman that I had become,
I stopped actually praying for direct help from my guardian angels. Yet
I began experiencing some interesting events.

I began suffering from lung congestion and sinus infections. I really
did not want to go to the old and dirty school where I had been
transferred way across town. All of the schools I had taught in were
very clean. I had to drive across a major bridge, through downtown,
through miles of warehouses and such. But it was test week for the first
quarter, and I didn't want my students to have a sub for their reviews
and tests. Each morning was a real drag.

Monday morning after a weekend in bed with a box of tissues, there was a wreck on the Matthews Bridge, and there I sat for what seemed forever. At least it was long enough for me to create a real big "pity trip". It was very foggy. All of a sudden a nice looking, clean-shaven man appeared. He was dressed in a dark suit, white shirt, tie, dark shoes, and no socks. He had a proud walk, and every time he stepped his ankle glared at the viewer. He was carrying an old beat up suitcase which was held together by a ragged, worn belt. He was walking from downtown Jacksonville across the bridge toward the suburb of Arlington at 6:20 AM on a Monday morning. One simply never sees anyone walking on this bridge. What circumstances ever brought this man to this point? I wondered. My "pity trip" immediately evaporated into appreciation for my transportation, my little apartment, my job, and my panty hose. I was filled with thankfulness for all of my many blessings.

Horns of the cars behind me roused me from my thoughts as I watched the man in the rear view mirror disappear into the fog.

All day the vision of the man kept haunting me. That evening I prayed that God would protect him and allow him to realize God's presence. During the night as I coughed myself awake, I prayed for him again. For months I prayed for this man. Each prayer brought a sense of well-being to me. Each prayer for him gave me reassurance that my own way was good and wise and correct. Each prayer for him gave me comfort and peace. Each time I prayed I wondered why the prayer calmed me.

Then one morning as I lay quietly in bed after first waking, it came to me that this man was an angel, an angel to remind me how fortunate I am and how very privileged I am to be a child of God.

Would I ever learn to recognize angels easily? I wondered why I was always so surprised when I recognized one.

Chapter 27

Not many months later I had to stop at the store after school to pick up some medicine. Although I was as usual trying to stretch those dollars, I decided that I was so sick that I would pamper myself. Dip and chips would be a real treat since I had had nothing junky in several months. However, when I reached the case of sour cream, guilt took over. I was bemoaning the fact that I should purchase yogurt for lunch the following day instead of sour cream for dip when a beautiful lady appeared beside me. I was leaning down into the case of dairy products, and when she spoke I stood erect. She was short with a mass of blondish, graying hair. There was a light around her head, and she had the sweetest voice. She was extremely clean and well-pressed. She remarkably began to audibly respond to my thoughts. Our brief conversation was astonishing. She told me that I had beautiful eyes where she could read the pain and joy of years. She told me that I should be pleased with my accomplishments thus far in life. I laughed as I thought that I really liked hearing that kind of talk and that she was saying exactly what I needed to hear. As she walked away, I was particularly impressed by the light around her. She had said that she was seventy years old, yet she had the walk of a thirty year old. She looked over her shoulder and said, "Yes, I know. You haven't heard this kind of talk often enough." She was responding to my thoughts. I was startled.

I paid for my chips, medicine and sour cream and rushed to the car through a sprinkle of cold rain. As I turned the key of the car, I realized that she was an angel. Notice that I was getting quicker recognizing them. I turned off the ignition and rushed back into the store, up and down every aisle. I searched frantically. She was nowhere to be found. I was just checking, but I really was not surprised.

As I winded my way home, I felt so warm and well and happy. I was assured again that there's a dimension of this world that I had read about and rarely seen which was now becoming real to me, as real as that dip and chips.

Angels can show up anywhere.

Chapter 28

I had worked hard, and I was totally comfortable when I bought the first house I have ever owned by myself when I retired from a long teaching career in 2000. My desire was to have a beautiful yard, so lifting hundreds of fifty pound bags of compost and Black Kow manure was a joy. It was only a minor concern the following year when I was struggling to lift the same bags that seemed easy the year before. I comforted myself by telling myself that the compost was wet and thus heavier.

My goal was to make the house comfortable and pleasant for my old age. After all, this was my retirement cottage. Purchases were made with much thought toward my future.

Considering my health and comfort, I decided that a major purchase was to be a Rain Soft water softener which I considered necessary here in Florida. I was delighted with the purchase. Wow! I had soft water for my hair and skin and for drinking; I had a different level of soft water for my laundry and dishwasher, and I had yet another level for watering the lawn. What a wise purchase! The first year a company delivered the salt for a small delivery fee, but they went out of business.

No problem for me. I would just pick up the 50 pound blocks of salt at Lowe's, which is only about a mile away. Then I realized I couldn't lift 50 pounds. I discovered that blocks of salt come in 25 pound blocks, but they cost almost as much as the 50 pound ones. Stubbornness kept me alert to the fact that this is ridiculous. The company advised against pellets. Every time I have to buy salt I get really grouchy just thinking about the price and my inability to lift 50 pounds of anything.

One day I was in the garden shop at Lowe's browsing the new plants, a trip I make often because seeing the plants makes me so happy, and the folks at Lowe's lift my spirit. Forgetting my increasing frailty, I stepped right inside the back door of the garden shop where they display the salt blocks. I was happy to see a male clerk standing there with a spare minute. I grabbed the opportunity and asked him to lift four blocks of salt into my cart. I was feeling very fortunate and grateful as I made my way to the checkout.

The problem came when I reached the car. How stupid I had been! It was around noon on a weekday. So hot that one could fry an egg on the pavement! There was no one in sight in the parking lot. I stood there with the trunk open wondering what to do when a woman in a navy business suit, white blouse, high heels, nice jewelry – dressed to the nines – approached me. She said, "May I lift those for you?" I laughed as she quickly lifted them into the trunk as if each was an ice cube. I was so shocked. Still smiling, she turned to me and said, "There you go!"

I stood there with my mouth hanging open. I was in shock. I closed the trunk and turned to say, "Thank you." But she was gone. I looked up and down the parking lot. She was just gone. She couldn't have reached the door of the store in that length of time, and she was not in any of the cars. She was just gone.

As I drove home, I had an eerie feeling. The feeling was actually indescribable. It was very comfortable and peaceful. I guess the best words would be happily relaxed. I realized that I had this huge smile on my face. I suddenly knew that the lady was an angel. That afternoon I opened a book which I hadn't touched in a while, and a bookmark fell out. On the bookmark was a quote from James Russell Lowell which said, "All God's angels come to us disguised."

Be not afraid to have strangers in your home
For some thereby have entertained angels unawares.
Hebrews 13:2

I became aware of a clue. Every time I have had an angel come to me that I know of, I have had the same calming feeling. If I was sick, I felt well. If I was worried, the worry disappeared. No other experience gives me the same feeling as the presence of an angel.

Chapter 29

If Only We Knew

Once Mike and I were returning home to Florida from a vacation in the beautiful mountains of North Carolina when we decided to stop over night to visit relatives in South Carolina.

In the afternoon a splitting migraine hit me with unusual force, so I excused myself for a short nap, hoping for relief before dinner. In the guest room it was warm and a little stuffy. I lay down with my head at the foot of the bed to get air from the only window and fell into a deep, refreshing sleep.

When I awakened an hour or so later, my eyes fell upon a picture hanging above the bed. As I gazed at the picture, Julie, my sister-in-law, came to the door to tell me that dinner was almost ready. I expressed my delight at the beautiful picture which showed five little angels in different poses forming a circle and asked Julie where she had found the picture. She responded, "Those aren't angels; they're just children".

I assured her that the forms were angels and showed her the wings. She was amazed and told me that the picture was in her room in her parents' home from the time she was small. We laughed that she had never noticed the wings. I found it rather strange that Julie had not known that these precious beings who had shared her whole life were little cherubs. For, you see, Julie was an intelligent, spiritual woman in her early fifties who was very fine tuned to her Lord.

Three years later I was shopping in an antique shop when I saw a piece of furniture I knew I wanted in my home. It was a sheet music cabinet. I had never seen one. I was writing the check for it when the dealer lifted it to take it to my car. There, over the piece of furniture, hung a copy of the same angels. How had I concentrated so hard on the little cabinet that I almost missed the picture? Needless to say, I purchased the picture also, and it now hangs in the same room which houses the two curios where my angel collection lives.

This picture has comforted me at the end of many a long, hard day. One day I was sitting on the couch quietly nursing a cold. It was sunset, and I had the blinds closed. Somehow one thin beam of sunlight shot across the living room and landed on a wall in the dining room. I was surprised. I followed the line of bright light to find that it was focused directly on one angel face on the picture. The room along with the other four faces were in dark shadow. The whole beautiful experience lasted perhaps a minute or two, but it will remain one of my most treasured memories for it was like a direct word from God saying, "I'm here with you, dear one."

Now years later there are so many angel books on the market, and I have discovered that the painting is Angels' Heads painted by Sir Joshua Reynolds. It is actually not five angels, but one little angel in five poses.

It was just recently as I smiled up at the little angels that it occurred to me that Julie had missed years of joy of these precious angels, and at the antique store I had completely failed to see the picture at first. How many of us are surrounded in times of need by the very comfort which we seek and don't even realize it?

Chapter 30

A Christmas Angel

Probably everyone has suffered from holiday blues to some extent. The Christmas season 2002 was especially hard for me. It seemed like I had been sick forever. And tired – the exhaustion overwhelmed me. I had done nothing toward decorating or shopping, and it was the 18th of December. I was moving like a zombie, sitting long periods of time in the recliner just staring into space. I tried hard to break out of the blahs. Then it happened.

The artificial tree was finally out of the attic. Boxes of decorations were scattered across the living room couch and floor and out into the garage. But I could hardly force myself to move. It was just all too much for one person to handle, and I was all alone. Finally, I decided to tackle the mantel first, thinking that one small step and then another would ease me into the holiday spirit.

There are two curios full of angels in the large foyer of my home. Years of collecting angels, mostly gifts from people who love me, has provided me with a gift shop display worthy of showing off. I immediately spied a beautiful white bisque Madonna with Child. She shone in the light of the curio in a strange way, but the strangest thing was that I didn't remember ever receiving her as a gift. Where on earth did she come from??? She really wasn't an angel. Why was she in my cabinet? Oh, well, the fact is that she is perfect as a centerpiece for the mantle. I figured out a way to set her high above the mantel, surrounded her with red poinsettias, and placed a white candle on each end of the board. "Simple, but beautiful!" I thought to myself.

The project took most of the day. This was unusual for a fast-moving, energetic woman that I thought myself to be.

As I sat in the recliner staring at the scene for a couple of nights, I enjoyed the serenity and peacefulness of the display. However, I was being plagued by the urge to find an angel to look over the Madonna and Child.

The second afternoon I dragged myself to the curio and began on the top shelf. Angels, angels, angels --- too tall, too short, too small, too large, blue, pink, silver, gold, too cutesy, too modern. The lights in the curio seemed to make each angel talk to me, blessing me as I slowly rejected each one. On the second shelf, then the third. Why couldn't I find an angel to join the Madonna and Child? I sat down on the floor of the foyer to surely find an angel on the bottom shelf.

Just as I had rejected each one there, someone knocked very hard and loud on the front door. I jumped, and my heart started pounding. I was a few feet from the door, so I crawled over to the door and reached up to unlock it as I wondered why any visitor would not ring the doorbell. With the door finally open, I saw the UPS man already hopping into his truck, and there was a package.

I brought the package in and set it on a chair thinking that I would put it under the tree if I ever got the thing decorated. It was from a cousin in North Carolina. We exchanged gifts sometimes, and sometimes we didn't. I would open this gift on Christmas morning. It would be my only surprise because both of my sons had asked me what I wanted, so I didn't figure there was any surprise there.

Receiving the package didn't really lift me out of the doldrums. That night I seemed to be getting more tired and deeper into the blues. I went to bed, but couldn't sleep. So I crawled out of bed and restlessly walked the floor. Walking through the living room, my eyes fell on the package. Heck with a surprise for Christmas morning, I needed a lift right then! I hurriedly opened the package. To my delighted surprise it was a white bisque angel, exactly the right size and height, exactly the right reverence shown on her face. I quickly redesigned the mantel display. Perfect! The flood lights over the mantle lit the faces so beautifully.

I sat in the recliner the rest of the night, reveling in the marvel of Christmas ….. the first one, and yes, every one since.

Part XI

Designing My Own Curriculum

College was such a wonderful time in my life. If I could get paid enough to live on to just attend classes, I would still be a college student. I love the campus, the bustle of the students trying to get to class. But those days are over. I was forced to design my own studies, and that I was capable of doing. I had chosen every course I took in college to count toward a degree. I had never studied Comparative Religions.

Chapter 31

Hinduism

I had recently seen the movie "Ghandi" which moved me deeply. He was such a gentle, peace-loving man. I decided that I would study Hinduism. I studied everything I could find – books, movies, the internet. Finally, I didn't think I could learn any more from these sources. I began going to convenience stores for the purpose of finding a real Hindu. I thought that I would find the answers to my questions by discussing their religion with them. This method only gave me more questions. I realized that Hindus do not know their own religion. Just like Christians!

When I arrived back to the apartment one day late, I had a message on my phone. It was my friend telling me that a Hindu Swami was speaking at the University of North Florida. I didn't wait to eat dinner. I just walked my sweet little Lhasa Apso, Samantha. Then I headed for UNF. I didn't realize that I had no money to get me into the parking lot. I begged the attendant to let me in. I promised her that I would bring the money to her the next afternoon. She let me in, and I drove to UNF the next afternoon to pay her.

Swamiji (great holy teacher) was speaking in a large classroom. There were so many people there that the chairs were removed, and we all sat on the floor. He spoke of his early years in India when his wealthy parents sent him to a Christian school because it was the best school in his village. Beginning in his early teens, he lived in Ghandi's ashram. This caught my attention immediately because I had studied the life of Ghandi. When Ghandi died, Swamji went up into the Himalayan mountains many miles above the tree line. This meant that he would have to walk miles to get fire wood to keep warm. He lived a solitary life in a small hut until he became an old man. I didn't understand at the time, but later I realized that he wanted to be in the mountains because of the pure air and pure water. He was moving closer to Vishnu who was the Hindu God who lived on the highest peak. Like Vishnu, I loved the mountians so.

One day a group of mountain climbers from Canada stopped at Swamiji's hut. The group of mountain climbers went there yearly. One of the men became a real friend. It took this mountain climber several trips before he convinced Swami to come to Canada to speak in different colleges. This was the beginning of many years that Swami spoke in colleges around Canada and the United States.

At the end of the meeting at UNF, Swamiji said, "I am so happy to have had the opportunity to be with you. Now I need to speak with this woman four rows back." That was me. I was shocked. People moved out, and I moved forward toward him. When I reached him, he took my hand and said, "I feel strongly that you have many questions and that you are seeking answers." I immediately had a real bond with this holy man. For the next four years, he was in the area for about a month each year. I was privileged to study with him. He told me that I was a very old soul. I accepted that, not really understanding what he meant.

Through Swamiji, I met many Hindus in Jacksonville. I went with him to the Hindu Temple. The people there were very friendly. Their services were very worshipful, but I never figured out who they were worshiping. During these years I felt that I was learning wonderful methods to become a better person. Meditation alone changed my life completely. Knowledge of the chakras (energy fields) and methods of moving toxins have served me well. I have never been able to prepare food as taught there. Not because I didn't like it, but because I had such a difficult time finding the ingredients.

About the same time, the same friend who told me about Swamiji's visit to North Florida told me that Deepak Chopra was speaking in

Orlando. We drove down. I was amazed at this man. He had just written *Ageless Body, Timeless Mind*. I read it and got absolutely nothing out of it. It was beyond me. This was very irritating to me. I read this same book over and over. Since then he has written many books. I've read all of his books. When I met him, I knew little about meditation, chakras, or Ayurvedic food or healing. I was an empty sponge eager to soak up the new.

Soon after Orlando, I attended a Chopra Seminar in Tampa. I was learning so much. One day Chopra himself walked down an empty hallway toward me. In the prior session he had announced that there were scholarships for medical professionals who wanted to study further. There in the hallway I explained to him how much I admired him, how much I was learning, and my concern that the scholarships were only for medical professionals. He told me that any time I could attend a seminar, I could have a scholarship. This was wonderful news because the seminars were way too expensive for my pocketbook. For many years I would attend these seminars. He would start the day with a two hour meditation. Before he taught me to meditate, I had tried it, but I couldn't sit still for more than ten minutes. To really meditate you must empty yourself and stick with it for sometimes hours.

His knowledge of Ayurvedic medicine was all new to me. He was trained in America. His father was a doctor in India. He recalled many times that his father at the dinner table would discuss a case that seemed to have no answer. He would be fretting about the situation telling his family of everything he had tried. The father's mother would remind him of Ayurvedic methods; he would use them, and the patient would be healed. At this time I had never heard of premordial or sutra meditation. Neither had I heard of Ayurvedic cures.

During this time I was suffering from severe back pain and going to a doctor near my apartment. One Friday afternoon he told me to see him Monday morning. He said if my back was not better by Monday that I would need surgery. I had loaned a friend the book "Many Lives Many Masters" by Brian Weiss. She allowed the book to get wet, so she paid me for it. Late Friday I went to Books A Million to purchase another copy of the book. Right beside the book I was looking for there was a book called "Working with your Chakras". I bought it. When I got back to my apartment, I began studying this book and doing all of the things I was instructed to do. By Sunday night my back was healed; no pain. Monday the doctor was shocked. He was from India. I showed him the book. He immediately sent one of his staff to buy the book.

I was also impressed with Chopra's knowledge of the Holy Bible. He told us of a habit of his. He quoted my scripture saying "Be still, and know that I am God." He emphasized the importance of quietness. Every month or so he would find a place to be quiet for a whole week. He would listen for God's directions. He did not voice a word.

At Grove Park Inn in Asheville, North Carolina, a staffer walked to the stage and gave him a note about nine o'clock one morning as he was speaking to about 500 attendees. He stopped what he was saying and started quoting scripture and poems by Rumi and Tagore. I will never forget one of the first quotes he said. It was something like, "When I die, I shall soar with the angels. When I leave the angels, what I shall become I cannot understand." I wondered what was going on. After about twenty minutes his staff stood ready to hand out stickers. The sticker simply said, "I'm observing silence". He asked us to wear these stickers all day. Then he announced that Princess Di had been killed in an accident. He wanted all of us to remain silent until dinner in honor of her life. We did. We even ate lunch without speaking. It was one of the most awesome things I've ever known. The employees at Grove Park Inn were astonished. When have you ever eaten lunch with five hundred people and not heard a sound – not even the clinking of a fork or the step of a server. The servers were in shock, but not more than I.

For good reason, three Hindus are at the top of my list of people I admire most. They are Swamiji, Ghandi, and Deepak Chopra. Honestly, I am not sure that any of them were truly Hindus. I have studied books about and by each. I stand in awe of all of these spiritual models.

Chapter 32

Buddhism

About four years after the beginning of my study of Hinduism, I received a letter from Richard Gere. Yes, Richard Gere of the movies. It was not a personal letter, but I was impressed. The letter was asking for money to help the Tibetan prisoners. Since the Dalai Lama is only a few months older than I am, I had always felt drawn to him. The movie "Kundun" gave me the story of how the Dalai Lama was found. It's an amazing story. About that time Brad Pitt made the movie "Seven Years in Tibet". This was a true story of Heinrich Harrer, an Austrian mountain climber and World War II prisoner of war who wound up in Tibet and befriended the boy Dalai Lama. This is most amazing since no outsider was allowed to enter Lhasa, the capital of Tibet. The Dalai Lama escaped out of Tibet and into Nepal as the communist overtook his country.

I began to study Buddhism.

The most important thing for me was to study the compassionate nature of Buddhist followers. In Tibet it had been the nature of the Buddhists to show compassion to all animals. The animals, never having felt a threat of danger, would respond to the Buddhist likewise. So an animal, considered to be wild and dangerous in other parts of the world, could walk right beside a person in Tibet. Neither the person nor the animal would have fear. This is part of Tibetan Buddhism.

There are several kinds of Buddhism, just as there are many denominations in the Christian faith. I studied Tibetan Buddhism most.

At that time I was horrified of snakes, and it seemed that every time I went out into my garden I would come across a snake. This fear took the joy out of gardening. One day I made up my mind that I would use Buddhist compassion on any snake I saw. I had the opportunity that very morning. I opened the gate into my butterfly garden. About 3-4 feet to my right lay a black racer. I stopped and announced to him or her in a very calm voice that I owned this property and that he/she must let me have space to do what needed to be done in the garden. Then I slowly followed the stepping stones the fifty foot length to the back yard. I turned into the back yard, all the while I was speaking softly to the snake who was following me, but staying three feet to my right. The back door was about twelve feet from the turn into the back yard. Although I wanted to run for the door, I slowly walked the last twelve feet talking softly telling the snake how important I was as he/she moved along right beside me. Even on the turn he/she didn't come any closer to me. As I opened the back door, I looked at the snake and told him/her to have a nice day. Then I ran for the recliner, sat down, and laughed for twenty minutes. Yes, Buddhist compassion really works. As with many elements in any faith, it's up to the follower to be able to follow the instructions. This was extremely difficult for me to do, but I was able to carry out my plan. It was a wonderful experience. This walk with the snake helped me to know that all I had to do to benefit from my own faith was to believe and act on my real belief.

Another example of the way I used Buddhist compassion was another day in the rose garden. I dug a nice hole to plant another rose bush; then I left to get the bush and some water. When I returned, there was a seven foot long glass lizard coiled up in the hole. I stood back and calmly explained that he/she should get out of my hole and allow me the space to do my gardening. He slowly slithered out of the hole to move about six feet away into a bush. He lay with his head in the air watching me. I kept talking to him. We were like that for almost two hours while I finished caring for a whole bed of roses.

These incidents sound simple, but this was not an easy thing to do. How I maintained a calm voice and composure is a miracle in my sight.

Remembering all the snakes in my life, I began wondering if they had been in my life to teach me a lesson. Animals seem to be attracted to me, especially snakes. Human snakes and the animal kind love me and want to follow me around.

It's been said that Buddhism is not really a religion, but methods for living. I could accept that. The four noble truths in Buddhism are:

1. Life is characterized by suffering.
    It seems to me that all people endure suffering which eventually makes them stronger. I have in my own life suffered to the point that I begged to just let me stay weak. Sylvie Boorstein said, "Life is painful, suffering is optional." I've been told many times that God will not allow you to suffer unless He gives you the ability to survive it. Many times I was sure that I could not handle what I faced. But I did because God knows me better than I know myself.

2. Suffering is caused by attachments.
    I can go along with this usually, but not always. Physical suffering is just there. I was never attached to my gall bladder. But it caused a lot of suffering before it was finally removed. On the other hand, my younger son has had many ailments and disappointments. Because I am so attached to him, I truly suffer when something bad happens to him. I also suffer when bad things happen to my older son. Watching them struggle through difficulties hurts me more than struggling through my own.

3. We can overcome attachments. We can do this through detachment. I don't want to be detached from my family. I don't want to be a "I don't even care" kind of person. I have feelings. Why would God let me have feelings if I turned away from the needs of this world. Although I believe this, I have come to realize that when one can "remove oneself

from a bad situation", the suffering is reduced. For example, many comfortable Americans would rather not know about the homeless, the hungry, or the sick because they don't want to be involved in finding a solution. Giving nothing or an occasional monetary gift is all they can manage.

4. You must release your ego by following a holy path.
   I don't understand this holy path at all. Is everyone to become a Buddhist monk? So where do women fit into this? I feel like following God's will daily is a holy path, but I don't believe a Buddhist would agree. Interestingly, Lord Shiva who is the destroyer of all evil and sorrow is thought to live on the summit of Mt. Kailash in western Tibet. This mountain is the source of four of the longest rivers in Asia. Here is another example of a god who lived in the mountains. I am drawn to the mountains. Why am I in Florida? There are many things in Buddhism that I think are wonderful. Subduing one's ego is a wonderful thing to try to do. In my lifetime, I have wasted much time trying to build my ego. There must be a balance there somewhere, and I will try to find it.

Chapter 33

Islam

It was time for me to move on to Islam. Everything I read scared me. This was around 1993. I didn't know then what I know now about Islamic extremists. Korans accepted by Muslims are printed in Arabic. I don't know Arabic. I suspect that the majority of Muslims don't read Arabic either. It is amazing to me that Islam originated from the descendants of Ishmael, the son of Abraham and Hagar. Christianity originated from the descendants of Isaac, the son of Abraham and Sarah. Abraham is the father of both, just as God had promised. There are many similarities. I think the problem comes when people of both faiths fail to know their scriptures. Although I studied this religion less than the others, I realized that there is much to desire in this faith. For example, the praying five times a day. I believe that it behooves us to develop the habit of always being in an attitude of prayer. We can all appreciate this practice of Islamic people all over the world. I wonder if the extremists pray five times a day? What do they pray?

Chapter 34

Judaism

My mother became ill in North Carolina and refused to go into a nursing home. She was in the hospital and had used up her insurance. She agreed to come to Florida although she hated Florida. Within six weeks she had to be put into a nursing home in Jacksonville. We were fortunate that we got her into River Garden which is a Jewish home near my house. I had already studied Hinduism and Buddhism and Islam to the extent of my ability. One night I sat in the dining area of River Garden alone eating my dinner and wondering how I should go about studying Judaism. I laughed when it finally occurred to me that I was sitting inside a Jewish Center.

I collected my books and articles to study. Then there were four synagogues and a large Jewish Community Center in the suburb where I live. I found the Jewish people I learned to know very knowledgeable and desirous of sharing their faith. I also found them very, very stubborn and narrow minded, but intelligent. They were not willing to listen to any Christian view about anything. They didn't even want Jesus' name mentioned. I attended Beth Shalom synagogue and several others. I read many books and studied the history of the Jewish people. It's so sad that they cannot accept the New Testament. Again much is to be admired about the Jewish people who conform seriously to their religion. For example, the men have minion daily where they pray.

Mother lived at River Garden for two years. Her next-room neighbor was a Jewish woman as were most of the patients. This woman had a son. He was a mess. Some time after she died, her son became a patient at River Garden. I went to visit him. He was very ill. He asked me to read Rick Warren's *Purpose Driven Life* to him. At the first reading when I read a portion about Jesus, he informed me that I could not say that word in his presence. So the first three chapters were read to him skipping the word Jesus every time it appeared. Of course, the reading made no sense what so ever. Reading this book took many visits because he had many questions. Giving answers without saying Jesus was a challenge. Finally while reading the fourth chapter to him, I accidentally voiced the word Jesus. He didn't yell at me. So the rest of the book was read as written. This was a wonderful opportunity for me. If it's true that Jews today accept Jesus as a prophet, why does His name upset them?

I looked into the Mormons, the Theosophists, the Bahias, and the Unitarians. I studied the *Book of Mormon* and the life of Joseph Smith and Brigham Young, the life of Helen Blavatsky who started the Theosophists, and the *Book of Miracles* taught by the Unitarians.

Chapter 35

Christianity

My conclusion at the end of all this study which covered about seven years is that I am where I belong. Without doubt, I am a Christian. Although I have studied the Bible my whole life, I continue to study. No matter how many times I read a chapter, each time I learn something new. I had used devotion books for years. Although they are handy and quite interesting, I believe that they are shallow. So I decided some years ago to study the Bible itself.

Of this I am sure:

- I believe with all of my heart that God put His son here on earth for the purpose of showing us humans how to live our lives and to die on the cross, to be buried, to rise, and to ascend into Heaven to sit next to His father, God.
- I believe that the Holy Spirit and our guardian angels are here with Christians today and that it is up to each of us to develop a rapport with them.
- I believe that the Bible, although written by human beings just like you and me, is inspired by God.
- I believe that God's mercy and forgiveness are the absolute best gifts we humans have ever known.

⅄ I believe that the grace of God is available to all who will accept it. I have.

⅄ I believe that it is easy to say that we accept all of the above, but to really put it to the test is a different story. I know that having these facts in one's head is not enough.

I also believe that we are here for a purpose. The Jewish man whom I met at River Garden often said to me, with tears in his eyes, "If I could only know my purpose." Whether I am in my first life or my tenth life here on earth, I know my purpose because Jesus came to earth and ministered three years to show me my purpose. Matthew wrote it down for me.

> "I was hungry, and you gave me something to eat;
> thirsty, and you gave me something to drink.
> I was a stranger, and you invited me in.
> I needed clothes, and you clothed me;
> sick and you looked after me.
> In prison, and you came to visit me.
> Truly I tell you that whatever you did for one of the least of
> these brothers and sisters of mine, you did for me."
> Matthew 25: 35-40

If you take these verses to heart, you might become overwhelmed.

> "I was hungry, and you gave me something to eat,
> thirsty, and you gave me something to drink."

There are so many hungry people. I don't think that I have the ability to take a few fish and loaves of bread to feed thousands. If I believed enough and if Jesus wanted me to feed thousands, I think that surely it would happen. But I am sure that monetary gifts to Feed the Children and City Rescue Mission help to feed the hungry. I am sure that giving food to the Mandarin Food Bank actually feeds the hungry near me. I am sure that loaning money through Kiva actually helps thousands and thousands of people to feed themselves. I am sure that the bags of rice, mango, papaya, and coconuts which I take to my Burmese family when I go to teach them English is exactly what Jesus meant in this verse. My friend Kathi prepares small bags holding a bottle of water, an energy bar, and some toiletries which she carries all of the time. When she sees a homeless person, she is ready. She is acting on this scripture. I know that when we send a flock of chickens for meat and eggs or any of the animals through Heifer International, we are activating this scripture. I am positive that when we send money to UMCOR and other such organizations to sink wells in countries where people have had to walk miles daily for a drink of water that those people are sure that somewhere in this world there is someone who cares about their daily lifes. How great it is that we can be a part of these things! How great that God provides these opportunities for us to act on the scripture Matthew wrote so many years ago.

www.feedthechildren.org
www.kiva.org
www.worldrelief.org
www.heiferinternational.org

"I was a stranger, and you invited me in."

Although I don't personally know the women around the world who need help, I am sure that my loan to them through Kiva helps them to realize that I have invited them to have a successful life using my small donation. I know that a mere $25.00 in America turns into much more in other countries. I am sure that the children I send monthly support to through Children International will be able to go to school and have health care. Their lives will be better because I cared. Their letters to me tell me that we have become more than strangers. I am sure that the women in Africa who receive corrective fistula surgery because my mission unit has paid for it through Global Ministries have a better life with thankfulness in their heart. I am sure that our gifts to pay for a cleft lip repair changes a child's life forever. I am sure that women at City Rescue Mission who are getting job training but have no bras are thankful that we collected bras and took to them, so that they will look nice for their job interview. I am sure that the people I have invited to visit my church or the Mandarin Senior Center know that that invitation is not to a building, but an invitation to come be my friend. I know that the refugees who come into Jacksonville know that they are invited to have a better life as we help them become acclimated to this new land which is to be their home. I believe that when we support our troops through Wounded Warriors or Homes for Troops, we are saying, "We have your back. Thank you for fighting for my freedom."

<u>www.childreninternational.org</u>
(<u>www.smiletrain.org</u>) or (<u>www.operationsmile.org</u>)
<u>www.woundedwarriors.org</u>
(<u>www.homefortroops.org</u>)

"I needed clothes, and you clothed me."

I am sure that the clothing given to those in need is greatly appreciated. Sometimes I wonder why I have so many clothes. I want to carry them to City Rescue Mission or Salvation Army or the Veterans groups. It's beyond my comprehension that I could live with just the clothes on my back. Some churches and the Mandarin Food Bank also have clothes closets. World Relief has a clothes closet which helps refugees who come with only the clothes on their back. I love to drive a refugee woman to Kohl's or Penney's and watch them pick out what may be the first new item of clothing they have ever had. This is my reward for reaching a certain goal in learning to speak English.

"....sick, and you looked after me."

I am sure that the dying patients at Hospice know with gratitude that their visitors care about them. Through Stephen Ministers the sick in our own community have contact with caregivers. For sure, the contributions to Memorial Sloan Kettering Cancer Research , Wolfson's Children's Hospital, St. Jude's Children's Hospital, and such are used for the sick. Our many, many visits to the hospital and to homes carrying food to the sick are worth while expenditures of our energy which comes from God.

<u>Www.mskcc.org</u>
<u>www.stjude.org</u>
<u>www.wolfsonchildrenshospital.com</u>

"In prison, and you came to visit me."

Earl's mother was a perfect example of acting on this scripture when she went to jail every Sunday morning to teach God's Word to those who were behind bars. Not many of us have been that brave.

I am positive that tutoring and mentoring help children and their parents know that someone cares. Everyone needs to be loved. By giving love, you receive love. This works because it is His plan. Following His plan, our obedience brings His favor to us.

I am sure that the refugees who mostly come from terrible chaos in their own countries know that they are loved by those who volunteer their time to teach them English or provide supplies for them or share prayers with them. When they get over being suspicious of our motives, the love pours out of them like milk pours into a glass. Good and nourishing.

Don't let the fact that you may not have much to give stop you. Your contribution added to the small contributions of many others will make a difference. This is the reason working in small groups is so helpful. Your prayers are needed and cost nothing. Use your time and talents to create a way to do something "hands on" to help those in need.

It's often dangerous now in our country to try to help someone. We have to be careful. But we must not be stopped. Say a prayer as you move forward to do His work.

Part XII

Chapter 36

Becoming Methodist

I was seeking a church home. For three years, my dear friend Shirley assured me that I should join Mandarin United Methodist Church. I sloughed her off saying, "I'm a Baptist." When a Lutheran Church was built near my home, I joined. I even went through catechism, but the members of the church weren't very friendly. So finally one morning I went to the Methodist church. I've stayed about ten years now because I like the small group studies, but mostly because I truly believe in the purpose of the United Methodist Women. The purpose is to serve women, children and youth around the world. In order to serve wisely, we need to keep up with what is needed and where it is needed, and then we must figure out a way to help. To me this is exciting. The facts I discover daily about those who need to be served are often unbelievable.

I studied the life of John Wesley and agree with him in every way. As Jesus worked with His apostles (a small group) to help thousands, I believe in working in small groups. I definitely believe that a small band of caring people can help thousands. I believe this because I see it happening constantly. Those who are wrapped up in their own problems are missing a great opportunity to have real joy in their lives through serving. Frequently serving is actually the answer to one's own problems.

I began taking small group studies. First, I took Alpha and enjoyed it tremendously. My next course was Disciple I. We had about eighteen people in the class, and it was about eight years ago. The class lasted thirty-four weeks. Today I consider the people in that class my most loyal supporters. I care deeply for each of them. Now I'm convinced that there are actually happy marriages because I can see them. Almost the same people spent another thirty-four weeks together studying Disciple III. Then some of us tried Disciple IV.

About this time my friends Val and Charlie became servant leaders of the worship team. One Wednesday night in the dining hall, Val asked me to serve communion on the following Sunday. Of course, I immediately explained to her that I was not worthy of such an honor. One of our pastors was walking by as I said that. He turned to me and said, "Kitty, no one is worthy." I agreed. This has been one of the most enlightening statements ever made to me. I often think of how unworthy I am. So what! Serving communion to the people of my church one by one was a touching experience. Every communion since that first time has meant more to me.

I was asked to update the church history. This work was a fascinating project. I learned so much about Mandarin, the suburb where I live. The church is truly a blessing in the community. Mandarin has Methodist, Presbyterian, Catholic, Episcopalian, Lutheran, and non-denominational churches. We also have several Jewish synagogues, a Greek orthodox church, a Mormon church, Jehovah's Witnesses, and a Hindu Temple. The really good thing about this diversity is that there is so much cooperation from church to church. For example, our Methodist church often collects food for the Mandarin Food Bank which is a Catholic project. Actually at present the Methodist church gives more food than any other denomination. This is a good thing. The women of the church also contribute to Divine Mercy House which is a Catholic project.

I'm convinced that the people at my church are the most eager Christians I've ever known. We have so much going on that one person cannot participate in everything. I often think of the many, many times that my friend Shirley told me, "Kitty, you really need to try Mandarin United Methodist Church." I was so determined that I was a Baptist that I wouldn't even consider her suggestion. Now that I am a member I see things more clearly. Ironically, there are many use-to-be Baptists at my church. So often one-half of the couple is one denomination and one-half is another denomination, so both of them decide to become Methodist. This is fine. But to protect myself and to celebrate my retirement, I initially decided to just attend church and try to avoid involvement. My friends in Disciple I wouldn't allow me to be inactive.

Shortly after I began going to Mandarin United Methodist Church, a friend from work invited me to go to the Walk to Emmaus. This was an amazing experience. On Saturday afternoon the youngest of the many speakers was talking. I was very tired. There was nothing great about her speech by comparison because they were all great. I was thinking just this when all of a sudden she said something that rocked my world. She said, "An isolated Christian is a paralyzed Christian." That's what I had become —a paralyzed Christian. When I returned to my church, I began to get involved. John Wesley was absolutely correct when he encouraged Methodists to work in small groups. As a group we can accomplish more than any one person could ever do. I hope that in serving in groups I have been seen as a good example because I have witnessed many group members doing great work for our Lord.

Part XIII

Chapter 37

What Is Retirement?

I retired from the school system when I was sixty-five. After the experience of being the Vice-Principal of the elementary school for one year, I was sent to be Assistant Principal of a new, large High School. I was there two miserable years. The principal and others on the staff definitely did not want me there. When the school system appoints someone to the school rather than allowing the principal to make his/her own choice, it frequently causes trouble before the transferred person even arrives. It was the farthest school north in Jacksonville, and I was living the farthest point south in St. Augustine.

After two years of misery, I went back to the classroom where I belonged. I was transferred to one of the worst schools in the county. I was teased that this was punishment for leaving administration. So be it. The last eight years was the best teaching I'd ever done. When I retired, the principal told me that he was glad I was leaving because the other teachers became irritated trying to measure up to me and my colleague Kim. I've never figured out if that was a compliment or not. I think not.

Retirement did not suit me. The next fall when I saw the "yellow dogs" picking up the students in the mornings, I would cry. I truly missed my students. I saw no need to retire, except that I was sixty-five.

I could work circles around many of the young teachers, but that didn't matter. I was sixty-five, and I was expected to retire. I went back three times after I retired. Today at seventy-six I am tutoring ESOL students at one school near my house and mentoring two students at a school across town. I am helping refugees learn to speak English working with World Relief. I love it. It is work - enjoyable, worthwhile work.

Chapter 38

God's Work

M any mornings now I awake and feel worn out, often in pain. Since retiring, I have the leisure of lying in bed and saying to God, "Good morning, what would you like me to do for you today?" Shortly after I say the last word, He leads me to my mission of the day. The tiredness disappears until I have finished my assignment. God truly wants a personal relationship with us. If you don't believe this, please try it. You will never receive the blessing unless you are willing to try. It occurred to me recently that God is not really concerned that I'm tired or sick or old. The thing He is most interested in is that I am willing to follow His direction. We are His feet and His hands here on earth. Believe me, when I tell you that this is the most exciting, fulfilling part of any human life.

Frequently some of my good friends are involved. I have been provided with the most wonderful Christian friends who serve the Lord with gladness daily. We are blessed daily and assuredly when we do His will. All we have to do to gain God's favor is to obey Him. This requires a close relationship with him. One must know His will. How else can we obey Him? So often I have allowed my humanness (lack of confidence, laziness, illness, feelings of inadequacy, and many other) stand in my way. I wish I had not been human as much as I have.

I will share a couple of the many examples as to how this method of asking for specific assignments from God has worked for me.

Several years ago I had finished a big project the day before, so I lay in bed the next morning telling God that I needed a new, challenging project. At the time the computer was in the bedroom. Just a few minutes later I jumped up to check my email before I made the coffee. As I read the first email, I knew that God had answered quickly. There was a request from Chad, a young friend from church, asking me to help another young man at church. Doug had finished his studies to become a minister and turned in his final papers. His advisers asked him to redo the papers with more attention to the grammar. He needed help. Grammar? I could do that. Within a couple of hours I was reading his first paper. It was exciting for me to read this material, and it was challenging. God answers prayers. Yes, for sure He does. His answers are so often exact and quick.

For more than a year I would awake many mornings and during the night thinking about Community Hospice several miles from my home. I kept thinking that God wanted me to work there. I never had any desire to work with sick people. I certainly was not a person to work with dying people. I kept explaining to God daily for more than two years that there was something wrong with our line of communication, and that it was making me uncomfortable. He refused to hear my whining. One day my friend Rose who is a nurse called me and said that she was going to take the Hospice training and asked if I would like to take it also. For some reason, I said that I would. I would think every day about the people in the Bible who would balk at God's instruction to do something for Him. They, like me, did not have confidence in themselves. When finally they would follow instructions, great things were accomplished. So many times the stories of these Bible characters encouraged me and still do. If one never reads the Bible, how can they receive that encouragement.

After the training I started receiving my assignments. Some of them I shall never forget.

My very first patient was asleep when I arrived. I waited and waited. She never awoke. I went to the nurses' station and asked if that was normal for her. They said that it was not unusual for her to sleep all day and all night. I went back to her room and read some framed newspaper articles about her on her wall. Then I took her hands. She was gurgling; I was sure that it was the death gurgle. I prayed with her. She opened her eyes and said, "Thank you". I arrived home ten minutes after that prayer. The phone was ringing. It was a director from Hospice telling me not to go see the woman because she had died. She must have died as soon as she said, "Thank you". I was there when her own children were working, and the nurses were busy elsewhere. This really touched me.

There are seven nursing facilities just around the corner from my house. Many times I was lucky enough to service patients in these near by places. The first year on Christmas Eve I received a phone call about nine o'clock asking me to visit one of my patients. She had had a stroke that afternoon. Her adult daughter lived closer to her than I did, but refused to have her Christmas Eve ruined by a mother who may or may not have even known she was there. I was happy to go sit with her for a while. She did know that I was there, but I'm not sure if she knew who I was. I don't really care if she thought I was her daughter.

Sometimes I had eight or more dying patients assigned to me. It took almost all of my time to meet with each of these patients each week. One of the nursing homes was far from my house.

I met the family of one of my patients. Ms. Washington was comatose. Every week I would go in and read a psalm to her. Her adult daughters who were still working seemed to appreciate this. She had not opened her eyes or spoken in several years. One morning in a rush and in the rain I ran into the facility, but left my Bible in the car. When I arrived at her room, the nurse had just finished changing her diaper and was tidying up the room. I said, "Oh, Ms. Washington, it's Kitty. I left my Bible in the car, and it's raining. But I remember a scripture which is especially for you. In Psalms it says, "Be still, and know that I am God.' " She smiled. I nearly fell over as the nurse looked at me and said, "She smiled". I believe that she knew I was there every time I visited.

I was asked to escort musicians at the main Hospice building. About twice a month accomplished musicians, sometimes from the symphony, would visit and go into each room to play or sing a favorite song for the very ill patients. They had to have a guide. That was me. I really enjoyed this assignment. To see these dying people enjoy something so much was a rare opportunity for me. Sometimes one would climb out of bed and dance with the IV still connected.

One of the dearest men in my church showed up in Hospice. He was the most positive person I have ever known. He went in for a regular checkup where they found cancer in his kidney. It was removed, and he was told that they got it all. Only a month or so passed before he was in horrible pain. The tissue around where the kidney had been was found to be cancerous. The cancer spread rapidly. Although I had talked to many hospice patients, talking to Ray was too, too sad. I made a contribution to Memorial Sloan Kettering Cancer Research Center in Ray's honor. They sent him a note saying that the donation had been received. He had that notice with him in every hospital room, and now it was taped to the television in his Hospice room. I had a feeling that I needed to speak with Ray, so my friend Carole and I decided to go to thank him for how much he meant to us. When we arrived in his room, Ray began telling both of us how much we meant to him and others. He told us that we must continue serving the Lord. He said to me with love in his eyes, "Kitty, what if that donation you gave helped to pay the salary of the researcher who finds a cure for cancer?" His energy was so spent, that we left without telling him how much he meant to us. He died shortly after that visit.

It touched me so much that the contribution to Sloan Kettering meant so much to Ray that I have made a policy of donating a contribution for each person I know who has cancer. This habit has given me much joy. It has been a difficult policy of mine simply because so many people I know have cancer. But because it is God's work, I have financially been able to keep up. He multiplies my money in ways that I could never do on my own.

They would call me to cover a department when a special event called the regulars away. Amazingly I could handle anything they gave me.

Finally I was completely worn out. I began working on the desk at the main facility. I only worked one day a week. So now I had time to do other things. If you ever want to be sure that God is using you, work with the dying. You will be blessed beyond anything you have ever experienced.

God has taught me many lessons throughout my life. The most

important lessons I've learned seem to have come from doing things that I initially didn't want to do. But God knows how to convince a reluctant servant. It's when you obey that you are richly blessed.

It was around this time that a course was offered at church called Servant Leadership. It was a small class. Sometimes the teacher closes really small classes, but the teacher continued to the end for about six weeks. The concept was so helpful to me. It filled me up like a good serving of Key Lime pie. But it was a continuous, satisfying filling. I was eager to try this. When I began, I started to realize that I had been a servant leader for a long while. I must be on the right path. This was comforting.

Chapter 39

More Exciting Projects For God

One of my greatest concerns living in this big city is the number of homeless people we have. I have had many rewarding challenges with the homeless.

Teaching at an inner city school has its draw backs. No, it's not necessarily the students. When I was teaching there, the black cafeteria workers would not serve me because I was white. If I carried my lunch, I had no safe place to leave it. Often when I left school in the afternoon, I was hungry. One day I stopped at a Burger King down town. I got my food and sat down. Across the aisle sat two older black men with large brown paper bags. They had been panhandling on the downtown streets all day and had large amounts of coins and one dollar bills. They were counting their proceeds.

A dirty young black man who smelled terrible came up to them and asked for enough money to have a burger. The two older men started screaming at him saying to go beg his own money. The young man answered, "But I'm really hungry." I stood and took him by the arm. I ushered him to the counter and said, "Get whatever you want." He did, and he thanked me. I went back to my table to finish my meal. The two older men began making threatening remarks to me for helping him. I'm not sure how I did it, but I sat calmly ignoring them until

I finished my meal. I didn't rush, and I didn't either look at them or say a word to them. They didn't exist. As I left, I smiled at the young man with the full stomach. By the calmness I felt, I realized that my Guardian Angel was there with me. I could not possibly have been so calm on my own.

One afternoon after school, I had to drive way across the city, way out to the beach, to see my son after school. As I turned off the highway onto the off ramp, I saw a homeless man begging for money. I hoped the light would be green, so that I could just bypass him. I only had a ten dollar bill which I was planning to use to buy my dinner. The light turned red. He came to my window. I had been warned never to give a homeless person money because they would probably use it to buy cigarettes, liquor, or drugs. But I felt so sorry for him that I gave him the ten dollar bill. They don't make change, you know. I was not a cheerful giver. Neither did I want to go on knowing that I had denied a hungry man food.

The next afternoon I had to go look at an apartment I was thinking about renting. I was on a major highway, swung onto the off ramp, and lo and behold there was the same man I had given the ten dollars to the afternoon before. This was at least 15 miles from yesterday's location. I had picked up another ten at the ATM for my dinner that night. I determined that he would not get my money this time. As he approached my car, he recognized me. He patted my window and said, "God bless you, Ma'am," and moved quickly on to the next car. I smiled. He restored my faith in homeless people that afternoon.

I arrived home in time for the six o'clock news, so I settled down on the couch with my KFC. A pedestrian had been killed on Baymeadows Road that afternoon. When the camera caught the body lying on the pavement, I saw the homeless man in his plaid jacket. I cried as if I had lost a brother. I have often wondered if my ten bought his last meal.

One year I volunteered to go to the big Prime Osborn building downtown to serve lunch to the homeless. I was cooking dinner for both adult sons later that day. I began serving the gravy over the good smelling dressing. I had only worked a half-hour when the manager came and asked me to get a plate. I didn't want to, but I did. He walked me over to a lady and two late-teen children. She was trying to eat holding her head as low as she could. She was ashamed. There were

TV cameras everywhere. I began to talk to her. Her husband had left her. She was a professor at University of North Florida. Her car broke down, and she couldn't pay to get it fixed. So she lost her job. Because she had no income, she lost her house. She and her children were living at City Rescue Mission downtown. The son went to college right across the street, and her daughter caught a ride to her high school. I sat there listening to her story, and I knew that this could have been me. It could be anyone.

That night as I sat down with far too much food and my two sons, I appreciated my life more than usual. I could hardly swallow my food. I have never been able to get this woman out of my mind. I pray that she is doing well.

My friend Dawn and I attended the School of Christian Mission at Lakeland, Florida, several summers ago. The morning course I was taking was disappointing. The lady who sat beside me was not impressed either. She talked a lot during the class. One morning she said that she cooked dinner every Friday night for the homeless in her small south Florida town. Then she added that at Christmas she gave every homeless person a pair of socks. She explained that when one's feet are warm, they are warm all over. For weeks, maybe months, I kept thinking about this woman.

One Sunday night some months later I rode with my friends Lamar and Judy Wheeler down to Schulzbacher Center for the homeless. A group of us from Disciple I prepared dinner and served. On the way down I told them of the nagging memory about the socks. Judy told the story of Lamar serving dinner one Sunday night to the homeless, when a homeless man walked up and asked, "Sir, do you know where I could get a pair of socks? My feet are cold." When Lamar responded with a no, the man walked away disappointed. When Lamar finished serving, he found the man and offered him the socks off his own feet. I was touched by this story.

At the time I was president of the United Methodist Women. The ladies wanted to help the homeless. We sat up tubs to accept toiletries for the homeless. We collected thousands of shampoos, lotions, soaps, hand sanitizers, and many other trial sized items. We purchased five hundred pairs of socks. Lamar later gave us money to replace our expenditure. We had group meetings where we rolled one sock and stuffed it into the toe of the mate. Then we packed the sock with toiletries and tied a red ribbon around the top.

I found that people really wanted to be involved with this project.

The Children's Director had almost three hundred carry bags made by the children at our church. She asked me to deliver them to the Children's Ministry at Schulzbacher.

I was in Winn Dixie looking for the new manager when I ran into a stranger in the aisle. I asked if he was the new manager. He had on black pants and a white shirt and wasn't buying groceries. He answered with no, but assured me that he could help me. I assured him he could not. He kept nagging me about what the manager could do that he couldn't do. Finally I told him that I wanted the manager to donate some items to the people at a homeless center. He immediately became more alert. He had lived in Jacksonville all his life, but he had never heard of Schultzbacher. When I explained their work and location, he was shocked. He asked if they have children at the center. He owned a vending business within five miles of the center. He gave me his card and told me he wanted to donate boxes of animal crackers to the children. When I went to pick them up, I was surprised to receive 265 boxes.

One woman told her dentist about the project. The female dentist donated over a 140 tubes of tooth paste and as many brushes. The woman was pleasantly surprised. I was beginning to become shock-proof.

One hotel donated 200 bars of soap.

My lesson in this project was that many people want to be led into action. Most people want a leader. Actually they may be capable of leading a project, but they lack confidence or willingness or time or all three.

On the day that we carried the donations to the center, we took the church bus because I wanted to give as many people as possible the opportunity to participate. About twelve people went. Lamar left his CPA firm and met us there. As we were about to leave, one of our pastors approached me and said, "Kitty, don't forget to look these people straight in the eye."

The center is in downtown Jacksonville. The people living there eat inside. The street people line up at the edge of the property where a cart is situated to serve lunch. There is no place for them to eat, so they cross the street and sit on the curb. I remembered what the pastor had said. I walked down the line looking each person in the eye and said over and over, "Today when you get your food, we have a little surprise for you." I had said this same thing one hundred and twenty times, and I was still a long way from the end of the line when a man stopped me and said, "I hope to God that the surprise is a pair of socks. My feet are cold." I grabbed him from the line to take him to Lamar. The man repeated his plea for a pair of socks. Lamar just happened to have a fresh pair in his pocket. As the man lifted his pants legs to show his sockless feet, Lamar handed him a pair of socks.

About a year later I heard a representative from Schulzbacher speak. She explained that one never knows the extent of one's own actions. She told us of a woman who had brought a team to Schulzbacher to deliver socks. She said that they filmed these volunteers giving out the socks and put it on their website. Evidently many church groups saw the project in progress. She said that now many, many churches in Jacksonville are bundling toiletries in socks and delivering them to the center. I smiled, holding my tears until I got to the car. I wish I could contact the woman who gave me the idea, but I don't know her name. She would be delighted to know what she started.

My friend Kathi works for a division of the City Rescue Mission where homeless men and women can live if they are willing to go through a year or so of job training. Then they are placed in a job. She told me one day that none of these ladies have bras. When they leave the shelter, they are embarrassed. Most certainly when they go for the job interview, they need to look as nice as possible. When the UMW ladies heard this, they began handing me bags of bras when they would see me at church. I began carrying a big tote to hold them. Kathi reported to me that the posture of these ladies improved, and that she could tell who had found a bra by the way they walked. We collected over a hundred bras for about forty women. So simple, but this was an important project.

When we saw that these women are in class all morning and that they have nothing to do all afternoon except to play cards and watch television, we bought a bookcase and carried books to them. We had so many books that we couldn't carry them, so one of the men volunteered to push them in an old grocery cart to the sitting room in the upstairs part of the building. When he arrived at the women's sitting room, he said to me, "Are you giving these books to the ladies?" When I answered with a yes, he asked, "Could I read this here book?" It was Rick Warren's *Purpose Driven Life*. He took the book, and I thanked God that He's in control. What an interesting way for God to pull this poor man into the fold! God is everywhere. He is full of surprises.

The women's dorm at City Rescue Mission had twenty year old carpet. The walls needed paint. The building certainly needed help. The UMW furnished towels, bedspreads, sheets, furniture and much more to renovate two rooms. The old carpet was ripped out and new flooring was installed. The Youth at our church picked up on the idea and renovated a total of five rooms during their summer mission project. The Youth did the UMW rooms to help us out. When one sees a project like this through, it changes them forever.

The UMW has a library containing books which is on a Reading List from the Women's Division. I usually order these books. I was concerned when I came across a book on the list. It was *Not Just A One Night Stand*. I thought it was about prostitution. I couldn't imagine why the ladies would need to know about prostitution. But I did order it. I was wrong. The book is about homelessness. The book reported that a Methodist minister in California kept praying and praying, asking God to do something about the homeless in his city. He couldn't understand why God wasn't answering his prayer. After a long period of praying, he got his answer. He heard it clearly. The answer was something like this, "Why don't YOU do something about the homeless?" I suspect that God frequently answers our prayers with, "Why don't you?" I hope that those who don't understand this have a really good excuse. And I hope that when He asks me, "Why don't you?", I will be alert enough to move to action.

Part XIV

PEOPLE WHO GREATLY INFLUENCED MY LIFE

Chapter 40

Hal Shumaker

YOUTH PASTOR AT FIRST BAPTIST, NEWTON, N.C.

Hal Shumaker was the youth pastor in my home church. He was vivacious, young, and dedicated. The Youth were so involved in the Lord's work, mostly because of his leadership.

He organized a Youth Choir and asked me to play the piano. We had around seventy Youth. He actually taught these kids to sing. Choir practice was fun. But the real joy was when we sang at other churches.

Several summers we were the choir at the Baptist summer camp at Fort Caswell on the coast of North Carolina. Fort Caswell was built during the Civil War to protect the mouth of the Cape Fear River. It is located outside Southport, North Carolina, right on the Atlantic Ocean. Every night we would gather on top of the fort to have a "Sing". A short while after everyone had finished dinner and gathered there in view of the ocean itself, we would walk slowly down the fort into the auditorium all the while singing "Blessed be the Name. Blessed be the Name. Blessed be the Name of the Lord" over and over. This was so beautiful and inspiring that I felt like I might be lifted off the ground and swept away by the angels.

One night was very special for me. Our choir sang "Battle Hymn of the Republic" for the evening special. When I left the piano bench, the week's pastor called me back to play again. He wanted the whole congregation to sing the song. It was so beautiful. My heart was full of joy, and my eyes were full of tears. I don't know how I played the piano. Hundreds of voices singing, "Glory, glory, Hallelujah. Glory, glory, Hallelujah. Glory, glory, Hallelujah. His truth is marching on!", sounded like a heavenly choir. I knew the strength in my hands because I practiced everyday. But my hands were not this strong. I felt that I could take my hands off the keys, and they would play themselves.

Hal arranged for me to have organ lessons. The teacher came to our church to teach me because we had a marvelous organ. One day I handed her the quarter for my lesson. Our hands did not connect. The quarter went down between two of the pedals on the organ. She liked screaming over the least thing. When the quarter fell into the pedals, she screamed so loud that I was sure the beautiful stained glass windows would fall out of their frames onto the floor of the auditorium. Her voice kept going round and round the sanctuary like an echo which wouldn't stop. Even she was surprised.

Although the music participation was so good for me, Hal made the biggest impact on my life when I was twelve years old. He gave me a chance of a life time.

Every Sunday night our church had Training Union for a couple of hours. We were divided into departments just as we were for Sunday School on Sunday morning. The Junior Department was ages nine to twelve. I was being promoted to the Intermediate Department in September. On promotion day, I had only been in my chair in the Intermediate Department for a few minutes when Hal came to me to say, "Kitty, I need your help. The adult teachers didn't show up for the junior kids. Will you please go sit with them tonight? I'll find someone by next week." I went upstairs to find nine little kids – three, two, and one year younger than I. Hal never found adults to take the class. When I went to college five years later, I left the Junior Training Union.

By the end of the first year, we had seventy-some kids in Junior Training Union. We did memory work. The boys and girls won state contests every year with their Bible verses. We did Sword Drills. They knew their Bible backwards and forwards. They could win Sword Drills with anyone who would challenge them. At summer camp our students were outstanding. It was amazing what the contact with these children did for me. I studied and memorized verses to stay ahead of all of them. This experience has served me well over the years. I often thought that my grandmother would be so proud of me. She loved her Bible and taught me my first Bible verses. I knew that she was smiling at us.

This was a challenge and a delight for me. Nothing had ever meant as much to me as leading the Junior Training Union Class. Many adults would "visit" to see how we could accomplish so much. They were as amazed as I.

All through high school this was the best part of my life.

Chapter 41

Ms. Myrtle Rowe, Piano Teacher

The Reformed Church had opened Catawba College in Newton in 1851. This college initially was for males only, but the Civil War played havoc with funding and the student body. By 1890 the school was changed to a coeducational school. In 1923 land in Salisbury, North Carolina was given to the college, and the college moved to Salisbury in 1925.

One of the faculty members did not go to Salisbury with the college where she taught music. Instead she married a hometown man and stayed in Newton. When I began school at age six, Daddy decided that his daughter should learn to play the piano. He purchased a piano and sought a teacher. Mrs. Rowe was his choice, and a good choice she was.

The week I started to school I began piano lessons, and my last piano recital was within days of the day I graduated from high school.

I wasn't talented. But Mrs. Rowe and I really hit it off. Her house was full of books and magazines. She always encouraged her students to read as they waited for her to finish the lesson prior to theirs. She had big rocking chairs on the front porch where we sat in warm weather. But she allowed us to sit in her parlor when the weather was cold.

Mrs. Rowe was tall. She was the most patient and calm person I've ever known. She always wore beautiful, but conservative, clothes. Her hair was wavy; she kept it pulled back in a knot at the back of her head. She was so graceful when she walked. It wasn't her looks that intrigued me. It was her manner.

She had two daughters and a son all quite a bit older than I. As I learned to know them, I found that their manner was exactly like hers. They were friendly. Never did either of them seem too rushed to stop and talk a few minutes. Her son, although several years older, always waved or spoke to me at school as if I was part of his family. One daughter received state awards for her broadcasting skills. She never got cocky although if anyone in my town had the credentials to act uppity, she did. The other daughter was a first grade teacher who directed an operetta at the Elementary School every spring. When I was in grades first through fifth she always gave me a part in the play. In sixth grade the principal allowed me to cover her first grade class relieving her to practice the play. This was the first experience I ever had with lesson plans.

Mrs. Rowe's home was the only home I ever entered where a maid was present. Tot helped with the cooking and cleaning. She was a teenager. She was the first black person I had personal contact with. She entertained Ms. Rowe's grandson while Mrs. Rowe taught piano lessons. I loved Tot. She was so sweet. When she finished school, she went on to college and became a teacher. No doubt that Mrs. Rowe's presence in her life influenced this girl.

When I was about eleven, the Rowe family moved to North Newton – about six blocks closer to my own home. This was perfect for me. There were no music stores in Newton, so Mrs. Rowe ordered huge boxes of sheet music from a company in Charlotte, forty miles away. She had begun to suffer from arthritis in her hands. On Sunday afternoons about four times a year, she would invite me to come to her house and play the different sheets of music for her. She would sit at a table near the piano. When I finished playing each sheet, I would hand it to her. She would write a student's name in pencil on the front of the music. She had a lot of students, both boys and girls. We would go through fifty or so sheets of music on each of these visits. I loved to help her. I loved the fact that she asked me to help her.

She put together a recital every spring to show off her students accomplishments. The recital was always in the Elementary School auditorium. I would always play a solo from memory. I would pace and shake and almost dissolve in sweat back stage. When it was my turn, Ms. Rowe would send me onto the stage with an encouraging word. The older I got the nearer the end of the recital I would perform. This gave me more time back stage to fret. I would try to comfort the little ones. I would walk to the piano in the middle of the stage. I always felt like I couldn't make it to the piano stool. My knees would be trembling under my long dress. As soon as my fingers touched the familiar piano keys, I changed into a different person. A person I barely recognized. I didn't think; I just let my hands and body perform. Years later in dance I learned that this is called muscle memory. Many years I would also play a duet with Doris Ann Mauney. A couple of years I played trios with a couple of the boys. Three of us on the same piano bench was bad enough, but I learned that boys have no control over their elbows. Or maybe they had control and were purposely trying to injure me. Ken Cloninger and Kirk Brookshire had the sharpest elbows in the whole town. I was a handy victim always placed in the middle of these "all boy" types. Looking back, I know that I was brave.

Mother always made a beautiful dress for me to wear at each of these recitals. She would grow flowers in her garden in colors to accessorize my dress to the max. One year, when I was about twelve, she made a light blue floor length organdy dress with a bustle. She attached a pink bow under the bustle. Right before we walked to the school, she cut pink roses from her garden and attached them across my shoulder as if they were a strap holding the dress up. Another year she cut snapdragons to stitch around the neck of the dress. Mother was very creative. Mother always offered to put fresh flowers among the ivy Mrs. Rowe used to decorate the edge of the stage.

One year when I was in high school, I played a very difficult piece. When I finished, Dr. Cloninger who had two sons taking lessons stood to his feet and yelled, "Bravo". Mother was sitting right in front of him. He could have given her a hundred dollar bill, and she wouldn't have been happier. She talked about this for years.

There is no telling in how many ways the Rowe family influenced my thinking when I lived in Newton. They were very special to me.

Once when Mrs. Rowe was very old and in a Nursing Home in

Hickory, I was visiting Mother. I wanted to go visit Mrs. Rowe. Of course, Mother didn't want me to go. She assured me that Mrs. Rowe didn't even know her own daughter. I insisted, so Mother went with me. As we looked for her room, I saw a woman in a wheelchair sitting in the dining room. She was very stooped and tied into her wheel chair. Mrs. Rowe had been tall and willowy. When I told Mother that the lady in the wheelchair was Mrs. Rowe, Mother argued that it wasn't. I walked toward the lady. She looked at me with an apparent clear mind and said, "Oh, Kitty, I'm glad you are here. Play something for me." I rolled her wheel chair nearer the piano, sat down and played as tears flooded down her face.

After a while, she asked, "Where are you living now?" When I told her Jacksonville, Florida, she shared with me the most marvelous story.

She was a three year old girl living in Jacksonville, Florida, in July,1888 when the second Yellow Fever epidemic hit. Over 400 people, one tenth of the population, died during this epidemic. Within two days of the first diagnosed case, the city was quarantined with armed guards on the main roads leaving the city. The Florida Weekly Times News printed, "Your choice is one road which leads to Hell; the other to damnation. Whichever you take, you'll wish you had taken the other." During the first few days and before the city was quarantined, the mayor who later died of Yellow Fever told the people to escape. He provided trains and buses to take them out of the city.

Mrs. Rowe's mother gave birth to her brother at the beginning of this epidemic. She died of Yellow Fever and was buried in Jacksonville. Her father packed a wooden wagon, hitched the horses, and left the city taking with him his new-born son and three year old daughter. He pushed on till he reached Atlanta where he purchased a two-story house. They lived upstairs, and he opened a general store downstairs.

The house was across the street from Peter Marshall's church. She remembered three block long lines waiting to get into the church to hear Peter Marshall preach. Peter Marshall later moved to Washington, D.C., where he was pastor of the New York Avenue Presbyterian Church and Chaplain of the United States Senate. He was married to Catherine Marshall. He came here from Scotland because he thought that was what God wanted him to do. He died of heart problems in his forties.

I was so very happy to have this last contact with a woman who had inspired me for many years in many ways. She was the personification of patience. A perfect picture of what a lady should be. I've never reached this height of perfection, but I keep this marvelous example in my mind to remind me that perfection does exist.

Chapter 42

Reverend Alvin Walker

In 1949, Christian missionaries were put out of China. Rev. Alvin Walker was one of those missionaries. He came home to serve as associate missionary in the district that my home church was part of.

I was enamored with China at the time. Dr. Hill, a missionary in China, had visited our church years before. He was an interesting and knowledgeable speaker. A little old lady at the meeting said to him, "Dr. Hill, I prayed for you on your birthday. I prayed that God would keep you ever alert to the tasks He wanted you to accomplish." The missionary's birthdays were printed in the WMU (Women' Mission Union) magazine. Dr. Hill looked so surprised when the lady finished. When he responded, we all were pleasantly surprised. North Carolina is about one-half way around the world from China, so morning in my home town would be night in China. He said that he paced the floor all night on his birthday wondering what God needed him to do that he was not doing. As a young girl, I was very impressed with this. I pray daily for missionaries around the world and have most days of my life. Prayer is something to take seriously.

Rev. Walker asked two other girls and me from my church to help him with Vacation Bible schools in small churches that had never had a

Bible School. We did three or four churches the summer I was fourteen. I considered this the greatest honor.

At an association meeting in late August, he asked me to speak. The church was packed. I was not nervous because I had prepared and practiced. I had notes in green ink on index cards. By the time it was time for me to speak, I felt anxious. I stood behind the lectern and looked down at my notes. Every word was smeared. I could not read anything on the little cards, so I put them down and winged it. In the Baptist church no one ever applauded, but I could tell before the end of the program that my talk had been well-received.

I will be forever grateful for the contact I had with Rev. Walker. He probably knew that he was laying a foundation. I didn't realize it then. He taught by giving gentle guidance and opportunity. What a wonderful example of a great teacher! I have frequently used this method in my own teaching. Providing opportunities for those who would never have a chance to respond to such incidents in their day to day lives is providing life- changing moments. Giving another person the chance to see what could be is often all they need to become what they are meant to be. If teachers don't do this, who will? Rev. Walker did this for me. He gave me the know-how and courage to do this for others.

Chapter 43

Barbara Isenhour, Cousin

Bobbie was born to my aunt Rose when I was six years old. She and Aunt Rose lived with Grandma Hendrix. Aunt Rose worked in the Glove Mill just across the field, and Bobbie stayed with Grandma and me. She was the prettiest baby you could imagine. She was smart. It seemed no time till she was just talking all day long. I had to go to school during the days leaving this cute little baby with my grandma. She got all of the attention, even when I came home at three.

I was jealous of her. I loved her, but all of the fuss surrounding her left me out. All of my aunts and uncles showered her with attention, just as they had done for me at that age. In the summer Grandma would send me to Ed's Café to buy two ice cream cones – one for Bobbie and one for me. On the way home, walking the short distance across a field which Grandma could see from her front porch, the ice cream would start melting. Nothing to do, but lick both cones as fast as I could, walking very slowly in the summer sun. By the time I reached Grandma's front porch, my cone and over half of Bobbie's cone would be gone. Grandma never acted like she noticed. In adulthood, Bobbie teased me saying that the reason I was larger than she was because I ate her ice cream. I must say that I was really happy when she put on weight.

In adulthood, everywhere I moved or in whatever situation I found myself, Bobbie called me every Sunday. She was always the one who sent me a real surprise for Christmas. She was a dependable "sister". We never had a cross word. Oh, she would "tell it like it was", but when she blasted me, it was for encouragement. She was always right.

One Tuesday when I was seventy-three, I received a call from Bobbie. It was a Tuesday night, not the usual Sunday. I knew that something bad was wrong. She could hardly talk. The day before she awoke not knowing where she was or who she was. She had been going to different doctors for about three years. They always said she had asthma. Now at the hospital she was diagnosed with cancer in her bronchial tubes, her brain, her lungs, her pancreas, her liver, and one kidney. When she left the hospital, she went home on Hospice care.

She completely lost her voice, so we couldn't talk. No one at home really told me anything except she was diagnosed with cancer. I was alert to the fact that something was very wrong. After a week , I left my dog with my son, and I drove to North Carolina. I wasn't sure I could make it because I had so many health issues. When I arrived in Newton, I went straight for her house. Numerous cars surrounded her little home. I walked into a room full of strangers, her husband's relatives, and went straight to her room. She was hooked up to morphine, in a coma with no hair. She always had really full hair. I walked to her bed and suddenly it hit me that she was leaving us. It was real.

I had always thought that she would be the one to handle my funeral. That would not be happening. It hit me hard and strong, standing there seeing her like this.

Her husband yelled, "Hey, Bobbie, Kitty is here!" She didn't open her eyes, but she mumbled, "It's about time." The next day there was no communication with anyone.

The third day I sat on the side of her bed rubbing her hand. Several women were standing around her bed. All of a sudden she sat up and grabbed me. She whispered in my ear, "My back hurts." I rubbed her back a few minutes while she held me so tight that I thought we were one. Then she fell back into the bed.

I am not a singer. But I felt compelled to sing to her. I was not embarrassed to sing in front of the room full of relatives who had gathered. I said, "Bobbie, you know I can't sing very well, but I want to sing you a song." I sang "When You Get Where You're Going". I remembered every word. It was like someone with a beautiful voice was singing. I didn't recognize my own voice. Toward the end of the song, I stopped because I was sure that she was back in a coma. When I stopped, she said in a normal voice loud enough for all to hear, "Kitty, I can hear you." So I finished the song.

When I Get Where I'm Going

When I get where I'm going on the far side of the sky
The first thing that I'm gonna do is spread my wings and fly.
I'm gonna land beside a lion, and run my fingers through His mane.
("Buddhist compassion," I thought.)
Or I might find out what it's like to ride a drop of rain.
I'm gonna walk beside my daddy and he'll match me step for step
And I'll tell him how I missed him every minute since he left.
Then I'll hug his neck.
Chorus When I get where I'm going, there'll be only happy tears
I will shed the sins and struggles I have carried all these years
And I'll leave my heart wide open
I will love and have no fear
Yeah, when I get where I'm going
Don't cry for me down here.

So much pain and so much darkness,
in this world we stumble through
All these questions, I can't answer. So much work to do.
But when I get where I'm going and I see my Maker's face
I'll stand forever in the light of His amazing grace.
When I get where I'm going, there'll be only happy tears
Hallelujah! I will love and have no fear
When I get where I'm going, don't cry for me down here.
Written by George Teren and Rivers Rutherford

Performed by Brad Paisley and Dolly Parton

Two days later she passed away, and I lost one of the best friends I've ever known. On the way home, driving alone, I cried so much that I finally stopped drying my tears. I don't really know how I ever got home.

Every day I look at all the angels she sent me. Every morning I drink coffee out of mugs she gave me. She left part of her with me, and I am so glad. Her memories are treasures for my life. I'll be so very glad to see her again.

Chapter 44
Love Sent My Way

When one has a special slice of love sent their way unexpectedly, it is a real joy. It seems like I have lots of love coming my way. Maybe I was too busy to notice when I was younger, or maybe it's the people I hang with now.

One night when I was whining about getting old, my friend Judy asked me how old I was. I told her that I would be seventy-five in February. She asked me how I was going to celebrate this very special birthday. When I told her I never celebrated a birthday, she was shocked. A few days later she announced in an e-mail that she was giving me a birthday party. She wanted the names of twenty people to invite. I made the list and sent it to her. She planned the party as a luncheon on the very day, the fifteenth. I arrived to find a counter of good food, two large tables set with real flowers and beautiful dinnerware. The birthday cake itself was something I had never seen. It was twenty or so cupcakes with icing covering all of them together. It looked like a huge cake. She told me several days ahead of the party that the ladies were asking her what to get me for a present. I told her that I didn't need anything. All of the ladies wrote checks to Heifer International in my honor. It was a large gift. I was so honored. Where does one find such giving friends? This gesture will be one of my favorite things to remember for the rest of my life. Everytime I feel a little down, I remember this sweet friend would cared about me enough to give me a special day.

I had been in the hospital with a frozen shoulder. The whole thing was very painful. When I finally returned home, Terry and Karen came by my house and brought me a Buddha for my fern garden. I had had a Buddha in my garden years before I knew them. When the Lutheran minister saw the Buddha, he said that I was worshiping other gods and asked me to get rid of it. I did. By the time I met Terry and Karen, I regretted getting rid of my Buddha. They knew the story. The Buddha they gave me sits in my fern garden now. What wonderful friends!

I have been privileged to have had many influential mentors in my life who touched me deeply over a period of years. I have had many great teachers; several who have been known around the world for their learning theories and their books and seminars. I have studied under great, widely known theologians. But the ordinary people around me have meant the most. I have been blessed beyond all expectation.

Chapter 45

Short-Lived Influences

If the truth be known, I have learned many valuable lessons from many who were not well-known nor well-educated. These people were in my life for short periods of time

For example:

1. Andrew, the custodian in the high school where I worked in Raleigh years ago. He was a quiet man who cleaned the high school five days a week and preached on Sunday. One afternoon when I stayed late, he came in to clean my room. We had not had rain in weeks. Thinking of my garden I said, "Andrew, are you praying for rain?" He stopped and leaned on his broom as he answered me, "No Ma'am. He already knows we need rain. I just constantly thank Him for the rain we are going to get when He gets around to it."

2. Malcolm, an emotionally disturbed fifth grader, became my friend. When I was transferred to his school, he came up to me on the first day to tell me that he had learned to spell my name. What a wonderful gift! I doubted him because I have to spell my last name everywhere I go. I've known many who couldn't handle McCaffrey after years of friendship.

But Malcolm was proud to let me know that he had learned to spell my name. He lived with his grandmother who really did not have time for him. She worked as a cook at Olive Garden way across town. She never had time to come for a conference. One day I went to Olive Garden before the evening rush. She sat down at the table with me and was delighted to hear something good about Malcolm.

3. One day I was shopping in a Christian Book Store. There was a line at each cash register. There was a woman in the next line who had a lace hanging. In the lace was the form of an angel. It was $15.95. I asked the cashier if there was another lace hanging like the one the woman had. It was determined that she had the last one. She purchased it and hung out by the door. When I finished paying, I headed for the door. She was waiting for me. She said as she handed me the lace angel, "Here. I want you to have this." I wanted it, but I didn't expect her to give it to me. She didn't even know me. I have this token of a giving heart, hanging on the inside of my front door. I smile at it every day.

After I began this section, I realized that I have been blessed with hundreds of these quick blessings. I could probably write a whole book on this topic. Here is not the place. I won't continue.

Part XV

NOT PERFECT YET

Chapter 46

It seems that with all the trials I've endured, all the wonderful experiences I have had, and all the projects I've been involved with, that I would be perfect by now. What a joke! I am far from it. The more I serve the more I am aware of my shortcomings. I read the Bible thinking as I read, "Yes, I know." But in real life, I frequently have a hard time calmly accepting what I know is true. The following is an example of my not being able to accept the real truth.

IN HIS TIME

In August, 2004, we were told that a bad hurricane was headed straight for Jacksonville. We were fortunate to have several days to prepare.

I can't remember when I was not a Christian, but for some reason, my anxiety ran rampant when I listened to the news. I would have left, but it was unclear whether I should go south or north or west. I couldn't go east because I would soon run into the Atlantic Ocean. I prayed for God to calm me. It seemed that the more I prayed the more acute my anxiety became. I was embarrassed and ashamed that I was so upset. I couldn't understand how a Christian could fear a storm. Where was the faith I thought I had? I wanted to be an Abraham, not a Jonah. Mom had been such a worrier that I began to blame her for being a bad example. I kept repeating the scripture found in Joshua 1:9 which says, "Be strong and courageous. Do not be afraid or dismayed; for the Lord thy God is with you wherever you go." My mind believed these words, but somehow my nerves were not connecting. I felt disgusted with myself.

I spoke to my son, who lives near by, about boarding up the house. He shushed me saying that I was over reacting. We owned a truck together. I asked him to let me use the truck to pick up plywood. He refused on the grounds that plywood was too heavy for me to handle. I asked my young gardening partner to use her husband's truck to help me get plywood. She refused, using the same logic that my son had used. It's very hard for me to ask for help. Now that terror had forced me to ask, everyone around me was refusing to help me. This was very confusing to me. My prayers increased as did my anxiety.

I methodically did what I could do by myself. God gave me a good mind which has always served me well. But nothing was working at this point.

1. I went to the grocery store to buy supplies. With a multitude of illnesses, the decisions for food supplies was seemingly impossible. The shelves were emptying very rapidly.

2. I purchased batteries as advised. When I got them home, I had no idea how to install them in my radio or even the flashlight. Tears flowed for an hour or so as I suffered through my ignorance, putting the aggravating little things this way and that and back. Nothing would work. Success seemed unreachable. How could I be so stupid?

3. I tried to fill the gas tank in case we were told to evacuate. There were long lines everywhere I went. It would have been no problem to sit in line, but every line for miles around was going the wrong way. This was the first time I knew that my car's gas tank was on the opposite side of the car from almost every car in Jacksonville. Upon reaching home with an empty gas tank and a pounding heart, I made a plan to buy gas in the middle of the night. The

plan worked. Ordinarily I would consider this adventure dangerous. Now it seemed that I had to chose between danger and danger…a clear case of being between the Devil and the deep blue sea.

4. I checked on all of my medicines.
5. I packed all important papers in water proof containers.
6. I went to the ATM in the middle of the night to get cash, thanking God that I had money in the account and that I was the only person at the ATM. For me, this was a horrifying experience. I was very nervous.
7. I listed every valuable thing I owned on the computer, backed it up on two disks, and drove to the PO in the middle of the night to mail one disk to my cousin in NC. This trip was eerie – just me, my dog, the rain, and the wind. I felt so alone. I reached out to God, but He seemed to be busy. I yearned to feel His presence. I felt like God thought I was overreacting. He was right. The newscasters were telling us that the bridges would close when winds got to 50 miles an hour. We were warned that tornadoes would accompany the hurricane. I made a plan for my dog and I to seclude ourselves in the hallway. I moved supplies into the hall. I considered a shelter, but I couldn't leave my Sammy Girl. If they closed the bridges, I would be stuck on the island where I live between the St. Johns River and the Intercoastal.

Now I had done everything I could humanly do. I seemed to calm somewhat, but realized that my prayers were now being spoken in a loud voice. I prayed, "I've used all the resources I have, Father. It's up to you now." As I heard myself say this foolish statement, my mind told me that it was all up to Him from the beginning. I rationalized that God expects us to help ourselves. After all, that's why He gave me good sense.

That night we began getting the northern bands of the hurricane. People began to lose their electricity. My anxiety increased.

Early the next morning a man who lived about a block away knocked on my door. Actually I was afraid of this guy. He had the reputation of being the neighborhood "bad boy". He had never been bad to me. He said, "Kitty, would you like your house boarded up?" I was in shock. Lowe's and Home Depot had run out of generators and plywood. This man had driven to Lake City and brought back a truck load of plywood. He and another neighbor, whom I didn't know, had my house secured within a half hour. I asked how much I owed them. He said, "Oh, you don't owe us anything." I insisted on paying. He said, "Well, thank you, forty dollars will be fine." I knew that Lowe's last plywood was $14.95 a sheet. They used seven full sheets.

He also told me that if we lost electricity for any length of time, I would lose everything in the freezer, but not to worry, he had a generator. He assured me that he and his wife would cook for me.

Every morning for about eight days he showed up at my front door checking on me. He assured me that if we had to evacuate he had six rooms booked in Valdosta, Georgia. My dog and I would be moving out with his family and other neighbors. The neighborhood "bad boy" had become my caretaker. I was amazed at this good fortune.

Bands of wind and downpours of rain came, subsided, and came again. Half of Mandarin was without electricity for a week. I had several friends with family members on oxygen. I began praying hourly for them. My thoughts left me and went to others. There are many nursing homes on St. Augustine Road near my house. I prayed for them, concerned that some of the personnel wouldn't be able to get to work for many of them lived in the Westside across the bridge.

Homes in the Westside of Jacksonville lost roofs, Mandarin lost trees, but the brunt of the hurricane turned toward the west just south of us and then went north. I was thankful, but now I felt guilty that I was safe when others were suffering. Seemed that I was determined to suffer one way or another.

Another amazing thing happened that stormy week. A neighbor who was a pitiful alcoholic came to check on me with her drink at nine in the morning the first day I was in the "cocoon". We talked and talked. She would get so drunk that she would walk through the neighborhood naked. Her 16-year-old daughter and her husband would be so embarrassed. Her alcoholism caused such disfunction in her home. I was able to witness to her, clearly laying out the plan of salvation, in the mornings every day for a week. The more I spoke to her about her alcohol use, the more she denied that she had a problem. She kept coming back through the downpours. Shortly after the storm, she passed away at age 43, and her daughter shot herself.

I've said all of this to lay the groundwork for my night with a visual display of God answering prayer. Yes, He was there in the hurricane.

About one in the morning of the worst day, my little Lhasa Sammy Girl had to pee. I put the collar on her, and led her out the only way to get out, the front door. We walked to the end of the driveway. I saw the trees all the way down the street bent over almost reaching the pavement of the road in the strongest wind I've ever seen. Living at the end of the cul-de-sac, I could see the whole street. There were nine huge oak trees and a large maple on my property. When I saw the trees on the street in such frenzy, I turned to look at my trees; not a leaf was stirring. I had feared that one of these huge, old trees would blow over on my house. Never fear. God had His calming hand on my property that night. As I stood astonished, staring at my trees, I was suddenly aware of what felt like a warm syrup flowing through my chest. It was definitely the touch of God calming my weary heart. I stood there a long time holding onto the mail box looking at the wind swept trees down the block and back at mine. No, I was not imagining it. I was still sane.

The next day the man who had boarded up my house and his sons came to pick up tree limbs in my yard. They were amazed that there were no limbs on the ground. While the whole street was being wind blown and torn, my yard was perfectly calm.

In His time He handles all of our struggles, all of our fears. How wonderful is our God!

Part XVI

Chapter 47

What Next?

Every senior I know is plagued with many aches and pains. I am normal and have my share. But I have learned that when God wants you to do something, He takes all excuses away. So I know that He will use me, until He decides to take me home. This is good. This is my desire.

Recently I attended a musical with a friend. At the quick intermission, she asked, "Kitty, what do you think Heaven will be like?" Before I could answer, the play began the second act. On the way home, I tried to answer. Fact is I don't know. But I have glimpses.

I listen to many ministers faithfully on TV. I tape them if I'm not going to be home. I can't get enough. Each one gives me a need to study further, and I enjoy the follow ups every week. I watch Joel Osteen at Lakewood, Houston, Texas, faithfully although many of my friends caution me that he's just a prosperity preacher. Frankly, I need a little prosperity thinking almost every week. He makes me feel happy and grateful. I always like to hear Herb Reevis at North Main Street Baptist, Jacksonville, Florida. He tells it simply and clearly. And, of course, Mac Brunson at First Baptist, Jacksonville, Florida. I enjoy George Davis from Faith Family Center, Jacksonville, Florida. I learn from Charles Stanley at First Baptist, Atlanta, Georgia. Strangely it seems that Charles

Stanley preaches on a topic I've been thinking about all week, almost every week! This week he talked about what heaven is like. Of course, I attend my own church. All of these ministers bless my life and give me courage to get through another week.

In the podiatrist office the same week, I picked up a Time Magazine. I never read Time. There was an excellent article on Heaven. All of a sudden my mind keeps thinking of Heaven. Maybe I'll go there soon.

I see the rest of my life as a continuation of the activities I have been involved with for years. I realize that at some point I will be forced to slow down. As with all old people, I feel the deterioration of this earthly body. I chuckle when I take my medications because I think that I rattle when I walk, like a medicine bottle. I whine a lot about a pain here and a pain there. But I keep going. If God wants me to accomplish a task for Him, He will give me the strength to do it. He proved that to me a long time ago. He will also give me joy in doing His work.

Many of my days are filled with amazing surprises and opportunities. Many are just quiet days of gardening and aloneness. Now I recognize opportunities quicker than I used to. This has been a wonderful journey. I don't want to miss anything God has for me to do, so let me stop writing and continue His work.